STRANGE BEDFELLOWS, TRYING TIMES

FIRST NATIONS HOUSE
OFFICE OF ABORIGINAL STUDENT
SERVICES AND PROGRAMS
University of Toronto,
Borden Building North,
563 Spadina Avenue, 3rd floor,
Toronto, Ontario,
M5S 1A1

October 1992 and the Defeat of the Powerbrokers

STRANGE BEDFELLOWS, TRYING TIMES

BROOKE JEFFREY

KEY PORTER BOOKS

Canadian Cataloguing in Publication Data

Jeffrey, Brooke
Strange bedfellows, trying times: October 1992 and the defeat of the powerbrokers

ISBN: 1-55013-470-1

1. Consensus Report on the Constitution (1992). 2. Canada — Constitutional law — Amendments. 3. Federal-provincial relations — Canada.* 4. Native peoples — Canada — Legal status, laws, etc.* I. Title.

JL65 1993.J4 1993   342.71'03   C92-095632-7

Key Porter Books Limited
70 The Esplanade
Toronto, Ontario
Canada M5E 1R2

The publisher gratefully acknowledges the assistance of the Canada Council and the Government of Ontario.

Design: Annabelle Stanley
Printed and bound in Canada
93 94 95 96 97 6 5 4 3 2 1

Contents

"It should be borne in mind that there is nothing more difficult to arrange, more doubtful of success, and more dangerous to carry through than initiating change to a State's constitution."

— MACHIAVELLI, *THE PRINCE*

For the Captain and Carletto

Introduction: Anatomy of Defeat

On October 26, 1992, Canadians passed judgement on the Charlottetown Accord in a historic national referendum. This direct consultation with the public was intended by the political élites to be a mere formality, but it proved to be the accord's undoing, and their own. Instead of approval, the Canadian people delivered a stinging rebuke. For Brian Mulroney, who was ultimately responsible for the decision to hold the referendum, the accord's demise represented a crushing personal defeat and perhaps the biggest mistake of his political career.

The October vote was only the third time in the country's history that Canadians had participated directly in the governing of their country. An impressive 75% of eligible voters turned out, a figure that suggests citizens took the referendum very seriously.

The high turnout left no doubt about the legitimacy of the verdict. An overall majority of Canadians voted No nationally (54%); provincially, six out of the ten provinces and one territory voted No. In Ontario, originally thought to be a sure thing for the Yes forces, the result was effectively a dead heat. Despite the concerted efforts of virtually all the country's political, corporate, and media élites, the accord, as Prime Minister Mulroney declared late on the night of the referendum, was history.

The referendum vote itself made history in two ways. First, the result went against the government of the day. Second, it did not — for a change — have the effect of isolating Quebec from the rest of the country.

The national referendums of 1898 (on prohibition) and 1942 (on conscription) both resulted in victories for the government of the day. The 1992 campaign was at least as intensely fought as the previous two, a fact reflected in its cost. Simply to hold the vote cost the federal government $125 million and the Quebec government $45 million; more than $10 million more was spent in advertising and polling by the combined Yes forces. Unquestionably, the results were a major disappointment to those who had confidently taken the Charlottetown Accord to the people.

Unlike the earlier referendums, in which the national Yes vote had concealed a deep split between the voters of Quebec and the rest of Canada, the 1992 vote was much less divisive because the results revealed broad-based opposition to the government's proposal. No region was isolated. Substantial numbers of No votes were cast in every region of the country. This outcome undoubtedly reduced the political alienation a regional split might have produced. Indeed, the way in which the accord was defeated may well have been the best possible result the élites could have hoped for.

There were, nevertheless, some significant regional differences in voting patterns. The accord was most emphatically rejected in the very parts of the country whose concerns the constitutional package was meant to address. The Prairies (Manitoba 61.7%, Saskatchewan 55.1%, and Alberta 60.2%) and British Columbia (67.8%) had overall rejection rates considerably higher than the national average. And the No vote in Quebec, at 55.4%, demonstrated that a significant number of "pro-federalist but nationalist" Liberals had joined forces with the hard-core separatist vote (estimated to be roughly 40%) to defeat the deal. Evidently the attempt to partially please all regional elements had led to universal unhappiness.

The rejection was so widespread that the more frequent post-referendum question posed by some analysts was why three of the four Atlantic provinces voted in *favour* of the accord. Part of the explanation would appear to be the credibility of the political leadership in those provinces — Clyde Wells in Newfoundland, Frank McKenna in New Brunswick, and Joe Ghiz in Prince Edward Island — a factor at odds with the generally low standing of their counterparts in the rest of the country.

In the rest of Canada the lack of credibility of federal and provincial political élites was not the determining factor in most voters' decisions, but it was a tangential influence. Their lack of faith in the elected officials forced many voters to trust their own judgement, despite their discomfort with the technical and complex nature of the subject. Knowing they were not experts in the field of constitutional law they would have preferred their elected representatives to resolve the matter. But for those who already instinctively disliked the contents of the deal, their lack of faith in those elected officials who had agreed to it tipped the scales in favour of a No vote.

Conversely, in Atlantic Canada, the high level of trust in their elected officials may well have led voters who were unsure of the merits of the deal to resolve the matter in the accord's favour. In addition, there is some evidence to suggest that the economic arguments of the Yes campaign may have made more of an impression in the Atlantic provinces. Their traditionally heavy dependence on transfer payments and equalization grants may have made citizens of those provinces more responsive to the suggestion that Quebec separation, with all its economic consequences, would follow from the defeat of the accord.

The results were instructive not only from provincial and regional perspectives but also with respect to the various interest groups that had taken a position on the accord. Perhaps most significant, the results demonstrated that a large number of native Canadians had rejected the deal despite the fact it was supported by their leadership and expressly designed to address their desire for aboriginal self-government.

In a precedent-setting move, the Chief Electoral Officer had agreed that votes of status Indians on reserves would be tabulated separately. The results showed that well over 70% had voted against the deal. This number undoubtedly underrepresented the degree of opposition, since many band chiefs had refused to allow polls to be set up on reserves, thereby forcing their members either to vote at polls off the reserve or to abstain from voting.

As Grand Chief Ovide Mercredi of the Assembly of First Nations (AFN) said when these results became known, even if there had been a national Yes vote, his association would have been obliged to reject the deal on the basis of this clear rejection by the rank and file. The split within the Indian community did not come as a total surprise: there had been several major confrontations between Mercredi and band chiefs in Quebec and the west during the campaign. Indeed, the refusal of the chiefs to formally support the accord at a national convention in British Columbia only a week before voting day had left Mercredi and his advisers in an embarrassing situation from which they never recovered.

The non-status Indian and Métis vote was not reported separately. There is some evidence, however, that both groups broadly supported the accord. Informal polls conducted by the umbrella association for these groups claimed that some 60% voted in favour of the deal. Meanwhile the Northwest Territories, with its predominant Inuit population, gave overwhelming support for the deal.

Voting Behaviour in the Referendum

On the whole, Canadians' voting behaviour in the national referendum bore little resemblance to the demographic trends usually observed in federal elections. There was, for example, no discernible gender gap, but a significant age gap and a reasonably clear voting distinction on the basis of class. These findings lead to the inescapable conclusion that Canadians viewed the referendum as a very different exercise than a federal election campaign, which of course it was.

In recent years, a significant gender gap has emerged in national elections with respect to party support. In the 1988 federal election, for example, roughly 10% more men than women voted for the Conservatives. By contrast, there was no apparent gender gap in the national referendum results at all. The margin between men and women voting yes, and the margin between those voting no, was in each case a statistically insignificant 2%. Given the No position taken by the National Action Committee on the Status of Women and its high-profile spokesperson, Judy Rebick, this lack of gender distinction is somewhat unexpected.

If gender was not a factor in the vote, class apparently was. This was surprising to political scientists, whose studies have tended to show that class rarely plays a part in Canadian elections. A Decima poll conducted for the October 28, 1992, edition of *Maclean's* magazine found significant differences in voting behaviour on the basis of both education and income, the two standard measures of class. According to the poll, voters whose annual income exceeded $60,000 were more likely to support than oppose the accord. And similarly, university graduates tended to vote in favour of the accord.

While the evidence of a class distinction in the referendum vote is significant in and of itself, the 10% margin between Yes and No voters on the basis of education and income masks another important finding, namely, that the No vote was significant at all education and income levels. It ranged from a low of 46% at the lowest income and education levels to a high of 56% at the upper levels. In addition, the high levels of support for the Yes side among upper-income and well-educated voters in Quebec and Ontario tend to distort the national numbers, masking considerably less class-biased voting in the Prairies and British Columbia, where the No vote attracted a majority of voters at all levels.

The most decisive demographic factor of this referendum vote, however, appears to have been age. By a margin of nearly two to one, voters under 65 were more likely to oppose the accord than support it. At 18 to 24 years, only 38% supported the accord and 62% rejected it. At 55 to 64 years, some 68% voted against the deal and only 32% supported it. Yet at over 65 these numbers suddenly reversed, with 61% voting yes and only 39% voting no.

A striking exception to this pattern occurs in one of the six defined age categories of the poll. Those between 45 and 54 years as a group supported the deal. Some analysts have concluded that these individuals, likely the most financially vulnerable category with mortgages and children still in school, were also the group most likely to feel threatened, apart from seniors on fixed incomes. Both groups, the argument goes, were therefore more likely to vote for the package for fear of the economic consequences of its rejection.

Demographic trends were not the only area in which the referendum vote differed from national election trends. The October vote had nothing at all to do with party affiliation. Although the three main federal parties all campaigned for the accord, neither their leaders nor their machines were able to deliver their supporters. Canadians clearly decided that, in a referendum, party lines were simply irrelevant.

Across the country, ridings held by prominent federal Conservative, Liberal, and NDP members voted overwhelmingly against the deal. None of Prime Minister Brian Mulroney, Constitutional Affairs Minister Joe Clark, or Justice Minister Kim Campbell was able to deliver a Yes vote in his or her own riding. Audrey McLaughlin's Yukon riding voted massively No, as did many labour and NDP strongholds across the country.

Liberals fared somewhat better, but probably only because their sitting members represent ridings predominantly in the Atlantic region and Ontario, the two regions where a substantial Yes vote was registered for other reasons. Individual riding results such as the exceptionally high Yes vote in Willowdale MP Jim Peterson's riding or the large No vote in the Davenport riding of Toronto MP Charles Caccia, an accord opponent, may well reflect the additional influence of hard work or immense personal popularity on the part of incumbents, but these examples were clearly the exceptions to the rule. Neither the Liberal Party's western lieutenant, Lloyd Axworthy, representing a Manitoba riding, nor former prime minister John Turner, in the British Columbia riding of Vancouver Quadra, was able to buck the No trend in the region to deliver a Yes vote in his own riding.

As for the effectiveness of the Yes campaign message, the results also showed voters did not believe the Yes side's argument that the failure of the accord would have serious consequences. Some 56% of voters outside Quebec agreed with the statement that the defeat of the accord would have "no real impact," as did 49% of Quebeckers. Among those Canadians who voted no, fully 65% agreed with that statement. Only 18% of Canadians and 29% of Quebeckers believed a defeat would mean the eventual breakup of the country.

Despite the argument of virtually all the political élites involved in the campaign that a better deal could not be negotiated, and that no future attempts would be made to achieve a consensus in the foreseeable future, some 54% of Quebeckers and 51% of Canadians interviewed in the *Maclean's*/Decima poll indicated a strong desire to have "a new attempt to get a constitutional agreement begin within a year."

Yes campaign supporters attempting to find an explanation for the defeat of the Charlottetown Accord have argued that voters made their decision out of an intense dislike of Prime Minister Brian Mulroney and Conservative government policies, or for selfish regional or personal reasons. The results of the poll do not support these interpretations. Only 8% of those who voted no indicated Mulroney was the issue, and a mere 2% agreed their decision had been based on the fact that "my province did not get as much as it could have." Interestingly, identical numbers of voters on the Yes side selected respect for prominent leaders (8%) and provincial gains (2%) as determining factors.

Taken together these results lead to an inescapable conclusion. It wasn't partisan politics, regional rivalry, resentment of the government, or even contempt for individual politicians that led to the defeat of the accord. It was the deal itself, and the process by which it was achieved and promoted, that did it in.

An Explanation of the No and Yes Votes

Outside Quebec, some 74% of voters identified the contents of the deal as the factor that helped them to make up their minds. For these Canadians, the issues of equality of the provinces (27%), strong central government (15%), and the more general "the deal is a poor one" (13%) were crucial.

Only 4% of No voters believed aboriginal peoples were given "too much." This refutes the notion put forward by the native leadership that Canadians had rejected the accord because of racial bias or out of a lack of concern for aboriginal issues. Indeed, 70% of those who voted no believed the issue should be addressed as a priority in future negotiations.

Within Quebec, fully 56% of those who rejected the deal believed it was a "poor one." according to Decima vice-president Michael Sullivan, "Most Quebeckers rejected the notion that Quebec did not get enough concessions at the table."

The reasons given for their decision by the supporters of the accord are even more revealing. Most of the Yes voters outside Quebec focused on the consequences of rejection rather than on the contents of the deal. More than a quarter of all Yes voters (26%) made their decisions in order to "help keep Canada together," while 15% wanted to "put constitutional matters behind us," and 13% believed a No vote "would be very negative for the country." Of the 22% of Yes supporters who did base their decision on the contents of the deal, the reason given was not support for a particular measure or constitutional principle, such as decentralized powers or collective rights, but rather the more general and revealing reason that it "represents a fair compromise."

In sum, supporters of the accord were unlikely to be moved by the No leaders' arguments about the contents of the deal, and No voters were unlikely to respond to the Yes campaign's emphasis on the consequences of rejection.

Taken together, the referendum results suggest two immediate conclusions: first, that in almost all respects the referendum campaign bore little or no resemblance to a federal election; and second, that there were two separate campaigns fought outside Quebec, appealing to two different sets of concerns, while the campaign in Quebec was an entirely separate process, unlike the others.

The referendum battle outside Quebec was dominated by two competing visions of Canada, the Yes side's personified by Brian Mulroney and Joe Clark, and the No side's by Pierre Trudeau. Mulroney and Clark advocated the more decentralized, asymmetrical federalism with a greater emphasis on collectivities, as embodied in the "two nations" concept of Canadian federalism. Trudeau argued for a strong central government, equal treatment of provinces, and the primacy of individual rights expressed in the Charter of Rights and Freedoms.

The philosophies of the opposing sides were different and so, not surprisingly, were their campaign strategies. The Yes campaign outside Quebec was dominated by a process-oriented strategy that emphasized both the degree of consensus achieved in the deal (rather than the precise contents) and the dire consequences of its rejection. The Yes campaign, in sum, defined the referendum question as one of national unity, in which rejection would spell the end of the country.

The No campaign vigorously rejected the Yes approach and defined the question exclusively as one concerning the contents of the deal: the referendum was to approve or reject the package, and nothing more.

Within Quebec a completely different campaign evolved. In that province the battle was between separatists and federalists, complicated by the addition of a "nationalist federalist" component led by Liberal Party dissident Jean Allaire. Instead of Trudeau and Mulroney, the key figures of the Quebec campaign were Robert Bourassa and Jacques Parizeau. While the No forces outside Quebec argued that the deal went too far in accommodating various provincial concerns, the No forces in Quebec argued it did not go far enough. Ironically, both No teams suggested that a better deal was possible in the future, thereby rejecting the universally held Yes view that the accord was the best and only deal possible in the foreseeable future.

What were the determining factors in these two very different campaigns? What lessons, if any, can be learned from the actual referendum process?

Lessons about the Referendum Process and the Campaign

To begin with, the lesson of the referendum for the Yes *organizers* was painfully clear. A referendum is not like an election. Consequently, the usual analysis of voting behaviour, the organizing practices, and campaign techniques of a full-scale election don't work. Despite a huge advantage in financing and human resources, the Yes side was totally unable to mount an effective campaign, while a ragtag collection of grassroots No supporters mounted a guerrilla attack that was devastatingly successful.

As pollsters and Yes campaigners both learned, the definition of the referendum question in voters' minds was a crucial issue. Having decided that a No vote did not mean no to Canada, but rather no to the deal, Canadians voted against the accord with a clear conscience.

The lessons for the political élite who decided to hold the vote are equally clear. Referendums are difficult to control, their outcome hard to predict. In a federal state, embracing a number of separate political jurisdictions, these difficulties increase exponentially. The legislation that made the October 1992 referendum possible was not explicit as to what would constitute a victory, making matters far worse. Practically speaking, anything less than a clear win nationally and in every province would have amounted to defeat for the Yes side. In effect, victory may always have been impossible for them to achieve.

To hold a referendum on an abstract issue such as the Constitution is always difficult. If the Charlottetown Accord had been merely a single amendment, rather than a massive restructuring of two-thirds of the nation's Constitution, it might have had a chance. A referendum is best suited to simple issues. When the question is complicated, the probability of a positive response diminishes dramatically.

As polls consistently revealed, Canadians were extremely unhappy with the referendum question. Many argued that a multiple set of questions or options other than yes and no as a response would have made the process more acceptable. As it was, the issues dealt with in the package were too complex, and the time frame for making a decision too short to absorb the arguments and make an informed decision on such an important matter.

This in turn leads to the entire issue of timing. To hold a referendum in the middle of the worst recession since the Great Depression, when political élites at both the provincial and the federal level were held in low esteem, was clearly an act of supreme folly. As sociologist Reginald Bibby of the University of Lethbridge wrote in the *Globe and Mail* of October 26, "Times of fragmentation and frustration are not times when politicians are wise to invite the citizenry to speak their minds...." In retrospect, the politicians were forced to recognize that they were simply not on the same wavelength as the people, whose main concern was the economy.

The campaign itself exacerbated these problems. It was perceived by Canadians to be a one-sided affair in favour of the Yes forces. With more money, staff, and other campaign resources at their disposal than they knew what to do with, the Yes organizers adopted a disastrous strategy of shows of force and unity that served to alienate many voters. Attempting to present a unified front at all costs, they succeeded in giving the unfortunate impression that the Establishment had closed ranks in support of the deal, regardless of its merits.

All things considered, it is hardly surprising that an underlying current of popular rebellion emerged during the referendum debate. The theme of "the little people" against the élites, first raised by Pierre Trudeau in his Maison Eggroll speech in Montreal, and repeated over and over again by members of the Reform Party and other opponents of the deal, struck a responsive chord with ordinary Canadians.

It appeared to many voters that an essential element of a pluralist liberal democracy — legitimate opposition — was missing from the debate. Canadians were sceptical when the political and corporate élite, labour, aboriginal, and media leaders presented a virtually united front in favour of the accord. Their concern increased when it became clear the only groups or individuals to articulate opposing

views were outsiders. The fringe Reform and Core parties, representatives of disadvantaged groups such as women, native women, and
the disabled (all of whom argued that they had been excluded from
the consultative process that produced the accord in the first place),
and a handful of dissident academics constituted the core of the opposition to the accord. This opposition, in turn, was crystallized by the
intervention of the ultimate outsider, non-conformist, and non-political politician, Pierre Trudeau.

The sense of a one-sided David-versus-Goliath campaign was
heightened by the obvious financial and personnel superiority of the
Yes side and by their initial campaign strategy of referring to opponents of the accord as enemies of Canada or disloyal, unpatriotic
Canadians. This misguided attempt to neutralize and marginalize opponents of the accord from the mainstream of Canadian politics was a
fundamental error that backfired almost immediately. It was followed
by an equally unsuccessful attempt to ridicule the No side's unlikely
alliance of Trudeau federalists, separatists, Reformers, and feminists;
this ill-conceived tactic only served to draw the public's attention to
the strange bedfellows *supporting* the accord.

As the Yes side began to recognize that it was in difficulty, the campaign rhetoric intensified. Predictions of impending disaster were sub-
stituted for the personal attacks on the accord's opponents. The Yes
side forgot the lessons of Meech Lake and once again warned that economic and social chaos, and the eventual separation of Quebec, would
inevitably follow if the accord was not approved. This time, however, there was an apathetic reaction to their threats as many voters concluded the élites had cried wolf once too often.

Given the need to win in every province, the Yes campaigners also
made the fatal mistake of singing from different hymn books. Supporters
of the deal in the various regional campaigns across the country ignored
the realities of modern telecommunications when they tailored their
message to local audiences. B.C. Intergovernmental Affairs Minister
Moe Sihota's classic blunder — telling a local audience that Quebec

had received "nothing" because Premier Bourassa had faced a "brick wall" of opposition from western premiers — did more to damage the chances of the Yes side in Quebec than almost anything except the daily revelations of the premier's own bureaucrats.

In the end, the majority of Canadians found the whole referendum process unsatisfactory. They had demanded that they be consulted over the course of the previous two years, but they found the process by which this consultation was implemented to be inadequate and stressful. Many who voted yes felt they had to "hold their noses" to do so; many who voted no did so with sadness and regret. As the callers to open-line shows on the day of the vote asserted over and over again, there were loyal and proud Canadians on both sides of the issue.

Reasons for the Referendum Call and the Accord's Defeat

As the analysis of the events leading to the Charlottetown Accord in the first section of the book demonstrates, the prime minister had not originally intended there would be a referendum. Joe Clark and several premiers had argued strenuously against it. Hardly anyone except the leader of the Opposition was initially supportive of the idea. So why was the referendum ever called?

In one sense, Mr. Mulroney and the other sponsors of the Charlottetown Accord had no choice but to call for a referendum. With three provinces already committed to holding a referendum by their own legislation, the practical desirability of superimposing a national referendum was self-evident. But there were far more serious reasons why *some* type of direct public involvement was considered necessary to validate the proposed changes agreed to by the elected representatives of the people. These reasons were rooted in the events of the previous ten years and, in particular, in the failure of the Meech Lake Accord.

The underlying factors that made the referendum vote necessary are explored in the first section of this book. The failure of the Meech

Lake Accord is placed in the broader context of the public expectations raised by the 1982 constitutional amendment process, a process in which various interest groups participated in an inclusive parliamentary committee review and the final package contained an entrenched charter of rights that was seen to respond to their concerns. The subsequent emergence of a "Charter society" and the expectation of a more open, inclusive constitutional reform process are shown to have had significant implications for the 1990 rejection of the Meech Lake agreement and subsequently for the hesitation of the political élite to proceed once more without the appearance of public consultation.

At the same time, the élites' failure to learn the correct lessons from the Meech Lake débâcle caused them to cut short the consultative process that began in 1990 and return to closed-door sessions that excluded significant groups and interests. As a result, the final product — the Charlottetown Accord — was as lacking in credibility as the Meech Lake Accord had been. The truncated consultative process did not produce the broad-based and knowledgeable support among Canadians that the 1982 process had done.

This lack of support was then exacerbated by the élites' decision to respond to the artificial timetable of the government of Quebec, proceeding immediately with a referendum vote before parliamentary committee hearings could be held to modify and improve the document. This in turn led to a ludicrous situation in which Joe Clark and others speculated that changes might well be made to the document *after* the vote had been held. Although it is doubtful the referendum could have succeeded in any event, this decision to proceed prematurely with the direct consultation was undoubtedly a fatal error akin to putting the cart before the horse.

Having decided to call the referendum, the élites then moved to ensure its success, in blissful ignorance of this strategic error. Although Brian Mulroney had hoped to avoid a national vote, he had already taken steps to ensure one would be possible if necessary. Aware of some of the practical problems of the referendum process that Clark and others had outlined, the federal government had carefully drafted the referendum legislation, and even the question, to stack the rules in favour of those supporting the accord.

When public opinion polls taken immediately after the signing of the accord in late August 1992 showed substantial support for the agreement both nationally and in every region of the country, the federal and provincial élites took advantage of the situation to schedule the vote with the least possible delay. What, after all, could a disorganized and underfunded opposition hope to accomplish in six weeks?

And yet the campaign was a disaster for the Yes team. Outmanoeuvred and outclassed by the disparate No forces, the 40% lead in the polls that the accord enjoyed on August 28 melted away in weeks. By the half-way mark of the campaign, the Yes forces knew they were in trouble in at least three provinces and began to suspect the national results might not be positive either. How could a campaign that was so carefully orchestrated have gone so wrong in such a short period of time? How could the élites have misread the degree of popular support and the climate of "constitutional fatigue" so badly?

The second section of this book examines the reasons for the failure of the Yes campaign. In it the inability of the political élites to understand the expectations of the Canadian public about the process of constitutional reform is all too clearly revealed. The analysis of the referendum campaign also makes clear the direct link between the élites' miscalculations and their underlying failure to appreciate the two profound and deeply held competing visions of Canadian federalism that exist in Quebec and the rest of Canada. Their strategic errors and their attempts to ignore or downplay these competing visions led inevitably to the defeat of the Charlottetown Accord.

Future Prospects

The referendum of October 1992 was a decisive if unintentional watershed in the evolution of Canadian federalism. A referendum that should not have been held and whose failure was all but inevitable, it will clearly have significant consequences for the evolution of the Canadian political process.

The final section of this book explores the potential consequences of this decisive referendum vote, both with respect to the short-term implications for those involved in the constitutional drama, and for the direction the country is now likely to take on outstanding constitutional reform issues as well as the political process as a whole.

An examination of the immediate implications for political leaders, their parties, and the leadership of other élites is followed by an overview of the likely fate of many of the issues raised in the accord itself. On several issues — aboriginal self-government, interprovincial trade barriers, and the redistribution of powers being the most obvious examples — current conflicts may actually be resolved more easily through administrative arrangements and federal-provincial negotiation. In future, attempts to change the rules of the game will undoubtedly need to be put forward in modest stages, through an open and inclusive process of public consultation.

In the longer term, the referendum may well have significant consequences for the traditional Canadian practice of élite accommodation, the credibility of political institutions, and the promotion of national unity within the federal state. Changes to parliamentary procedure and reform of the electoral system, in some respects long overdue, are other non-constitutional measures that must be taken to enhance the overall credibility of our political institutions and restore Canadians' faith in the political process.

Many experts argue that in relatively young countries, where different segments of the population hold different sets of political values and traditions, the wisest course is to avoid constitutional tinkering. In Canada, where at least three distinct cultural and political entities — anglophone, francophone, and aboriginal — are clearly identifiable, attempts to resolve many differences in a single binding document are certain to fail. The more rational approach now is to focus on legislative and symbolic measures that highlight common values and issues on which there is broad agreement. The really positive message implicit in the referendum result may be that Canadians have far more in common with one another than their current political leaders believe. It is this commonality of interests and views that the leadership will need to draw on in outlining a unifying national vision for Canada in the next century.

Saying No to Closed Doors: Lessons from the Past

Constitutions are meant to endure, if not forever, then for a very long time. Unlike ordinary legislation, which can be changed by a government at any time or by any new government when it comes to power, the constitution of a country normally can be changed only with considerable difficulty. Change, in other words, is permitted but not encouraged. It should be undertaken only if it is believed to be essential to maintain the stability of the state.

Constitutions reflect the heart and soul of a people. They embody the fundamental principles, and shared values and beliefs on which the citizens of a country base their political institutions and laws. A country's constitution is the bedrock on which its entire political system rests and from which it draws its legitimacy. Put another way, constitutions provide the basic framework or rules of the game for the operation of a country. Once established, a constitution is not something that should require the attention of politicians or citizens as they go about their daily business.

Indeed, no country can survive for long if its constitution is constantly changing. As in an established sport such as hockey — where players may be traded, leagues expanded, and individual franchises folded or moved, but the actual rules of the game rarely change — so in most western democracies political parties, governments, and laws often change, but few attempts are made to modify or amend the constitution.

The Canadian Constitutional Obsession

In this respect, at least, Canada is different. The October 26 referendum on the Charlottetown Accord was only the latest in a long line of constitutional initiatives undertaken by federal and provincial governments of all political stripes over the previous 125 years. In fact to the rest of the world, and to many Canadians, the seemingly endless round of constitutional negotiations, which began shortly after Confederation and has continued to the present day, has become an integral part of the Canadian national identity. Constitutional negotiations are a unique Canadian preoccupation and, arguably, a favourite pastime for the phalanx of politicians, bureaucrats, and legal experts who participate in them.

Few of these negotiations have been successful, but failure has never prevented their resumption for long. An examination of the major constitutional initiatives of the past few decades reveals a striking pattern of negotiation followed by agreement followed by failure. The pattern can be seen in the lengthy series of constitutional meetings in 1960 and 1961, for example, which led three years later to a proposal for constitutional amendment known as the Fulton-Favreau agreement. Initially accepted by all provinces in October 1964, it died a short while later when one province, Quebec, withdrew its assent.

No fewer than seven first ministers' conferences on the constitution were held between 1968 and 1971. They culminated in the Victoria Charter, an accord that all provinces agreed to present to their legislatures for approval or rejection. Although eight provinces ratified the deal and the ninth, Saskatchewan, would likely have done so if a provincial election had not intervened, the deal was ultimately rejected by the then premier of Quebec, Robert Bourassa, after he was subjected to intense political and media pressure. The Victoria Charter died as well.

Undaunted, Canadian politicians began another round of federal-provincial negotiations six years later. In 1978 the federal government introduced another formal proposal for constitutional amendment known as Bill C-60. It too died without being implemented. Yet another federal proposal was put forward in the fall of 1980 by the government of Pierre Elliott Trudeau. This proposal formed the basis of the 1982 constitutional amendment, the first successful amendment of the Canadian Constitution in 40 years. This amendment finally "patriated" the Constitution, that is, it brought home the decision-making power so that all future constitutional changes would be made in Canada without the need for British parliamentary approval.

As virtually all Canadians over the age of 10 know only too well, the Canadian "obsession" with constitutional change did not stop there. Under Prime Minister Mulroney another series of first ministers' conferences culminated in 1987 in the ill-fated Meech Lake Accord. Meech expired in June 1990 after it failed to achieve ratification by the required number of provinces. This failure led, in turn, to renewed negotiations between the federal and provincial governments and, ultimately, to the Charlottetown Accord on which Canadians recently passed judgement in a federal referendum.

After a century and a quarter Canadians, it seems, are still preoccupied with establishing the rules of their game. Why is our approach to constitution-making so different from that of other western countries? Are Canadians, as Brian Mulroney once lamented, a naturally "disputatious and fractious" lot, inordinately difficult to govern? Do we take a perverse delight in constitutional wrangling? Have Canadian politicians been peculiarly and inexplicably obsessed with the Constitution, perhaps at the expense of running the country?

The simple answer to these questions is no. Until 1982 at least the Canadian focus on the Constitution was a matter of necessity. It was caused, in the first instance, by the lack of an amending formula in the British North America (BNA) Act, the initial constitutional document drawn up by the Fathers of Confederation in 1867.

While it is true that changes to a constitution should never be undertaken casually, it is equally true that, over time, minor changes to any country's constitution are unavoidable. No "founding fathers" can expect to anticipate all future developments. The authors of constitutions accordingly anticipate the need for amendment and spell out the way in which it can be accomplished to ensure that change, while difficult, not only will be possible but can be accomplished smoothly, accurately reflecting the will of the majority of citizens.

For this reason, the constitutions of all other western democracies contain an amending formula. When changes are required, the politicians of the day have a clearly established procedure by which they make them.

No such provision was written into the BNA Act. The negotiations that led to the creation of the new country were complicated by a variety of considerations, some related to the governing institutions existing in Upper and Lower Canada and some related to their status as a colony of Britain. The authors of the document were unable to agree upon the form that an amending mechanism might take. The result was that any changes to Canada's Constitution had to be requested by the government of Canada and approved by the British parliament.

Not surprisingly, it was not long before Canadian politicians and many other Canadians became uncomfortable with the notion that Canada, as an independent country, should have to approach the British government with cap in hand every time it wished to make even the most minor change to its Constitution. On the other hand, before requesting "patriation" of the Constitution, it was felt by most politicians and constitutional experts that there should be prior agreement on the amending procedure to govern future change.

Although there is every reason to believe that the Fathers of Confederation thought of this arrangement as a temporary measure, it proved to be a nearly insurmountable problem. Patriation of the Constitution, and the need to agree first on an amending formula, bedevilled federal and provincial politicians in Canada for more than a century.[1]

The Constitutional Impasse and Administrative Federalism, 1945-1982

The Fulton-Favreau accord, the Victoria Charter, and Bill C-60 all proposed different methods for amending Canada's Constitution but

22 ♦ Strange Bedfellows, Trying Times

none received the unanimous support of the federal government and all provinces.

The problem wouldn't go away. Indeed, it became increasingly important as time passed and issues emerged that the Fathers of Confederation could not have anticipated. The absence of clearly assigned responsibility to the federal or provincial levels of government for areas such as manpower training, forestry, urban affairs, and housing was a growing irritant. More difficult still, certain responsibilities *had* been addressed and assigned to the provinces, but were becoming impossible for them to administer. Social services, education, and health care, thought to be of little consequence by the Fathers of Confederation, had become very consequential indeed in the second half of the 20th century. These areas made little or no claim on government purses in the late 1800s but made huge demands on those of their successors. Because of the division of responsibility laid down in the BNA Act, the provinces had few sources of revenue to finance spending in these areas, primarily because most methods of taxation were assigned to the federal government.

The provinces attempted to alter the balance by appeal to the British Judicial Committee of the Privy Council (JCPC) and later to the Supreme Court of Canada. These appeals largely failed. An initial tendency on the part of the JCPC to increase provincial responsibility shifted decisively the other way after 1949, when the Supreme Court became the final court of appeal for Canada. From the 1950s on, provincial politicians abandoned most attempts to come to a judicial resolution of their jurisdictional disputes and settled them instead through cost-sharing agreements and other administrative agreements.

The cost and complexity of negotiating these administrative arrangements increased exponentially over time. Federal-provincial meetings, and the structures to support them, evolved into a three-stage process of negotiation beginning with officials, progressing to ministers, and finally involving first ministers. In 1957 there were five federal-provincial committees at the ministerial level and 59 at the level

of officials. By 1977 these numbers had risen to 31 ministerial committees and 127 involving officials. Both the federal and provincial
governments created intergovernmental units in their bureaucracies,
and at the federal level the Canadian Intergovernmental Conference
Secretariat was also established to provide background materials and
logistical support for these meetings.

The growth in intergovernmental bureaucracy was actually proof
that this non-constitutional solution to many problems of co-ordination and administration worked well. In many policy areas, the degree
of co-operation between federal and provincial governments was
extremely high and led to improved delivery of services and uniform,
nationwide standards.

The cost-sharing approach also worked well for a time, as provinces
accepted the conditions imposed by the federal government in exchange
for fiscal largesse. The Canada Assistance Plan, medicare, and funding for post-secondary education were all financed through programs
that received massive transfers in federal payments, allowing many
of the poorer provinces to establish programs that would otherwise
not have been available to their citizens.

Over time, however, for a variety of reasons, these arrangements
became a source of increasing irritation to the provinces, and especially to the wealthier ones. Although a number of adjustments were made
in an attempt to ease the irritation, certain provinces continued to object
to the standards that were imposed by Ottawa. This was particularly true
in the area of health care, where one of the federal conditions was the
prohibition of user fees. As health care costs rose, the governments of
Ontario, Alberta, and Quebec variously attempted to introduce forms
of user fees to augment the income for these programs, only to be chas-
tised by Ottawa in the form of reduced transfer payments.

On the other hand, the lack of conditions in the agreements on post-
secondary education led to federal complaints about the system and
the numerous abuses of it by provinces. A case in point was the
province of British Columbia, which for many years spent less on

post-secondary education than the amount of money transferred for that purpose by the federal government, despite the fact that the agreement technically required the province to contribute an *equal* amount to the program over and above the federal contribution.

In the end the provinces concluded that the issues of funding and jurisdiction were too important to leave to such agreements. They returned to the idea of constitutional amendment as a better method of resolving federal-provincial jurisdictional disputes and to "modernize" the Constitution, bringing it in line with new realities.

The agenda of the federal-provincial constitutional conferences of the 1960s accordingly listed an additional set of items; the issues of patriation and an amending formula were now competing with the question of federal-provincial jurisdiction, cost sharing, and tax revenues. Although this made negotiations more complex and more antagonistic, it must be emphasized that it did not change the fundamental nature of the negotiation process. From 1867 until 1978 virtually all discussions about constitutional amendment involved only two sets of players — federal and provincial politicians — in a standard format of ministerial meetings and first ministers' conferences. This process came to be known as "executive federalism."[2]

The closed nature of these discussions is hardly surprising as their substance was both technical and obscure. Ordinary Canadians paid little attention either to the meetings or to their outcome. They were not unduly concerned about their high rate of failure. To most it appeared that these deliberations among the political élite had little if anything to do with their daily lives.

All of this changed with the entry of Pierre Elliott Trudeau to the federal political arena. A lawyer, professor, and authority on constitutional matters, Trudeau entered federal politics firmly committed to federalism as a unifying force in Canadian political life. His pan-Canadian vision, and the centralist view of federalism on which it depended for implementation, were to become the driving force behind almost all the actions of his government over the next two decades.

His opposition to Quebec nationalism and his determination to promote the federal government as an alternative source of power for francophone Canadians led to the enhanced promotion of bilingualism and a growing desire to entrench linguistic rights in the body of the Constitution, where they would be impervious to the whims of future governments.

Trudeau experienced at first hand the frustrations of executive federalism when, as minister of justice in the final years of the Pearson government, he participated in another round of first ministers' meetings. Given this experience, it was perhaps surprising that, when he assumed power himself, he chose not only to revive the process, but also to add yet another subject to the agenda.

The new prime minister's proposal added a set of language and civil rights to the suggested amending and patriation formulas. This was a time when human rights were emerging as an important issue. Former prime minister John Diefenbaker had already attempted to protect certain basic rights in his 1961 Bill of Rights. But, as an ordinary piece of legislation rather than a constitutionally entrenched document, the Bill of Rights had largely failed in its intent.

At a time when increasing international attention was being directed to the importance of constitutionally guaranteeing the fundamental rights and freedoms of citizens, Canada found itself with a constitution that did not contain any recognition of these rights. This, in turn, was due to the fact that the British parliamentary tradition, from which Canada's Constitution was drawn, based its guarantees of human rights on the common-law tradition rather than on formal declarations such as those found in the American or French constitutions. For many Canadians, a series of negative decisions by the courts on aboriginal and women's rights issues after 1961 heightened awareness of the absence of constitutional guarantees, and led them to conclude that the informal ones in the common law were no longer sufficient.

When taken together with the unique linguistic and equality issues that Canada faced as a bilingual and increasingly multicultural country — issues that the British constitutional tradition had not been forced to address — popular support for some formal type of entrenched guarantee of basic rights was growing and the prime minister's proposal was timed to take advantage of it.

In June 1971, Trudeau's gamble appeared to have paid off when the participants in the seventh round of negotiations since 1968 gave their initial consent to the Victoria Charter. They agreed not only to an amending formula and patriation, but also to the entrenchment of a number of "political and linguistic" rights and to a series of provisions affecting the Supreme Court, regional disparities, and future federal-provincial consultations. Trudeau, who wrote the introduction to the published proceedings himself, stated at the time that he believed the package represented "the most significant and comprehensive development in the search for a basis of constitutional revision since Confederation."

Small wonder, then, that the Victoria Charter's rejection by Quebec soon afterwards led to a seven-year hiatus in which only a few dispirited attempts at federal-provincial negotiation took place while the federal government focused on other matters. It was not until 1978 that the federal government once again turned its attention to the unresolved issue of constitutional reform, and then only because of unavoidable political pressures. Indeed, many observers believed this second initiative was primarily intended as a symbolic response to the election of René Lévesque and a separatist government in Quebec in late 1976. Lévesque himself often referred to Ottawa's sudden renewed interest in bilingualism and constitutional matters after 1976 as "Operation Panic."

Trudeau felt he had to respond to the separatist threat, but he was wary, now, of attempting to achieve constitutional change by working with the provinces. The package he put before the country actually dropped both the amending formula and proposals respecting federal spending powers — both issues that required provincial approval. Instead, in an obvious attempt to deal exclusively with areas in which the federal government had (or thought it had) sole jurisdiction, the package focused on institutional reform at the federal level and the entrenchment of language and other human rights in a federal charter. All other issues he set aside for a later, "second round" of negotiations.

The premiers were not amused by Trudeau's attempted end-run. They pointedly examined the package in detail and rejected most of its contents at their annual meeting in August 1978. Their antagonism may not, in itself, have scuttled the prime minister's plan. When a number of prominent legal experts raised questions about the federal government's authority to proceed alone on measures related to institutional reform, however, Trudeau abandoned the proposal.

It appeared that Trudeau might adopt again the mechanism of executive federalism, but the election in 1979 of Joe Clark's Conservative government cut short the attempt. Clark's own response to the rise of separatism was a decentralized version of federalism that Trudeau disapprovingly dubbed the "community of communities" approach. But Clark's tenure was short-lived. Trudeau's Liberal Party regained power in February 1980 in time to fight Quebec's upcoming referendum on their own terms.

These terms included an offer of a "renewed federalism." When Quebec answered Premier Lévesque's call for separation in the referendum of May 20, 1980, with a resounding no, the federalist cause was committed to embark on yet another round of constitutional reform. Trudeau promptly announced that his minister of justice, Jean Chrétien, would tour provincial capitals to explore the possibilities.

Trudeau Breaks the Impasse: The New Approach of the 1980-82 Negotiations

Both his admirers and critics agree that Pierre Trudeau changed irrevocably the traditional approach to constitutional reform in 1982. This dramatic change resulted from two significant innovations, both of which evolved out of his experiences of the previous decade. First, he bypassed the established procedures of executive federalism to break the constitutional impasse. Second, he included an entrenched charter of rights and freedoms in the amendment package.

It is debatable which of these two initiatives was more significant, but both played a major role in changing the direction of constitutional reform in Canada. The Mulroney government's failure to come to grips with the implications of the 1982 amendment led to the Meech Lake débâcle and, subsequently, to the decisive failure of the Charlottetown Accord.

The chain of events that set these initiatives in motion began on June 9, 1980, when the premiers met with the prime minister in Ottawa to establish a timetable for negotiations leading up to a full-fledged constitutional conference. Determined to set the agenda, the prime minister announced the federal government would provide a draft "plan of action" for discussion at these meetings. Referring to the "solemn commitment" to change that had been made in the Quebec referendum campaign, Trudeau also implied that if the meetings were not successful he would proceed without them, acting unilaterally through Parliament.

He was supported in this approach by Joe Clark, now the leader of the Opposition, who stated at a meeting of the Conservative Party in Toronto in June that "the participants in the conference speak for eleven governments. Parliament speaks for 23 million Canadians. If the First Ministers of the Federation cannot make marked progress towards changes which fit the Canada of the 1980s, then the Parliament of the Federation may have to assert a stronger role."

At the First Ministers' Conference in September, after months of behind-the-scenes negotiations among federal and provincial officials, the federal government tabled a 12-point agenda agreed to by the provinces and a copy of the government's draft plan to respond to some but not all of these items. The premiers debated for three days, in publicly televised sessions, but were unable to arrive at a consensus. A further day of private talks led to little change in the provinces' positions.

True to his word, Trudeau then took the first of a series of dramatic steps. On October 2, he announced in a nationally televised address that his government would table its own constitutional reform package in the House of Commons in the form of a proposed resolution for constitutional amendment. At the same time, he indicated that a parliamentary committee would be established to hear testimony from witnesses and that it would be instructed to report back to the House by December. Ratification by both the House of Commons and the Senate, and a request to Britain for approval of the package, would follow in early 1981.

This timetable was rendered obsolete almost immediately. It was not until April 1982, nearly 18 months later, that a considerably modified version of the government's constitutional proposal — a document that nevertheless patriated the Constitution, provided for an amending formula, and entrenched a charter of rights and freedoms — became the first successful amendment of the Canadian Constitution in 40 years and the last to be approved by Britain.

The delay was, on the face of it, surprising. Trudeau had indicated that he intended the package be pushed forward as rapidly as possible. But even Trudeau was unable to control the process that he set in motion. By excluding the provinces, he shut the doors on one set of players, but by moving the debate to Parliament, he opened them to many others.

The wheels began to fall off the constitutional express almost immediately. The parliamentary committee reported back to the House in November that it would need more time than the government had allocated to hear testimony from experts and recommend changes. In the end, the committee received written briefs from 163 groups and individuals and heard testimony from another 97 witnesses who appeared in person. Representatives of women's groups, the disabled, ethnocultural communities, and aboriginal peoples, as well as human rights specialists, appeared to present their opinions and suggestions for

change. For the first time ever the hearings of a parliamentary committee were televised in their entirety. It was estimated that tens of
thousands of Canadians tuned in on a daily basis to follow them.

Mr. Chrétien appeared before the committee in early November.
He assured committee members that every effort would be made to
accommodate the committee's recommendations. On January 12, 1981,
he returned to the committee to table a new document that took into
account many of the changes that witnesses had suggested.

Chrétien read from a prepared statement entitled "Government
Response to Representations for Change to the Proposed Resolution,"
in which the minister said, "The Government of Canada will accept
major changes to the Charter of Rights and Freedoms and the amending formula as set out in the Proposed Resolution. I have studied with
great care both the written briefs and the oral testimony... and I have
taken into account the points of view which have been expressed by
all members of this committee. The government has listened to the
views of Canadians." An information kit was distributed publicly identifying not only the proposed changes but the names of witnesses who
had suggested them.

The clause-by-clause study of the revised package that followed
resulted in an additional 67 amendments, including several that had
been suggested by the Conservative and NDP members of the committee. By the time the resolution left the committee, it had received
the express endorsement of almost all of the special interest groups,
expert witnesses, and individuals who had appeared before it.

Although the resolution was returned to the House for debate in
February, it was still under discussion nearly two months later. Ongoing
opposition by eight of the premiers (Ontario and New Brunswick having supported the resolution) to the unilateral action of the federal government had prompted both federal opposition parties, despite their
basic support for the contents of the deal, to call for the federal government to refer the resolution to the Supreme Court for a ruling on
whether the proposed unilateral action was constitutional.

Mr. Trudeau reluctantly gave in to this request in April 1981. This caused a further delay as the Supreme Court did not render its verdict until late September. When it did bring down its decision, it conveyed a decidedly mixed message, which led to confusion and further delay. In essence, the Court ruled that the government's plan to proceed unilaterally was constitutionally legal, but contravened a longstanding constitutional "convention" or traditional practice of consultation with and approval by the provinces. The Court indicated that unanimous provincial consent was unnecessary, but failed to state the number of provinces that were required to agree. It implied, however, that the two provinces that supported the federal proposal were too few.

Although many advisers and legal experts urged Mr. Trudeau to proceed with the final vote on the resolution in Parliament and take the package to Britain for approval, he decided in the end to return once more to the federal-provincial negotiating forum. Many believe that this was a serious mistake. In the event, it led to more changes to the package.

Nevertheless this last meeting of first ministers in early November 1981 was in several important respects unprecedented. On this occasion, as on no other occasion previously, the 11 leaders met to discuss the details of a federal package that had already received the implicit approval of Parliament and the explicit approval of virtually all interested groups in Canadian society. Moreover, the agreement enjoyed the strong support — demonstrated by public opinion polls — of the Canadian people. Equally important was the fact that, this time, the premiers were limited to making changes within the parameters set by the federal government. Having said that he would not trade "fish for rights," Prime Minister Trudeau had limited the debate by tabling a package that addressed only three of the 12 original items on the provinces' shopping list in September. The provincial input, in other words, was limited to responding to the federal agenda.

After three days of meetings, Mr. Trudeau and nine of the premiers signed an accord based on the federal resolution while Quebec's premier, René Lévesque, refused to do so. There were three significant modifications to the federal proposal. At the insistence of the premiers, the amending formula had been modified, a notwithstanding clause had been added to allow provincial governments to override certain sections of the Charter if they chose, and a section (34) recognizing and affirming aboriginal and treaty rights had been deleted.

With these changes in place, the resolution was again debated in Parliament. Although all parties expressed regret that Quebec's separatist government had not chosen to approve the agreement, and Mr. Trudeau expressly offered to delay passage of the package while federal and provincial officials discussed what other changes might be made to accommodate that province's concerns, it was clear that both opposition parties and all other provinces believed the federal government should proceed with the package, without Quebec's approval if necessary.

Meanwhile, in yet another dramatic indication of the degree to which non-partisan Canadians had been able to influence the outcome through testimony and lobbying, the aboriginal community succeeded in having section 34 restored to the text after it had been reintroduced in Parliament, and women's groups succeeded in having their equality rights section (28) removed from the influence of the notwithstanding clause.

The resolution was approved by Parliament on December 8, 1981, bringing to a close a remarkable process of constitutional negotiation unlike any that had gone before. The final product received the overwhelming support of politicians and political parties, both federal and provincial, and the vast majority of Canadians.

The Charter and the New Rules of the Game

The 1982 reform package failed to achieve the support of the Quebec government, but it was nonetheless a success in two significant respects. First, it resolved the two longstanding issues — repatriation of the

Constitution and provision of an amending formula — which all previous efforts had failed to resolve. Second, the process was popular. The exclusion of the premiers, and the repudiation of executive federalism for much of the time, and the inclusion, for the first time and in such effective fashion, of representatives of virtually all major interest groups and elements of Canadian society, combined to form a process that Canadians followed with interest and viewed as legitimate.

Indeed, there can be little doubt that the legitimacy of the final product owed a great deal to the highly credible inclusive, open, and responsive process by which it was achieved. Two months after the proclamation of the constitutional amendment in April 1982, Gallup reported that "in a ratio of four to one Canadians feel... our Constitution will be a good thing for Canada." Despite the refusal of Premier Lévesque to sign the agreement, only 16% of Quebeckers believed the 1982 amendment would "not be a good thing" while fully 49% stated that they positively supported it.

Ten years later the popularity of the Charter of Rights and Freedoms continues to grow. It is an integral element of the Canadian political culture, as important in its way as medicare and the baby bonus. Along with its popularity as a national symbol, the Charter has proven to be a living document. Much has been written in the past decade about the influence that it has had on the evolution of Canadian politics and constitutional jurisprudence. It has led, literally, to the creation of a Charter *society*.

Some commentators, political columnist Jeffrey Simpson among them, have lamented what they view as an unacceptable intrusion by the Charter, and hence by the courts, into the law-making domain of elected officials. Others have celebrated what they view as an invaluable tool to achieve the equal treatment of all citizens. No one would dispute the considerable use that a variety of disadvantaged, minority, and special interest groups have made of its provisions. Few would maintain that its effect — as found in Supreme Court rulings of recent years — has been entirely as they anticipated.

Virtually all would agree, however, that the Charter has become embedded in the national consciousness. Subsequent constitutional negotiations that appeared to threaten or alter its terms aroused strong reactions on the part of those groups who were represented within it, and the public at large. Having been given a stake in the Constitution through the Charter, where their rights were clearly set out, none of these groups or individuals was prepared to stand idly by while a small number of politicians appeared to renegotiate or eliminate them.

Political scientist Alan Cairns of the University of British Columbia has studied this evolving phenomenon at length. Speaking in April 1991 to another parliamentary committee, Professor Cairns noted that before 1982 the history of Canadian constitutional reform was "a debate among governments about the role of governments." Put another way, the debate leading to patriation in 1982 was "not a debate about how citizens might participate in an amending process, but about how powers should be distributed among Canadian governments when we removed the role of the British government in that process."

The Charter, according to Professor Cairns, changed the acceptability of that approach dramatically and irrevocably. It created "charter constituencies" with a vested interest in maintaining their place in the Constitution. "The reality," he concluded, "is that governments are no longer the sole inhabitants of the constitutional playing field. The Charter and the aboriginal constitutional clauses have generated new constitutional actors." Perhaps even more importantly, "the Constitution now speaks directly to citizens. It pulls them into the constitutional order. I would go so far as to argue that we now have to think of citizenship as a constitutional category in the same way we think of courts, legislatures, executives and the administration."

The Failure of the Meech Lake Accord under the Old Rules

Seen in light of these developments, the Mulroney government's subsequent negotiation of the ill-fated Meech Lake Accord in 1987 could not have been less compatible with the expectations of Canadians. The prime minister ignored the lessons of 1982 and returned to closed-door sessions of executive federalism. He excluded interest groups and stakeholders over the next three years despite their loud protests of outrage. He refused to contemplate any changes whatsoever in the original text — the so-called "seamless web" approach in which "not one comma" could be changed to respond to legitimate concerns. All of these positions were seen by the Canadian public as totally unacceptable.

When coupled with the atmosphere of intimidation, panic, and fear-mongering that pervaded the final year of the débâcle, when Mr. Mulroney and several premiers began to sense that the accord was in real difficulty, the failure of the Meech Lake process can only be described as inevitable.

Canadians did not like the prime minister's attempts to manipulate the process for his own ends, an attitude epitomized by his infamous "roll of the dice" line. They sympathized with aboriginal leaders who rallied around Elijah Harper in Manitoba as evidence of their dissatisfaction with that process. When Harper refused to grant permission to allow the vote in the Manitoba legislature by denying unanimous consent, and Clyde Wells steadfastly refused to call a final vote in Newfoundland later that day, most Canadians cheered. The turning-point in the accord's fate has often been described as the result of a single incident or combination of discrete events. A more substantial analysis demonstrates that this view is superficial and misses entirely the significant shift in public attitude towards the entire process of constitutional reform.

Both the Meech Lake agreement and the process by which it was achieved were flawed. The Canadian people rejected both the process, which excluded them, and the agreement, which diminished the effect of the Charter of Rights. The underlying problem was neither the prime minister's propensity for gambling nor the principled obstructionism of individual politicians, but the prior failure of the political élite to come up with an agreement that reflected the values and aspirations of Canadians.

In sharp contrast to the 1982 process, public support for the Meech Lake Accord fell throughout the three-year period of debate. By May 1990 fewer than one in four Canadians believed the deal would be "a good thing" for the country, and even in Quebec, for whom its acceptance was described by the prime minister as crucial to national unity, it received the support of less than half (41%) of the population.

The federal government would later claim that the 1982 amending formula was partly to blame for the failure of the Meech Lake agreement. Stephen Scott of McGill University emphatically rejected this suggestion when he testified before a parliamentary committee in August 1990. Scott identified three problems with the Meech process: "The perceived substantive defects... the methods by which the package was devised... and third, and most important, the extreme methods employed in the attempt to secure its passage."

Several witnesses who appeared before the same committee emphasized the need to build on the lessons learned in Meech before embarking on future constitutional reforms. "Absolute government control of the total process of the kind attempted in Meech Lake is no longer possible... There must be significant time and occasion for public input," declared Allan Cairns, who called for public participation not only during the discussion stage, but also "at the ratification stage via referenda." The feeling that the prime minister and the premiers had lost credibility was widespread, and the call for public approval of any future agreement was taken up in many quarters. The fateful word, referendum, had been spoken, but few yet thought that it would be necessary or wise.

Opening Up the Process?
From Spicer to Charlottetown

The day after the Meech Lake agreement died, the sky did not fall, as some supporters had said it would, nor did the stock markets crash, nor did the country come apart. It was business as usual, and yet, in certain respects, the country would never be the same.

The failure of the Meech Lake agreement *mattered* to Canadians as no previous constitutional impasse had. Ordinary Canadians felt that the deal would affect them directly. They saw themselves as having a stake in the outcome. They actually had taken sides on the issue, as if it were an election campaign rather than a dispute over constitutional amendments. They came to see the failure of Meech Lake as the political élite had encouraged them to see it — as a failure of the country and of national unity. The agreement's demise produced a sense of crisis that had never been present before.

There were several reasons that this failure was taken to heart. First, all the groups and individuals involved in the 1982 process had expected automatically to participate in 1987. They had been astonished to find themselves shut out. Representatives of women, aboriginal peoples, and the ethnocultural community, for example, had tried to have their views influence the negotiations in a variety of ways, but time after time they had been rebuffed. In the end, many came to see the Meech Lake process as one involving only "11 white males in suits."

If those on the outside of the Meech Lake process felt excluded, then many of those on the inside felt betrayed. From Brian Mulroney's point of view, he had tried his best to cut a deal that gave something to everyone. Unable to understand that his brokerage approach to constitution-making was totally unsuitable, when that approach failed he simply could not believe it. Many others who had supported the deal followed Mulroney's example and became cynical and withdrawn.

Thus failure, for both supporters and opponents, left a bitter taste in the mouth.

A second reason that the failure of the Meech Lake Accord had such an impact on the country was the vacuum that followed its demise. Parliament was in recess, the prime minister went into seclusion at his Harrington Lake retreat, and scarcely any statements were issued from the PMO. With the near total absence of the federal government from public view over the next two months, the bitterness that existed on June 24 was allowed to simmer and come to a boil over the summer. As federal politicians disappeared, Quebec nationalists and western extremists filled the void, dominating the nightly newscasts.

Throughout the summer, the Reform Party increased its profile and credibility in western Canada. On July 25, 1990, Prime Minister Mulroney's former friend, ally, and cabinet colleague, Lucien Bouchard, who had already resigned from cabinet and the Conservative caucus over Meech Lake, announced that he was creating a new federal political party — the Bloc Québécois — committed to achieving Quebec's independence. Bouchard was joined when he made this announcement by several disaffected Quebec Conservative backbenchers who were prepared to cross the floor. Two Liberal MPs from Quebec also appeared at Bouchard's side. Their motives were less clear, but undoubtedly were based in part on their unhappiness over the recent election as Liberal Party leader of Jean Chrétien, an opponent of Meech Lake.

The appearance of two new protest parties was significant. But it was the Oka crisis that dominated the national scene in the summer of 1990. The incident that started the trouble was apparently minor: a municipality set aside disputed Indian lands for a golf course. The result, however, was an international incident made worse by the failure of Meech Lake and its bitter aftermath.

At the same time that the political élite was in retreat, the native leaders were very much in evidence, still furious over their exclusion from the Meech Lake process and eager to support the Mohawk claims at Oka. The extent of their unhappiness had already been demonstrated by their support for Elijah Harper, a native Canadian and member of the Manitoba legislature who had blocked passage of the accord in that province. Aboriginal representatives from across the country had lent their support to Harper's undertaking, making it clear that he spoke for more than his immediate constituents when he refused the necessary unanimous consent.

Over the summer the dispute at Oka was allowed to mushroom from a minor incident to a full-blown crisis of national proportions. Natives wearing masks and carrying automatic weapons blocked a major road, causing havoc to commuters. The Quebec provincial police were finally withdrawn and the army was called in. Confrontations between the two groups became the stuff of nightly newscasts.

Groups such as the Canadian Council of Churches and the Canadian Human Rights Commission condemned the government's inaction as a total abdication of responsibility and called for the appointment of a federal mediator as well as the recall of Parliament.

As the situation deteriorated further, embarrassed Canadians were treated to the spectacle of representatives from Amnesty International, the United Nations, and the European Human Rights Commission paying visits to observe Canada's handling of the affair and report to the world. Despite this unwelcome notoriety and the threat of violence that was looming large, Parliament was never recalled. Few aboriginal Canadians failed to conclude that their concerns mattered little to the federal government.

The vast majority of Canadians were equally dissatisfied with the performance of their political leaders in this affair. By fall 1990, a national poll indicated that more than 70% of Canadians believed the federal government had mishandled the Oka crisis and fully 75% believed Parliament should have been recalled.

The Canadian public had no difficulty discerning the link between the failure of Meech Lake and Oka. Three months after Meech died, some 85% of Canadians still approved of Elijah Harper's decision to oppose it, and more than 50% described aboriginal rights issues — not the resolution of the "Quebec round" — as the most important outstanding item on the constitutional agenda.

At the end of the summer, support was also growing in all regions of the country for some type of formal consultation process, both on the regular issues confronting Parliament and the provincial legislatures, and on the specific issue of constitutional reform. One major nationwide poll reported that 77% of Canadians wanted to see governments "obliged" to participate in "full public consultation processes" before making "major" decisions. Some 55% were in favour of being able to remove elected representatives from office by petition before the expiry of their term.

Establishing a Consultation Process

When Parliament was finally recalled in late September, a subdued prime minister was faced with the prospect of a lengthy winter of discontent among not just native peoples but Canadians generally. Unable to ignore any longer the visceral climate of unease and national despair that was sweeping the country, and acutely aware of the continuing criticism of Meech Lake as a closed-door exercise in deal making, he responded by acknowledging the need for widespread public consultation to restore Canadians' confidence in their politicians and their political system.

Mr. Mulroney indicated that his government would take a number of initiatives to facilitate public consultation. He announced the creation of the first immediately: the Citizens' Forum on Canada's Future. Speaking in the House of Commons, Mulroney described the forum as an "independent body of eminent Canadians" whose mandate would be to "launch a dialogue with people across the country and help create a consensus about Canada and our future." The forum was given eight months in which to conduct its work and was instructed to report back to Parliament by July 1, 1991.

Keith Spicer was named chairman of the forum. Spicer, a colourful former academic and journalist, at the time of his appointment was chairman of the Canadian Radio - television and Telecommunications Commission (CRTC). His co-chairs represented a wide range of backgrounds, skills, and views, as he was soon to learn. Unfortunately the government's bold new experiment did not get off to a good start, largely because of the haphazard way in which it was put together.

Within weeks, the forum was in difficulty. It lacked organizational coherence, an overall plan of action, and most of all, agreement among the 12 commissioners. Public disputes at members' organizational meetings became the rule rather than the exception. Some members resigned. There were questions about the expenditure of funds and the propriety of the financial arrangements. Finally, the government sent in a team of senior bureaucrats to assist him, and Spicer's Citizens' Forum began to achieve some measure of coherence.

By the time the Forum Report was tabled on Canada Day of the following year, 1991, some 400,000 citizens had participated in its deliberations through group discussions, community meetings, the toll-free telephone hotline, and student forums, and by submitting briefs and letters.

In fact, the forum's impact began to be felt long before the final report was issued. By early February 1991, a leaked summary of the contents of hotline calls revealed a level of discontent across the country that was still astonishingly high. It could not be denied, however, that two of the most significant recurring recommendations of hotline callers were impeaching the prime minister (a device not available in our parliamentary system of government) and ensuring that a constituent assembly, referendum, or other form of direct consultation be a compulsory part of any future constitutional reform process.

Not surprisingly, the final report of the forum reiterated these recommendations. Chairman Spicer wrote that "some variation on the assembly idea and on citizens' ratification of our constitutional ground rules seem necessary to restore our people's sense of owning their democracy." Without referring directly to the strong-arm tactics and doomsday scenarios of the Meech Lake supporters, which had led to the post-failure crisis, Spicer also noted that "a political system at least partly designed by the people and broadly approved by them will be far easier to trust, as will the politicians representing us within it." Spicer ended the report with the warning that the need to consult must be taken very seriously by politicians. "No hyperbole or political hedge," he declared, "can screen any member of any legislature who thwarts the will of the people on this matter. The voters are watching and waiting."

Even while the forum was conducting its hearings, the federal government was already planning a renewed effort at constitutional reform. To the astonishment of some, spokespersons for the prime minister put forward the proposition that only Brian Mulroney could lead Canada out of the constitutional wilderness.

Shortly thereafter the prime minister himself began speculating on the possibility of a new agreement based on a much broader range of topics than the Meech Lake Accord. It would be, he suggested, a more inclusive process that would resolve not only Quebec's outstanding concerns but also those of the western provinces, native peoples, and other special interests — a "Canada round" rather than a "Quebec round."

These references to a possible new round of constitutional negotiations increased throughout February and March. The theme was picked up and reinforced by senior cabinet ministers. By April the idea of a new attempt at constitutional reform was firmly entrenched; speculation among premiers, academics, and the media was now focusing on possible items of negotiation, not on whether there would in fact be discussions.

On April 21 Mulroney announced a cabinet shuffle. It had been expected for some time and was rumoured to have been delayed more than once because of the reluctance of senior cabinet ministers to leave their portfolios. In an obvious move to shore up support for his government among alienated western Canadians and Quebeckers, with whom Joe Clark still had considerable personal credibility, the prime minister appointed his minister of external affairs to the newly created post of minister for constitutional affairs. Clark evidently sensed that the task might easily lead to a political graveyard and was known to have vigorously resisted the appointment. (More than a year later, when victory appeared to be within his grasp, Clark alluded in the House of Commons to his initial reluctance to accept the portfolio: "As the prime minister will attest, I did not exactly volunteer for this assignment.")

At the ceremonial swearing in of the new cabinet later that month, the prime minister clearly indicated that his government had a constitutional game plan. The "Unity Cabinet," as he called it, was being appointed to deal with the "vital" issues of "national reconciliation" and national unity. To that end, he declared, the federal government would build on the consultative process already underway in the form of the Spicer Commission.

The Throne Speech that followed in May 1991 continued to stress the importance of public consultation. The speech contained the announcement that the cabinet would "formulate new proposals to focus public discussion on the goal of a more united and prosperous Canada." These proposals would then be referred to a special parliamentary committee in September. The committee's mandate would be to "hear the views of men and women across Canada," as well as provincial legislators and representatives of aboriginal peoples. The committee would report back to Parliament by the end of February 1992. After consideration of the committee's report, the government "would propose a plan for a renewed Canada for consideration by the people of Canada." To that end, legislation would also be tabled to allow the federal government to hold a national referendum on the proposals.

This plan was well-received by most observers. They contrasted it favourably with the ad hoc negotiating tactics and pressure-cooker scenario that had characterized the Meech Lake process.

The sense that the federal government had again taken charge of the constitutional agenda was undercut to some extent by the publication of the final report of the Spicer Citizens' Forum on July 1. The report described the government and the prime minister as "very, very unpopular people" who were not trusted by many ordinary Canadians. Spicer suggested in the foreword to his report that it would be difficult to overestimate the importance of this discontent. Although he noted that much of it was directed at Brian Mulroney personally ("There is fury in the land against the prime minister"), he also remarked that Mr. Mulroney was serving as a lightning-rod for widespread unhappiness on a range of issues. And he emphasized again the need for every step of the new process to be taken only after lengthy consultation and consensus building.

The government apparently took the lecture in stride. The federal cabinet's priorities and planning committee met many times over the summer of 1991 to attempt to put together a package that could find favour with most Canadians. The meetings of the committee were high-profile, public relations events in which jovial ministers posed for photo opportunities. As time passed and the deep internal divisions between Quebec ministers, led by Benoît Bouchard, and western ministers, led by Joe Clark and Don Mazankowski, became evident, however, the meetings became more secretive and the ministers more subdued. Internal feuds erupted into public view more than once.

In early August, the prime minister addressed the national unity issue publicly at the annual general meeting of the federal Conservative Party in Toronto. Referring many times to his illustrious predecessor Sir John A. Macdonald, Mulroney told a receptive audience that he would engage in an "all-out fight" against a "disastrous" breakup of the Canadian federation. Referring to the threats posed by the Bloc Québécois and the Reform Party, he declared, "My only enemies are the enemies of Canada." There would be no national election before 1993, he announced, so that the government could formulate its proposals and resolve the national unity crisis.

The proposals were more easily promised than delivered. On September 3, Graham Fraser reported in the *Globe and Mail* that "although Mr. Mulroney has been trying to lower expectations in Quebec and increase flexibility and openness to change in the rest of Canada, he still has to forge an agreement that his own cabinet can live with." This was still the case two weeks later when Parliament reconvened.

Finally, on September 24, 1991, the government tabled in the House of Commons a package of constitutional proposals. The following day, the formation of a special all-party parliamentary committee was announced. It was to be chaired by Manitoba Conservative MP Dorothy Dobbie and Quebec Conservative Senator Claude Castonguay. The government also issued a glossy brochure, "Shaping Canada's Future Together," which it made available to individual Canadians on request.

Like the Citizens' Forum before it, the Dobbie-Castonguay Committee had problems getting off the ground. Early rumours of infighting among members became public rows barely two weeks after the committee was formed. NDP and Liberal committee members accused the co-chair, Dorothy Dobbie, of patronage appointments of staff, exorbitant expenditures, and hopeless disorganization. It became apparent that at least the last of the three charges was true when, in early November, the committee travelled to Manitoba to hold hearings, which no one attended. The spirit in which the meetings were being conducted also came into question when, at several venues, witnesses with testimony likely to be unfavourable to the proposals were prevented from speaking.

The issue climaxed with the committee's abrupt cancellation of its schedule and return to Ottawa on November 6. Almost immediately, co-chair Claude Castonguay resigned, citing ill health, and was replaced by Senator Gérald Beaudoin. After two weeks of sparring in which both opposition parties called unsuccessfully for Ms. Dobbie's resignation and threatened to boycott any future meetings of the committee, the crisis was finally resolved and the committee resumed its program. But the damage had been done.

Constitutional Affairs Minister Joe Clark attempted to salvage the situation by announcing on November 13 that five policy forums open to the general public would be held across the country in January and February. The proposal struck some as redundant, with the Beaudoin-Dobbie hearings back on the rails, but support for it grew. When it became apparent to Clark that the criticism of the aboriginal leaders about their exclusion from the process would continue if they were not accorded some measure of consultation, the possibility of using the conferences to achieve this objective added to their appeal. In the end, the five conferences were convened in Halifax, Toronto, Montreal, Calgary, and Vancouver between January 17 and February 28.

These conferences were widely viewed as a significant public relations success. They gave a much clearer impression of citizen participation and consultation than the Beaudoin-Dobbie Committee ever achieved. Behind the scenes, however, some observers were distressed by the obvious attempts on the part of the organizers to manipulate the final results. It was noted, for example, that the "general public" participants at each conference were carefully selected; the meetings were packed with representatives of the business and political élites favourable to the government's package; and moderators or "facilitators" in some workshops blatantly shepherded the participants towards a prearranged objective.

Nevertheless, in at least three of the conferences, the "ordinary Canadian" participants were perceived by many observers to have seized the agenda from the government. As columnist Deborah Dowling of the *Ottawa Citizen* wrote after the third conference in Montreal: "This weekend they killed the government's ideas for a strengthened economic union, last weekend in Calgary they shot down an equal Senate, and in Halifax the weekend before they murdered wholesale decentralization."

The positive spin on these conferences was heightened by the release on February 28, 1992, of the Beaudoin-Dobbie Committee's report, which was submitted with the agreement of all three federal parties.

Although many interested observers were critical of certain aspects of the report, it had obviously attempted to remedy some of the problems with the original proposal that had been identified by witnesses in their hearings. Almost everyone was prepared to view its recommendations as a "good basis" for discussion. The consultative approach and the carefully crafted game plan appeared to be working.

Responding to the Quebec Timetable

The world, of course, was not standing still while the federal government's consultative mechanisms shifted from low to high gear. After the defeat of Meech Lake, Quebec Premier Robert Bourassa had borne separatist taunts that Quebec had been "rejected" by the rest of Canada and nationalist-inspired accusations of weakness from within his own party. In Bourassa's view it was now clearly impossible to promote the status quo. His first move was to refuse to allow Quebec ministers or officials to attend any federal-provincial meetings. When the conventional wisdom developed that it would be impossible in future to accept anything "less" than Meech Lake had offered, Bourassa did nothing to discourage that line of thinking. Since Brian Mulroney was in no position to offer anything to Quebec at that time in any event, Bourassa may well have considered his support for the nationalist position to be somewhat academic and therefore harmless.

At about the same time that Mulroney set in motion the Spicer Forum, Bourassa appointed a special internal committee of the Quebec Liberal Party to consider the minimum requirements for any further round of constitutional negotiations. Bourassa doubtless hoped that the Allaire Committee (named after Liberal backroom organizer and lawyer Jean Allaire) would dispel some of the support for separatism. He also established the Campeau-Bélanger Commission. This was a bipartisan (Liberal and Parti Québécois) public inquiry, which invited participation from leaders of the business and labour communities to examine "the political and economic future of Quebec."

The Allaire Committee report was made public on January 28, 1991, while Spicer was still consulting. Its recommendations undoubtedly came as a shock to Robert Bourassa. In effect, it appeared that the committee had been won over entirely by the extreme nationalists. As more than one critic of the report noted, its exhaustive list of recommendations for the transfer of powers from the federal government to Quebec would have left the national government with little to do except wage wars and handle postage. Reaction from moderate Quebec federalists and other premiers was swift and highly critical. Unfortunately for the premier, he could not simply dismiss the report out of hand. The contents of the report, while not yet party policy, would have to be discussed and voted upon at the party's upcoming general convention.

The report of the Campeau-Bélanger Commission, released March 27, 1991, was tamer. It was nevertheless clear that neither commissioner harboured any firm attachment to Canadian federalism as it had been practised to date. Their principal recommendation was that Quebec should proceed promptly to hold a referendum on the sovereignty issue if no acceptable agreement could be reached with the federal government and the other premiers on a replacement package for Meech Lake. They even described the nature of the legislation that the government should table to establish the referendum.

The premier found himself between a rock and a hard place. Both commissions were his creations, after all. On the one hand, many of his party militants wanted to pursue the extremist recommendations of the Allaire Report immediately. On the other hand, the separatists under Jacques Parizeau seized upon the proposal for a referendum on sovereignty and pushed for it mercilessly. Bourassa viewed both options as either unacceptable or unworkable, or both, and so engineered a compromise.

He introduced referendum legislation to the provincial legislature on May 15, 1991. In this legislation hc committed the government to hold a referendum on sovereignty-association if the federal government had not made an appropriate proposal within the coming year.

His comments shortly thereafter, however, made it clear that he would be prepared to amend the timing or the question "if necessary."

These events in Quebec led to the dramatic intensification of the Mulroney government's constitutional efforts in May 1991, as reflected in the throne speech. The impetus for the federal government to proceed with its national reconciliation agenda therefore came not only from the high level of public discontent in other parts of Canada, but also from the perceived clear and present "danger" that the Quebec government's agenda presented.

Both governments came to be impelled to ever more frantic efforts by artificial timetables. The federal government was driven by the Quebec agenda and the Quebec agenda was driven by a self-imposed deadline.

The galvanizing effect of the developments in Quebec on the federal government can hardly be exaggerated. The open, participatory process that began in early 1991 was transformed, by February 1992, into something quite different. The Mulroney government was seized by the conviction that a Quebec referendum on sovereignty must be avoided at all costs and that the only way to avoid it was to present a set of federal "offers" to Quebec. The entire tone and tenor of the federal government's constitutional initiative changed dramatically. With only a few months to go before the Quebec deadline, the government returned to closed doors and executive federalism.

Returning to Closed Doors

On March 12, 1992 the traditional approach of federal-provincial constitutional negotiation resumed. Sooner or later the federal government had to go to the provinces with its proposals. That much was inevitable. The credibility of the negotiations that followed would have been greatly enhanced, however, if the meetings had been televised and the various provincial negotiating positions made public.

But this was not to be. Indeed, for the next several months little was known of the behind-the-scenes negotiations among the premiers and their officials. The one dramatic departure from the Meech Lake process was the inclusion in some of the meetings, after prolonged resistance, of representatives of native peoples. This decision, which was clearly a coup for Grand Chief Ovide Mercredi of the Assembly of First Nations, was a highly positive step in the view of ordinary Canadians and may have done much to prevent a critical public reaction to the return to closed doors. In a sense, with the inclusion of Mercredi and representatives of the Métis and Inuit peoples the doors, for many Canadians, remained at least slightly ajar. Representatives of women and ethnocultural groups continued to complain about their lack of a presence at the bargaining table, but their government steadfastly refused to include them.

Progress was slow. Premier Bourassa let it be known that he was extremely anxious about the upcoming referendum deadline. By June 24, when the House of Commons went into recess, the prime minister lost patience. He declared that he would recall Parliament by mid-July and table a unilateral federal package if the premiers could not agree to one of their own before then.

Mulroney had already tabled legislation to permit the federal government to hold a national referendum "in one or more provinces" if it wished. Although at the time he did not expect or want to make use of it, particularly as his advisers were cautioning that its potential dangers were many, the legislation served as a convenient reminder to the premiers that the failure of one or two to comply with an emerging consensus could always be dealt with by appealing over their heads to their constituents.

The first ministers met again in Ottawa on June 29, but reached no agreement except to meet again. Several of the premiers objected to the increased pressure and pace. Premier Bob Rae of Ontario in particular complained about the continued absence from the negotiating table of Robert Bourassa, which he regarded as an almost-impossible hindrance to effective consensus building. Saskatchewan's Roy

Romanow, a newcomer to this post-Meech round of talks, referred to the prime minister in a CBC interview near the end of one of these sessions as "the quintessential deal maker" and a man with "no specific vision as to the nature of Canadian federalism." Clyde Wells, the deal breaker on Meech, left in an obvious huff with no comments.

On June 30 the changes to the Quebec referendum legislation were passed in the National Assembly. In Ottawa the premiers reached a tentative agreement on Senate reform and then, in a matter of days, on a number of other issues. The meetings followed one another now at a breakneck pace. Premier Bourassa finally agreed to attend a "lunch" at Harrington Lake with the prime minister and the other premiers, but it was strictly understood that no content would be discussed, only the question of whether there was enough of a consensus to justify his return to the table!

Anatomy of a Deal

This ludicrous situation led to no agreement but some subdued expressions and vague comments from the premiers as they left. Many now believed for the first time that no deal was possible. Despite their misgivings, the nine premiers agreed to meet again without the presence of Bourassa, determined to avoid a scenario in which the federal government proceeded without them, something they suspected was being planned behind the scenes. This in turn led to the now infamous series of meetings between the premiers in Toronto at which Joe Clark was present along with federal officials, while the prime minister was in Europe on government business.

The next few days saw "miracle breakthroughs," "dramatic interventions," and "patriotic" compromises made by all of the players at the table. In an atmosphere eerily similar to the final Meech Lake negotiations in Ottawa in June 1990, the image of a pressure cooker and a sense of urgency prevailed. By now the original federal proposals, Beaudoin-Dobbie, and the five policy conferences had been long forgotten. The first ministers were in uncharted waters, improvising solutions — as Bob Rae later admitted — at the drop of a hat, using laptop computers.

To the astonishment of almost everyone, the participants emerged from several days of intense closed-door negotiations to announce that a firm deal had been reached. Several of the elated premiers indicated that the deal had the tacit approval of Quebec, a belief that sprang from their understanding of the role that Clark and his officials had been playing during the meetings, apparently keeping in constant touch with Quebec spokespersons.

Brian Mulroney was as astonished by the announcement as everyone else. This deal was not supposed to have happened. As several senior officials later indirectly confirmed, the prime minister had left for Europe confident that no deal would be possible. Moreover, rumours abounded that he and the Quebec premier had already agreed on an alternative strategy just as the other premiers had suspected. In this plan, the federal government would proceed to table its own package in the House, a package to which Quebec would have already given its tacit approval.

Whether Joe Clark had not been informed of this strategy, or had chosen deliberately to ignore it, remains a matter of considerable controversy.

What was only too clear was the fact that there had been a second game plan, a hidden federal agenda, which had come to grief. A furious Mulroney was now obliged to scrap the second plan and attempt to forge out of the package to which Clark and the premiers had agreed a consensus that Quebec could accept. Mulroney personally considered this package to be unsaleable.

Meanwhile Robert Bourassa was also having considerable difficulty putting the best face possible on the unwanted agreement. Consultations continued for several days between Ottawa and Quebec City before either leader was able to say anything reasonably positive about the deal. For Bourassa, the timing was critical. He was bound to hold a referendum on October 26, and he firmly intended that the question on the ballot would refer to a set of federal offers for renewed federalism, not sovereignty-association.

In the end, all the premiers attended another meeting in Ottawa with the prime minister. By now some were threatening to withdraw their support for the package if a comma were changed, and many were furious with the prime minister and Bourassa for having allowed them to believe they had reached this deal with the tacit approval of Quebec only to be told that, in Quebec's view, this "firm deal" was only "a draft proposal for discussion." B.C. premier Mike Harcourt had already found himself in hot water over provisions on the Senate and House of Commons that appeared to work to the disadvantage of his province and would have been only too happy to have a reason to back out.

In the final analysis, the deal had to be one that Robert Bourassa could return home and "sell" in the referendum campaign. The other premiers, in return, now believed they had to be able to show that they, too, had achieved something for their province in exchange for the compromises with Quebec. Although some premiers, notably Newfoundland's Clyde Wells, continued to have misgivings with respect to certain sections of the agreement, the perceived need to achieve a deal at almost any price overcame caution.

For his part, the prime minister again resumed his self-imposed role of "honest broker," in which there was no federal position nor parameters set on the debate. Rather than a consensus-building exercise based on such an initial federal vision, and input from the public consultation process, the whole deal was coming down to another set of trade-offs for political expediency.

But public opinion was still generally supportive of the process. The early rounds of public consultation and the presence of native leaders at the bargaining table had a lingering positive effect. The speed with which the final negotiations took place, and the fact that they occurred over the summer months, may also have helped. Add to these factors the "constitutional fatigue" that many observers ascribed to the public, and the elements suggest an explanation for the muted but initially positive popular response to the agreement. More than 70% of Canadians expressed support for the accord in polls at the time it was announced.

When they signed the final Consensus Report of the Charlottetown Accord on August 28, 1992, the prime minister and the premiers believed they had a winner on their hands. They believed the final validating exercise of a "national" referendum campaign in nine provinces — to be held simultaneously with the Quebec referendum campaign of October 26 — would put the final seal of approval on a remarkable exercise in nation building.

Earlier fears about the dangers of the referendum mechanism and the ongoing concerns expressed by Joe Clark and senior federal officials could not dampen the enthusiasm that the prime minister was now beginning to feel for hitting the campaign trail. He announced that Parliament would be recalled on September 9 to pass enabling legislation on the referendum question. Secure in the knowledge that this campaign would last six weeks, not three years as Meech Lake had, it must have seemed to the first ministers that the universe finally was unfolding as it should.

Letting the Genie Out of the Bottle: From the Quebec Round to the Canada Round

The package of proposals that the Mulroney government put before the Canadian people in the fall of 1992 was unlike any that had come before. Its many provisions covered an extraordinary range of issues. Its effects were to a great extent incalculable.

The Charlottetown Accord was also remarkable because of the broad support it enjoyed among members of the political and business élite. What opposition there was came initially from those who were excluded from the negotiating process and, significantly, from individuals within the academic community who were wary of the accord's far-reaching ramifications. Those who were excluded from the process perceived, in many cases, that the accord would hurt them. Academic critics suggested that the overall effect of the accord would be to make the country less democratic, less coherent, and perhaps less governable.

Even its proponents agreed that the Charlottetown Accord would change the nature of the country. But the debate over relative merits of the accord was coloured by political considerations, economic grievances, and personal enmity. It was also obscured by a series of popular misconceptions about the historical context in which the accord was formulated.

The Charlottetown Accord can be seen, and has often been presented, as an attempt to correct the flaws in the Meech Lake agreement, which, in turn, was an attempt to address the flaws of the constitutional amendment package of 1982. But the historical record is more complicated. Each new round of negotiations actually embraced an expanded range of issues. Following its "exclusion" from the 1982 agreement, the Quebec government presented the federal government with a list of five subjects on which it required satisfaction. Meech Lake addressed eight substantive issues. The 1991 proposals covered 12. And the Charlottetown Accord dealt with no fewer than 18 substantive changes to the Constitution in more than 60 clauses.

This expanded agenda was not only unnecessary but impractical. It resulted solely from the prime minister's view of constitution-making as a process of brokering competing claims. Instead of setting parameters to the debate and excluding some issues as either unacceptable or premature to the discussion at hand, he appeared prepared to listen to all proposals and merely mediate among them. With each failure, the stakes were therefore raised and more subjects were placed on the table to achieve an agreement — an approach that flies in the face of both logic and historical precedent.

The most successful examples of constitutional reform are those in which only one or two issues have been addressed at a time. No country has successfully restructured so many fundamental aspects of its constitution at one fell swoop as the Charlottetown Accord proposed to do.

But logic had little to do with the debate that unfolded in the fall of 1992. Proponents of the accord, for example, argued that it was a well-integrated, progressive package of proposals for change that would take Canada into the 21st century. At the same time, they suggested that it was an imperfect set of compromises that were temporarily necessary in order to save the country from disintegration. What both arguments had in common, however, was an implied criticism of the status quo, and in particular of the 1982 constitutional amendment that had produced an "unacceptable" state of affairs. The Quebec Round that produced Meech Lake was believed by the élites to be essential to save the country from the disastrous situation that had existed since 1982. The Canada Round, in turn, was necessary because Meech Lake had failed.

Many Canadians could be forgiven if they were misled by this line of reasoning to conclude that the country had been operating in a constitutional vacuum for nearly a decade. Many Canadians in Quebec and elsewhere *did* believe, according to several national polls in the fall of 1990, that the failure of the Meech Lake Accord earlier that year had left the country with no rules of the game, and with Quebec excluded from the game entirely.

The reality is very different. The constitutional amendment of 1982 was exactly that — a constitutional amendment. No more, and no less. It was not a new constitution that replaced the old one. On the contrary, the original constitutional document, the BNA Act, remained in force. So did the other amendments that had already been passed before 1982 by appealing to Britain. In other words the amendment of 1982, while it was unquestionably the most significant amendment to the Constitution since Confederation, simply added to the existing body of the Constitution.

Apart from finally achieving patriation, the *Constitution Act, 1982*, contained two major measures: an amending formula and an entrenched charter of rights and freedoms. It made no changes to the distribution of powers between the federal and provincial levels, nor did it alter any of the fundamental institutions of government, such as the Senate or the Supreme Court.

Yet it remains a common misconception that Canada's whole Constitution changed in 1982. Separatists and federalists alike have tended to promote this view. Everyone from Jacques Parizeau to Brian Mulroney and Joe Clark has inadvertently (or deliberately, in the case of the separatists) described Quebec's constitutional situation as one of "exclusion" or "isolation." Even the first throne speech of the Mulroney government in 1984 declared that it was "obvious" the constitutional agreement was "incomplete as long as Quebec is not part of a constitutional accord." As the former president of the federal Conservative Party and Alliance Quebec, Peter Blaikie, has noted, "The implication is that Quebec's 'legitimate' aspirations have been rejected."[1]

The origins of this mistaken impression are rooted in the way in which the 1982 amendment was achieved, namely, without the consent of Quebec. Although the amendment package of 1982 received the approval of the federal government, nine provincial premiers, and most interest groups and constitutional experts, it was not supported by the government of Quebec, which at the time was in the hands of René Lévesque and the Parti Québécois. Despite efforts by the Trudeau government to negotiate some changes to the deal that might make it more acceptable to Quebec, it proved impossible to do so. With the encouragement of the provincial premiers and the federal opposition parties, and the blessing of the Supreme Court, to say nothing of 73 of the 75 members of Parliament from Quebec, the federal government decided to proceed anyway.

The Origins of the Quebec Round

Quebec didn't sign the 1982 agreement, but its provisions applied to Quebec just as they applied to all the other provinces. Technically and constitutionally, the process was complete. Nothing more had to happen. Politically, however, many believed the widespread idea that the amendment package was "imposed" on Quebec against its will. In practical terms it meant, among other things, that little or no progress could be made on issues such as aboriginal rights, or in other areas where federal-provincial administrative agreements were pending, since Quebec refused to participate. Still there was no urgent necessity to embark on another round of constitutional debate. Pierre Trudeau repeated on several occasions that he believed the issue of future constitutional reform should be shelved for a decade or more.

Nevertheless the Mulroney government embarked upon the Quebec Round of negotiations in 1987, supposedly to redress the wrongs inflicted upon Quebec in 1982. For this reason the subjects under discussion in this round logically should have reflected the concerns expressed by Mr. Lévesque when he repudiated the 1982 package. But this was not, in fact, the case.

Lévesque had three objections to the 1982 proposals. First, he did not approve of a Charter section on official language rights guarantees, which he felt would have the effect of overruling a Quebec law on the language of education. (In this he was correct: a provision of Quebec's language legislation, Bill 101, which restricted admission to English-language schools, was subsequently found to be unconstitutional by the Supreme Court on the basis of the new Charter provision.) Second, he had concerns about the guarantee of mobility rights in the Charter, which he believed would mean that Quebec could not protect jobs for Quebeckers. Third, and most important, he believed the amending formula eliminated what he considered to be Quebec's traditional veto over constitutional changes.

In the initial months after the 1982 amendment came into force, relations between Ottawa and Quebec were frigid. The Lévesque government announced that it would boycott all future first ministers' conferences until its concerns were addressed. At the same time it invoked the notwithstanding clause to protect all of its legislation from the potential effects of the Charter.

It was not until early 1985, with a new government in power in Ottawa, that the government of Quebec made any concrete proposal to bridge this political chasm. In a surprising departure from tradition, the Lévesque government abandoned Quebec's longstanding insistence on a veto in favour of a proposal that would provide for full financial compensation to a province when it chose to "opt out" of amendments that transferred powers.

Before the federal government responded to this proposition, the Lévesque government was defeated by the provincial Liberals under Robert Bourassa.

In May of the following year (1986), Mr. Bourassa's minister of intergovernmental affairs, Gil Rémillard, issued a five-point proposal — a set of minimum conditions that would have to be met if Quebec were to come back to the table. With one exception, these conditions bore virtually no resemblance to the initial concerns of Premier Lévesque. Instead they requested the symbolic recognition in the preamble of the Constitution of the nature of Quebec as a distinct society; the limitation of the federal spending power; a guarantee of increased provincial powers over immigration; and a guarantee of Quebec's participation in nomination of judges to the Supreme Court. Lastly, in an about-face from the 1985 position of the previous government, the Bourassa government returned to the pursuit of the right of a veto.

Ironically it was Brian Mulroney, a Quebecker and strong supporter of the 1982 amendment package, who was now in power in Ottawa and obliged to respond to these five conditions. And it was his decision to do so as a matter of priority that led to the federal-provincial constitutional negotiations of 1987, which he dubbed the "Quebec Round," negotiations that ultimately produced the Meech Lake Accord.

The Meech Lake Accord

The brokerage politics and deal making that produced the Meech Lake Accord have been described by a number of authors.[2] The process was flawed and so was the document it produced. Most significantly, perhaps, the contents of the Meech Lake Accord reflected the many bargains struck between the federal government and the provinces in return for their consent to Quebec's five conditions. As a result, the final product did far more than respond to these five concerns. As Robert Bourassa publicly admitted shortly after the deal was first struck, Quebec had received far more than it had asked for, and there were several items in the deal that were of no interest to that province.

Not only did Quebec receive recognition of its distinctive character, but the relevant section was placed in the *body* of the Constitution rather than the preamble as Quebec had requested. This was a legal nicety but one that most constitutional experts agreed would have far more than a symbolic effect. Many observers expressed concern that the "distinct society" clause might even affect the Charter and hence the fundamental rights and freedoms that were guaranteed within it.

In addition, an existing federal-Quebec arrangement on immigration (Cullen-Couture agreement) was written into the Constitution; Quebec was guaranteed its role in the selection of judges for the Supreme Court and given the veto it had asked for; and considerable limitations were placed on the federal spending power with respect to national standards for cost-sharing programs.

But this was not the end of the matter. In a move that determined the shape of things to come, the federal government resolved the problem of regional jealousies by not only giving all the other provinces the same concessions Quebec received, but also acquiescing to many other provincial demands. This brokerage approach to constitutional reform meant that the veto as well as the immigration provision and the spending power were applied to all provinces.

With respect to the federal spending power, the ability of a province to opt out of new programs with compensation was to be tied to its agreement to "carry on a program or initiative that is compatible with the national objectives." The federal government maintained that this wording meant a national child-care program, for example, would still be possible. Opponents of the deal were sceptical. Their scepticism was heightened when Mr. Rémillard indicated his interpretation of the vague phrase "national objectives" meant that Quebec could build bridges with money intended for sidewalks or highways.

The use of the unanimity principle (that all ten provinces and the federal government would have to agree) to resolve Quebec's veto demand was, of course, an extreme extension of the limited role assigned to it in the 1982 amendment formula, where most future changes to the Constitution were possible with the consent of seven provinces with 50% of the population. Only in a few exceptional cases did the 1982 formula apply the unanimity principle, for the obvious reason that such a requirement might well make future change impossible. Indeed, no other federal country in the world has an amending

formula based on unanimity. (Ironically, it was the first ministers' decision to voluntarily apply the concept of unanimity to the passage of
the Meech Lake Accord itself that eventually led to its failure.)

As for the Supreme Court, not only Quebec but all provinces were
to be allowed to submit a list of names to the federal government from
which it must choose. Apart from the obvious requirement to have
judges trained in the civil- as well as common-law code, the notion of
regional representation had previously been an informal one, based
on the assumption that judicial decision making should be impervious to regional biases. Critics of the Meech Lake provision also noted
that there was no deadlock-breaking mechanism; should a province
refuse to provide names, or the federal government refuse to choose
from a list, there would be no way to ensure positions would be filled.
Eventually, it would be possible for the vacancies on the bench to
increase to the point where no work could be done.

The Meech Lake Accord addressed two other issues that had not
been raised by Quebec. The first was a measure to provide for compulsory annual first ministers' conferences on the economy and other
matters. While proponents claimed this would make the federal government more "accountable," and national planning and co-operation
more successful, critics argued it was merely an institutionalization
of another order of government — executive federalism — which
would complicate the decision-making process and make it less
accountable to the people by marginalizing Parliament and provincial
legislatures still further.

Lastly, the Meech Lake Accord contained a measure intended to
placate western premiers led by Alberta's Don Getty, who had been
calling for an elected Senate. Failing agreement on that, the proposal
provided in essence for Senate appointments to be made by the
provinces rather than the federal government. Those provinces who
chose to do so were, it was understood, free to hold an election to
determine whom they would appoint. This measure failed to please
the proponents of an elected Senate, and especially those favouring a

triple-E Senate, at the same time that it infuriated critics who preferred the status quo, abolition of the Senate or, at a minimum, a federal rather than provincial election plan for a federal institution.

The Canada Round Begins

When the Meech Lake Accord died, many thought the issues of interest to Quebec would be dealt with in other ways. In particular, it was assumed that administrative agreements would take the place of constitutional amendments. Indeed, one of the first acts of the federal government after Meech was to sign a bilateral agreement with Quebec on immigration, which resembled almost identically the agreement that was to have been entrenched in the Meech Lake text.

But after this initial effort, the process faltered. The politicians were hunkering down as the public was seized with a general malaise about the political system and politicians. Several of the participants in the Quebec round, notably David Peterson of Ontario, succumbed to this pent-up frustration and the voters' wrath in provincial elections. The Spicer Commission provided an outlet for virtually every complaint, not merely those related to the Constitution. As time passed, public opinion grew harsher, rather than mellower.

Polls in January 1991 demonstrated that the Canadian public was in no mood to compromise. Provincial politicians took note. Don Getty began to articulate a more hard-line approach to a triple-E Senate. He was supported not only by western interest groups but also by Clyde Wells of Newfoundland. Bob Rae in Ontario, Peterson's successor, advanced the idea of a social charter. And native peoples, emboldened by their public relations success at Oka and the election of the highly credible Ovide Mercredi as Grand Chief of the Assembly of First Nations, adopted a more aggressive tone on the issue of aboriginal self-government.

By the time the Unity Cabinet had finished its deliberations over the summer and the government had tabled its formal proposals in the

House of Commons in mid-September, the list of items on the constitutional shopping list had grown once again. Now the ante had been upped from eight to 12 areas of discussion in some 28 separate points. To the original five concerns of Quebec and the three add-ons of Meech Lake were added four completely new topics. There were measures on aboriginal self-government, economic union, the division of powers, and a hodgepodge of Charter issues such as the inclusion of property rights and limitations on the notwithstanding clause, which permitted governments to override certain sections of the Charter.

These proposals, in turn, formed the basis for the deliberations of the Beaudoin-Dobbie Committee and the five policy forums organized by Joe Clark, at which the social charter, interprovincial trade barriers, and the federal powers of disallowance and reservation were also thrown into the constitutional hopper. A document prepared by the Research Branch of the Library of Parliament, juxtaposing the contents of these various proposals, required 116 pages.

Every effort to solve problems in the previous round tended to create new problems. Every attempt to dispose of one contentious provision tended to spawn new provisions that were no less contentious. The distinct society clause, for example, had been one of the most controversial in the Meech Lake agreement. In the Canada Round, the aspects of Quebec's distinctiveness were spelled out, with reference its "French-speaking majority, unique culture and civil law tradition." This wording, in turn, caused new concerns about elements that were left out, such as the existence of the anglophone minority, and about elements that were vague, such as the term "culture."

The new proposals placed the distinct society clause in not one but two separate locations: in an interpretative Canada clause within the body of the Constitution (a solution that many critics had been calling for since Meech), and *within the Charter itself*. Although the government argued that limitations on individual rights protected in the Charter would be minimal, critics of these new provisions believed they would have a considerable, negative impact on individual rights and freedoms.

For all these complications, the lesson of Meech Lake's veto for every province appeared to have been learned. This set of proposals required the approval of only seven provinces with 50% of the population to amend the Constitution. In fact, the question of Quebec's veto was only peripherally addressed in a statement that indicated the federal government would be willing to support the amending formula of Meech Lake "if a consensus on this matter were to develop."

The issue of Senate reform had been transformed from a matter of permitting provincial appointments to the creation of an elected legislative body. Under the terms of this proposal, the Senate was assigned specific responsibilities, including the ratification of appointments to boards and agencies. While this obviously went much farther than the Meech Lake provisions, the triple-E supporters were still unhappy that equal representation and efficacy were not addressed.

An equally expansive approach was taken in areas unrelated to Meech Lake. A section was included on aboriginal self-government, for example, in which the recognition of a "justiciable" right was proposed, along with a 10-year implementation period to allow for negotiations on the definition. There was also a commitment to some unspecified type of aboriginal representation in the Senate.

Unfortunately for the government, these provisions did not quell the criticisms of native peoples. On the contrary, the Association of First Nations (AFN) under Ovide Mercredi launched a massive public relations campaign in which they exhorted Canadians to "break the pattern, not the promise" by calling for "meaningful" proposals on aboriginal self-government. Describing the government's proposal as a "hoax," Mercredi linked his claims on behalf of aboriginal people to those of Quebec, arguing that native peoples were a distinct society as well and demanding equal recognition.

But unquestionably the most significant new areas of proposed discussion were those relating to the economic union and the transfer of powers. Here there were seen to be both positive and regressive measures. Unlike the Meech Lake process, this time the federal government outlined some conditions of its own. These included the elimination of interprovincial trade barriers (which it referred to as a common market clause) and the "power to manage the economic union," as well as a proposal to limit the use of the notwithstanding clause. More than once the prime minister referred to the common market issue as a bottom line for the federal government, without which there could be no deal.

While the conditions outlined by the government were considered an improvement over its laissez-faire approach in Meech Lake, the latest federal initiative also opened up a whole range of new areas of responsibility for possible adoption by the provinces, most of which the Trudeau federalists considered regressive. Worse, the federal plan suggested no areas in which provincial responsibilities might be transferred to the federal government. It was a one-way street involving training, immigration, culture, and what have come to be known as the "six sisters": tourism, forestry, mining, recreation, housing, and municipal/urban affairs. The proposal also provided for the federal government to divest itself of two of its few remaining tools for national economic management, the residual and declaratory powers. (Although both of these powers had been expressly assigned to the federal level by the Fathers of Confederation to ensure federal supremacy, they had been little used in the second half of the 20th century. Essentially they gave the government the power to claim responsibility for any areas that were not specifically assigned to the provinces, and to intervene in areas where its power was in question if it was for the national good.)

Supporters of the package argued that such a transfer of powers was necessary to "streamline" government and reduce waste and inefficiency. It was appropriate for power to be transferred to the provinces because they were best able to administer these areas. Some of the areas listed were already exclusive areas of provincial jurisdiction in which the federal government had intervened through the spending

power. Others were areas of de facto shared jurisdiction that supporters claimed would be more efficiently administered by the provinces.

This argument about duplication had become the conventional wisdom. It was always couched in terms of economic efficiency; the
transfer of powers was necessary to avoid costly and inefficient "duplication" and "overlap" of government services. The assumption that
such duplication existed was taken for granted by virtually all the federal and provincial participants. No one suggested, however, that if
such duplication existed, it could just as easily be eliminated by trans-
ferring powers to the federal level.

Oddly enough, a team of experts assigned by the government to
study the whole matter refuted the duplication argument. The study,
which examined programs expending a total of some $96 billion, was
released on November 26, 1991 — the same day the revamped
Beaudoin-Dobbie Committee reconvened to review the government's
proposals. According to the study, there was "no evidence of outright
duplication." In those areas where federal and provincial programs
appeared to be providing similar clients with similar services (fewer
than 45%), "in every case the participation of the second level was
adding value, not duplicating work."

The Response to the Federal Proposals

This type of evidence had little influence on the proposals, however,
since the debate on this topic had now become — once again — a
debate about broader issues rather than the actual contents of the deal.
In the case of the duplication argument, the conflict was really between
two competing visions of the federal state. The government's 1991
proposals, aptly entitled "Shaping Canada's Future Together," revealed
a clear trend towards greater decentralization. The question was
whether this was a positive or negative development.

Virtually all the government's economic-based proposals came in
for substantial criticism by those who claimed the changes would lead

to a weak central government and render it unable to manage the economy. Similar criticism was aimed at the opting-out provision on the federal government's spending power with respect to national social programs. As one analyst summed it up, "The limitation will severely constrain the federal government's ability to initiate new programs and impose critical national standards."[3]

Proponents of the proposals did not deny that the effect would be greater decentralization. They did argue, however, that this was the more efficient and responsible way to administer a number of programs. They also argued that provincial programs were more likely to be responsive to the needs of the people and better tailored to regional economic conditions and realities.

In the end, the actual content of the government's package became less important to the political élite than their determination to arrive at a consensus at the bargaining table. The efforts the federal drafters had made to incorporate the findings of the Spicer Commission and the lessons of Meech Lake, together with much of the input of the Beaudoin-Dobbie Committee report, fell by the wayside.

As the five national policy forums sponsored by Joe Clark demonstrated, and as countless polls in the months leading up to the deal confirmed, Canadians outside Quebec were not always interested in the details of constitutional reform, but they had a reasonably firm set of underlying goals and objectives that they wanted to see incorporated. Among these was the principle of equal treatment for individuals and provinces or regions, which led them to reject overwhelmingly the concepts of the distinct society clause and asymmetrical federalism, and to support the concept of an elected and equal Senate.

Another fundamental principle was the necessity for strong central government. Although Canadians approved of the transfer of certain areas of responsibility to the provinces, their approval was moderated by the caveat that such a transfer should have no effect on the ability of the federal government to establish new national social programs or to set standards and guidelines for existing ones.

But public opinion and the results of all the consultative commissions and forums faded into insignificance in the second half of 1992. The overriding concern of the government was to arrive at a package the premier of Quebec could sell on October 26 and the other first ministers could live with.

What emerged on August 28 in the Charlottetown Accord was a document that bore the marks of having passed through many consultative bodies, but in several key areas it was a repudiation of their findings. In certain respects it was a totally new endeavour, as the attempts of the political élites to accommodate what they believed to be provincial minimum demands led to new and "innovative" solutions with many unexpected provisions.

Debate on the Charlottetown Accord

Both supporters and critics of the Charlottetown Accord have referred to it as Meech Plus, and with good reason. The Consensus Report announced by the first ministers on August 28, 1992, contained provisions that responded to each of Quebec's original five conditions, as well as the two basic add-ons of Meech Lake, but it also outlined a whole new set of proposals for institutional and economic reform that most observers believed would have far-reaching effects on the operation of the Canadian political system. The more than 60 clauses of the text represented changes or additions to roughly one-third of the existing Constitution. The Charlottetown Accord, in sum, was not a minor amendment but a proposal to massively rewrite the rules of the game.

Despite the immense significance of this proposed set of changes to the Constitution, political rhetoric overwhelmed the debate during the actual six-week referendum campaign, often ignoring reality and perpetuating or creating myths in order to capture the hearts and minds of Canadians. Although a certain number of substantive arguments were put forward on the relative merits of the deal, they were overshadowed by the second level of debate, in which the real issue was defined as the future of the country.

Most supporters of the deal tended to argue their case in terms of the political implications of a No vote. For them, the failure of the accord would spell the beginning of the end of Canada. Deteriorating economic conditions caused by lack of investor confidence would be only the first step on the rocky road to Quebec's separation. Conversely, support for the accord would lead to a period of economic and political stability in which politicians could turn their attention to the more pressing issues of the day. In addition, support for the deal would demonstrate the innate generosity and tolerance of Canadians and their willingness to compromise, attributes supporters believed essential to the maintenance of national unity.

The supporters of the accord were in fact fighting a different campaign, framed around a different question from that of their adversaries on the No side. Opponents of the accord were more intent on addressing the contents of the deal and criticizing particular aspects of it. Although they were sometimes obliged to respond to the Yes agenda by outlining their views on the consequences of a No vote, they avoided it as much as possible.

This conflict between the two views of the debate was epitomized by the comments of Pierre Trudeau and Brian Mulroney. Trudeau's exhaustive analysis of the contents of the deal in his Maison Eggroll speech — in which he concluded, "They have made a mess, and this mess deserves a big NO" — was attacked by Mulroney the next day without his ever referring to the contents of the deal or rebutting Trudeau's criticisms. Instead, Mulroney focused on the reasons why the accord was "necessary," namely, that in his view "Canada's constitutional mess was created by Pierre Trudeau and was not created by the Charlottetown Accord."

Part of the reason for these two different campaigns was strategic, but the qualifications of the individuals leading the debate on each side may also have been a factor. Supporters were drawn from virtually every branch of the country's élite — politicians, the business community, the arts, and the media. With some notable exceptions, members of those political or business élites lacked constitutional expertise. It followed that most avoided debate on the issues. Most of the substantive criticism of the accord came from the academic élite, and more precisely from constitutional experts — lawyers, political scientists, and historians.

With one side talking about broad issues, and the other focused on detail, it was difficult for ordinary Canadians to compare the positions of the two, or to obtain objective opinions in support of the deal itself.

It was also difficult for both supporters and critics to address issues squarely because of the absence of a legal text. Until two weeks before the end of the campaign, all those wishing to discuss the merits of the deal were obliged to refer to the document released shortly after the August 28 meeting, a document referred to as a "consensus report." When a legal text was finally released in early October, it was labelled a "best efforts draft" that would be "subject to approval" by first ministers and could therefore be changed at will.

Indeed, as the campaign progressed, Constitutional Affairs Minister Joe Clark indicated publicly that changes might well be made to the Consensus Report and the legal text *after* the referendum. In fact, changes were being made on an ongoing basis in response to premiers' concerns with the draft wording. This degree of uncertainty about the final product heightened the anxiety of all Canadians. It was particularly difficult for experts, for whom the importance of the precise wording could not be overestimated in forming a reasoned view of the package.

A great deal of misinformation about the legal effect of the accord was perpetuated during the campaign. The removal of interprovincial trade barriers, for example, was an issue that many Canadians were led to believe had finally been resolved. In reality, the issue was simply addressed as a matter of importance for future discussion among the premiers. Indeed, much of the accord — some 26 provisions —

was still subject to future federal-provincial negotiation and agreement. This meant that, if the deal were approved, certain measures would become constitutionally entrenched immediately, while many others merely constituted an agreement to proceed with further talks. Still other measures were to be constitutionally entrenched but would have no real legal effect (in constitutional terms, were not "justiciable") because they represented only statements of principle or philosophical commitment. The social charter was the most obvious example.

Myth and Reality in the Substance of the Charlottetown Accord

The remainder of this chapter attempts to separate the myth from the reality in the Charlottetown Accord by examining the major issues raised and the potential constitutional implications. The debate on the *political* implications of the accord's success or failure is outlined in the following chapters on the conduct of the referendum campaign.

These substantive concerns are analyzed in the context of their origins, beginning with the issues that flowed from Quebec's original demands and concluding with those that emerged as the result of the final, closed-door session of first ministers in August. As with any complex document, this strictly chronological approach is not always feasible, but it serves as a basic framework for the analysis.

The Distinct Society Clause and the Canada Clause

Of all the provisions in the Meech Lake Accord, the distinct society clause was the one opponents of the deal were most likely to reject and least likely to be flexible about. Nevertheless the importance of the issue had grown dramatically in Quebec with its perceived rejection by the rest of Canada. What had once been a lesser item among Quebec's five conditions had become a non-negotiable bottom line. Yet any clause that would convey perceived special status remained anathema to the overwhelming majority in the rest of Canada. Joe Clark recognized this dilemma at one point in his travels with the policy forums in early 1992 when he declared that, since such opposition was not likely to go away, or demand for the clause's inclusion to decrease in Quebec, "another way will have to be found to express the same idea."

This led to the government's acceptance of the widely recommended "Canada clause" concept in the 1991 federal proposals — a clause in which the distinctiveness of Quebec society was included within a list of other basic or fundamental characteristics of Canada such as a federal parliamentary system, official bilingualism, and multiculturalism.

Supporters of the Charlottetown Accord outside Quebec consistently argued that by defining the term clearly, and by placing a second reference to the distinct society within the Charter, the importance of the phrase was greatly diminished and its implications for the rest of the Constitution, and individual Canadians, were minimized. This was especially the case, they maintained, because the new Canada clause would be what in legal terms is called an "interpretive clause" — something less than a specific provision but far more than a preamble. In Quebec, of course, supporters of the accord made a very different case. The fact that there were not one but two references to the distinct society in the accord made it an obvious "improvement" over Meech Lake.

Opponents of the clause pointed to the actual language of the text, which stated at the beginning that "a new clause should be included as section 2 of the Constitution Act, 1867," which would "guide the courts in their future interpretation of the entire constitution, including the Charter of Rights and Freedoms." The Constitution, it read, should be interpreted "in a manner consistent with the following fundamental characteristics." One of the eight characteristics that followed was that "Quebec constitutes within Canada a distinct society."

The treatment of the distinct society issue gave rise to three broad concerns: first, that it would give the government of Quebec different powers than other provinces, and possibly powers over other provinces; second, vis-à-vis the interpretation of the Charter, that citizens in that province might not enjoy the same rights as other Canadians; and, third, that it would give collective rights, and especially language community rights, primacy over certain individual rights.

It was not certain that even francophones in Quebec were in favour of such recognition. A 1992 CROP poll found that more than 70% of Quebeckers identified with the federal Charter of Rights and did not believe that its provisions should be overridden. Although they overwhelmingly supported the concept of a distinct society clause, they did not believe that it should or would be used to deny minority rights. Earlier polls indicating a high level of discomfort among francophone Quebeckers over the sign legislation (Bill 178), which the Bourassa government had introduced in violation of the Charter, appeared to confirm the CROP findings.

Most if not all of the critics' concerns would have been eliminated if the recognition of Quebec as a distinct society had been put in a *preamble* to the Constitution, as Quebec had originally requested in its five conditions. Most expert critics were not opposed to such recognition, viewing it as a political fact of life. What they objected to was the conferring of additional powers on the government or legislature of Quebec, since they believed these powers could have no other purpose than to implement some unspecified agenda. As Toronto lawyer and civil rights activist Clayton Ruby succinctly put it, "Quebec is beyond doubt a distinct society, but it does not need the power to oppress its own minority to preserve its distinctiveness."[4]

Responding to this criticism, constitutional lawyer Katherine Swinton of the University of Toronto, a supporter of the accord, stated that the wording now made it clear "no new legislative powers are conferred on Quebec vis-à-vis other provinces." While agreeing with those who claimed that citizens of Quebec might not enjoy the same rights as other Canadians, she defended this provision by noting that "many would argue that it makes express what the Supreme Court has already indicated... that rights are not absolute, that the factors of federalism or provincial diversity can be a factor... and that Quebec can legitimately act in certain circumstances to protect the French language and culture," provided that the "infringement of rights is no greater than is reasonably justified in a society that is free and democratic."[5]

As for the collective rights issue, Ms. Swinton argued that only "those who argue that collective rights are not a legitimate concept in the constitution will still have reason for unease." Put another way, it seemed clear to Ms. Swinton that collective rights would indeed prevail on occasion over individual rights if the new text were to come into force. Although some proponents of the accord refused to agree with this interpretation, recognition of its validity was made by several supporters with legal or constitutional expertise, including Justice Minister Kim Campbell.

For those experts who supported the accord, the infringement was seen as an acceptable balance between two competing sets of claims. For opponents such as Professor Anne Bayevsky of the University of Ottawa's law faculty and an author of several books on the Charter and its jurisprudence, "the issue is whether the preservation and promotion of the collectivity should be done at the expense of individual and minority rights.... Overall the distinct society clause will have the greatest impact on the Charter, and federal and provincial cheerleaders simply must not pretend otherwise."[6]

A large number of prominent legal and academic experts agreed with Ms. Bayevsky and disagreed profoundly with the perceived need to accommodate collective rights at the expense of individual ones. They also agreed that the effect of the clause would not be minimal. A group of 12 constitutional lawyers, including Loraine Weinrib of the University of Toronto and John Humphreys, a former Canadian chair of the United Nations Human Rights Commission, declared categorically that "the distinct society provisions have the potential to erode existing protection of Charter rights and freedoms in Quebec."

In a sense, they agreed with Swinton as to the effect of the clause, but disagreed that this was an acceptable situation.[7]

Professor Weinrib and her 11 colleagues were joined by several noted civil rights lawyers, such as Julius Grey of Montreal and Clayton Ruby, in their criticism based on the third issue, the relationship between collective and individual rights. While for Loraine Weinrib the question was really "Why do so many people who are proponents of a distinct society clause assume that Quebec's distinctiveness must be ensconced at the expense of individual rights?" others such as Clayton Ruby stated categorically that "individual rights are more important than collective ones." Moreover Ms. Weinrib argued that the issue was not really one of individual rights versus collective rights, but of individual rights versus "collective *power*, majority power."[8]

When former prime minister Pierre Trudeau, a constitutional scholar and lawyer long before entering politics, joined the fray in his celebrated speech to the *Cité Libre* dinner at La Maison Eggroll in Montreal, it was to reiterate these longstanding concerns about the distinct society clause and also to add a new one based on the Charlottetown Accord's wording of the Canada clause. In a 20-minute speech in which roughly 60% of his time was devoted to a detailed dissection of the flaws in the Canada clause, Mr. Trudeau identified what he referred to as a new "hierarchy" of rights and "categories of citizens" that the agreement would create by virtue of the different language used in different sections.

He observed, for example, that Quebec's distinct society was to be "preserved and protected" by the government and the legislature of Quebec. Aboriginal peoples and their governments, meanwhile, were to "have the *right* to promote" their culture, while Canadians and their governments "are only *committed* to the vitality and development of official language minorities." Worse still, in Trudeau's view, was the fact that only the word "Canadians," not the phrase "and their governments" appeared in the text in the last three categories — only Canadians were committed to "racial and ethnic equality" and

Canadians were merely to "confirm" the principle of "the equality of provinces."

Making much of the fact that "committed to" was not a legal term of any significance in English, he then noted that in French the term used to translate Canadians' "commitment" was the even less firm *attachement* (an emotional impulse). Lest anyone argue that this was simply a case of disagreeing over the choice of wording in a translation, Mr. Trudeau pointed out that later in the same constitutional text, "when it comes to equalization payments, the translator of the English word 'commitment' suddenly discovers the French word '*engagement*' (a solid commitment)."

Although many supporters of the clause heatedly denied that the different wording did indeed have significance, few offered an alternative reason for the distinction. In a final CBC "Journal" debate only days before the vote, Justice Minister Kim Campbell responded to these concerns when they were expressed by accord opponent and Manitoba Liberal leader Sharon Carstairs, explaining the apparent "hierarchy" of rights was a deliberate "balancing" of the rights of governments, individuals, and collectivities."

Aboriginal Rights and the Charter

A second new issue that had arisen with the accord's handling of the Charter concerned its application to aboriginal peoples in the event of self-government. Here again the conflict between individual and collective rights was a prime concern. After a lengthy legal process in which native women's organizations had attempted to delay the referendum itself by claiming in an appeal to the federal court that their rights had been and would be denied under such an agreement, a change was made to the accord and reflected in the draft legal text. Nevertheless, the real possibility remained that aboriginal governments would have access to the notwithstanding clause and/or be exempt from the Charter's provisions with respect to democratic rights and gender equity.

According to constitutional lawyer Bryan Schwartz of the University of Manitoba, author of several books on aboriginal self-government, "The question that is most overlooked [in this debate] is the protection of local individuals and minorities from their own aboriginal governments."9

For Professor Stephen Scott of McGill University, another key concern was the fact the accord would include aboriginal governments along with provincial and federal governments in the unanimity provision to repeal the notwithstanding clause. "The Charlottetown proposals," according to Professor Scott, "would further extend the 'override' [notwithstanding] power — giving it to dozens, even hundreds of aboriginal legislative bodies.... The scheme will make it almost impossible to get rid of the notwithstanding clause because it creates an uncontrollable momentum for proliferation, not abolition."10 Needless to say, these possibilities did not instill optimism in the minds of those who already opposed the potential violations of individual rights posed by the distinct society clause.

In short, disagreement on the distinct society clause was profound and deep-seated, grounded in two very different philosophical perspectives that appeared irreconcilable. No minor change in wording would be likely to move either side, and the depth of feeling attached to the two positions argued against a cheerful compromise.

The Quebec Veto/Amending Formula

On the issue of the veto, opinions were equally firm. In essence, the accord abandoned the federal government's original proposal and acquiesced to Quebec's request by returning to the concept as found in the Meech Lake agreement. If Quebec was to have a veto, then all other provinces would have one as well. The accord added to the number of categories where unanimity was required, notably in the case of institutional reform. Thus a constitutional agreement that proposed to dramatically alter the functioning of the Senate, the House of Commons, and the Supreme Court would, after the fact, in all likelihood be unassailable.

For many experts the concept of unanimity was anathema. To them the likelihood of further change in areas where one or more provinces would have nothing to gain and everything to lose was slim indeed. Constitutional lawyer Deborah Coyne, a former adviser to Newfoundland premier Clyde Wells, took this position in her brief to the Beaudoin-Dobbie Committee and in subsequent articles. "If we discover that this or that reform is not working well in the future," she wrote, "it will be virtually impossible to change since all provinces now have a veto over federal institutions."[11]

Justice Minister Kim Campbell, in the CBC "Journal" debate of October 23, dismissed this argument out of hand by noting that unanimity had already been reached twice in a five-year period, in both the Quebec and the Canada rounds, and hence there was every reason to believe it could be achieved again.

The Supreme Court

The provisions of the Charlottetown Accord on the Supreme Court essentially reaffirmed the formalization of the consultative process that Meech Lake had already recommended. Three of the Court's judges would continue to come from the province of Quebec. (It was the absence of the Supreme Court and its appointments process from the Constitution, not the actual practice of appointment, that had concerned the government of Quebec in the first place.) Thus the proposal to entrench the existing practice of representation from Quebec did not cause undue concern elsewhere. However many critics expressed dissatisfaction that all potential appointees would now be drawn from provincial lists. Supporters noted that this proposal did not differ substantially from the actual (but informal) consultation process already in place, but opponents argued that the federal government must retain control or the potential for regional or even political bias on the bench would be greatly enhanced.

However, unlike the other Meech-related issues the Supreme Court received little attention in the Charlottetown debate. The technical issue raised in the Meech Lake Accord concerning the lack of a deadlock-breaking mechanism was resolved in this agreement and, apart from the concern of Clyde Wells that the legal text did not formally identify the Supreme Court as the final court of appeal, virtually no serious objections were raised.

Senate Reform/House of Commons

Although the degree of institutional reform was relatively innocuous in the case of the Supreme Court, it was becoming more substantial for the Senate with every new round of constitutional negotiation. By the time the Charlottetown consensus was reached, it could be argued that Senate reform played a leading role, almost equal to that of the distinct society/Canada clause debate.

The provisions on the Senate in the Charlottetown Accord could only be described as "innovative" and dramatic, since they in no way represented the thinking of the participants in the previous Quebec round or the consultative process in the current Canada round. Small wonder, then, that these provisions, and the consequent changes to the structure of the House of Commons that they precipitated, were among the most intensely debated and heartily disliked elements of the August 28 agreement.

Essentially, the debate here was another uncompromising philosophical one between those who believed in strict representation by population (and hence equality of individual voters) and those who supported the notion of regional (read: provincial) equality as a type of check and balance. It was therefore not the *election* of senators, but their basis of representation and their powers that caused the major dispute.

The issue of Senate reform in the Canada round in a very real sense could be described as the west's equivalent of the distinct society clause in the Quebec round. Since the failure of Meech Lake it was frequently declared by Premier Getty to be a non-negotiable item. His position was echoed by Premier Filmon of Manitoba and by Premier Wells of Newfoundland. When the premiers sat down to dicker for the final time in late August, the compromise they achieved was nevertheless far from what most observers expected.

A major stumbling-block to Senate reform in the past had been thrown up by the provinces of Quebec and Ontario, both of whom had clear numerical superiority in the Senate and neither of whom believed it was politically feasible for them to relinquish it. The example of former Ontario premier David Peterson, who had offered to give up a handful of seats in a previous round and was pilloried for the gesture, was salutary. This time, however, the drive to achieve a deal was even stronger than some premiers' instincts for self-preservation.

At the suggestion of Bob Rae, the premiers agreed to a provision in which Ontario and Quebec would lose their Senate majorities entirely, in favour of equal provincial representation, but they would gain seats in the House of Commons to compensate for those lost in the Senate. Meanwhile, the suggestion of New Brunswick's Frank McKenna to guarantee Quebec 25% of the seats in the Commons in perpetuity, regardless of population, while grounded in some historical precedent, was one that served only to further enrage opponents of the deal. This decision to intervene in the structure of the other major institution of Parliament to rectify problems in the first was novel to say the least and led to a series of unanticipated consequences.

As Premier Mike Harcourt of British Columbia soon discovered, the arrangement was one that had the potential to leave his province seriously underrepresented, given its ever-growing percentage of the total Canadian population. But the 25% solution also became a fundamental reason for hard-core opposition to the deal in western Canada, and especially British Columbia, because it was perceived to violate the principle of equality by giving Quebec preferential status. Given that Quebec did not ask for this provision and, indeed, that it had never raised the issue of Senate reform, the provisions accorded to Quebec in this deal proved disproportionately controversial.

As to the actual functioning of the Senate, another attempt to accommodate Quebec had left the accord with the probability of elected senators in nine jurisdictions but appointed senators, or senators elected by the National Assembly, in the case of Quebec. Put another way, the government of that province could conceivably control the actions of its "representatives" in the federal Senate, a matter of no small significance, given the ability of francophone senators in the new, improved Upper Chamber to veto any matters relating to "language" or "culture," terms that in turn were seen to be dangerously ambiguous.

Meanwhile the huge added membership of the House (members increased from 295 to 337 to compensate Ontario and Quebec for their loss of senators) was in itself criticized as likely to make the machinery of government even more cumbersome, costly, and unworkable. It would also have the effect, according to triple-E proponents, of making the Senate a far less effective regional voice than they had hoped since disagreements between the two chambers were to be resolved ultimately through joint sittings, in which the House with its Quebec and Ontario majority would clearly dominate over the interests of western or Atlantic Canada.

Ironically these complex provisions for Senate "reform" came in for criticism by many academic experts for going too far — rendering the system unworkable and the country ungovernable — at the same time that proponents of the triple-E option were lamenting that they did not go far enough. While (mostly) elected, the Senate, in their view, would be no more effective and its equality would be rendered meaningless by the changes to the House.

Political scientist Robert Jackson of Carleton University described the proposed changes as a "Rubik's Cube" of institutions that would "cause more trouble than it is worth." Citing in particular the possibility of a separatist government in power in Quebec that would take advantage of the new provisions to sabotage federal legislation and produce constitutional deadlock, Jackson concluded that this arrangement was "much worse than not perfect. It will only perform efficiently and effectively when we have perfect politicians and perfect parties" of goodwill and majority governments in power.[12]

Nevertheless proponents of the accord described these new arrangements as a major breakthrough. The government's own literature argued that "the reformed Senate's powers should significantly increase the role of elected Senators in the policy process."

Michael Bliss of the University of Toronto, an overall opponent of the accord, was prepared to recognize some possible merits in these provisions. Describing the resulting Senate as "bound to be better than the one we have," Professor Bliss also noted that "it's hard to see how it could seriously hurt us. I suspect, for example, that the people of Quebec will soon force the election rather than the appointment of their Senators..."[13]

Limitations on the Federal Spending Power

The issue of limiting the federal spending power provoked considerable disagreement, just as it had at the time of the Meech Lake debate. Once again the debate centred on two differing visions of federalism — that favouring strong central government and that favouring provincial rights.

The Charlottetown Accord, like the Meech Lake agreement, took the provincial rights/decentralization approach, which meant that any province, not just the province of Quebec, would be able to opt out of any "new" national shared-cost program and receive compensation from Ottawa if its own program "was compatible with the national objectives." This wording led critics to argue that no national *standards* would be possible, an objection reminiscent of the various critiques of the Meech provisions.

In an article dealing with this issue, Deborah Coyne concluded that "the federal government will be reduced to the sterile role of chief cashier, required to provide fiscal compensation to provinces not participating in a program."[14] Two other problems were articulated by critics — first, that new social programs such as a national child-care scheme would be impossible to implement, and second, that "old" programs such as welfare and medicare could be in jeopardy if major changes were to be defined as, in reality, the creation of a "new" program. In the latter case, the example most often used was the reform of the national welfare programs (such as the Canada Assistance Plan) to create a universal guaranteed annual income.

Critics argued that in practical terms the rich provinces would withdraw, taking substantial compensatory funding with them and leaving the federal government to fund national programs in the poorer regions of the country. Supporters of the accord pointed to Clyde Wells. The premier of Newfoundland at first had opposed such opting-out provisions in the Meech Lake round precisely because provinces such as his own would be seriously disadvantaged, but he had agreed to the Charlottetown proposal.

Supporters also argued that, unlike Meech Lake, the accord contained a clear recognition of the legitimacy of federal spending in areas of provincial jurisdiction. They also pointed to the clause on the economic and social union to refute the argument that social programs could be in danger. In his brief guide to the accord, *Still Thinking*, Manitoba law professor Bryan Schwartz agreed with these arguments, stating that the social union clause "makes it clear that the basic features of our medicare system are a permanent and integral part of the Canadian system." In his view, this clause "should encourage the federal government to continue to play a leading role" in the funding of this program.

Nevertheless a former top federal public servant — who had advised the prime minister and cabinet, implemented numerous shared-cost programs, and participated in negotiations with provincial officials — indicated that he shared the view of those who believed no new programs would be possible. Al Johnson, retired Secretary of the Treasury Board, said, "The probability of a [new] federal program being adopted by enough provinces that it could be launched, or called truly national, is so slim that no Government of Canada would be likely to start one...." Moreover, in Johnson's view, "Every premier and every provincial minister of finance would have a no-lose incentive for opting out. They would be compensated by the federal government whether or not they conformed with the proposed national standards; they would be in a position to get at least some 'free money' for other objectives by opting-out, simply by mounting a less-costly but still 'conforming' program; and they would avoid any real accountability for the spending of the 'equivalent compensation' they received from Ottawa."[15]

Economic Union/Elimination of Interprovincial Trade Barriers

The elimination of interprovincial trade barriers was one of the few new issues introduced by the federal government itself in its 1991 proposals. Unfortunately the federal proposal to strengthen the national role in economic planning and establish a "common market" did not survive the negotiations of the final closed-door sessions. Although Prime Minister Mulroney had earlier declared this item to be a federal "bottom line" in the negotiations, it was reduced to a statement of intent and an agreement to further provincial negotiations.

Like the federal proposal to limit the use of the notwithstanding clause, this federal "principle" fell victim to the horse-trading that characterized the final negotiations. A senior federal official explained how the government's plans to settle interprovincial trade disputes through a special, independent tribunal were scuttled because of fears that the delicate "balancing act" on Senate reform, aboriginal rights, and the transfer of powers would come unglued. "With everything else in place, it was not worth risking the whole accord in a continued fight on economic management," the official said.

As even Gordon Robertson, retired former Clerk of the Privy Council and strong overall supporter of the accord, was moved to write, "It is most unfortunate that the clause on the economic union is not stronger and that Section 121 [interprovincial trade/common market] of the Constitution Act, 1867, has not been strengthened."[16]

In defence of this failure, Robertson could only muster the argument that the situation after the accord had been ratified would be no worse than the status quo and did not prevent future improvements in that area. Ironically, the presidents of the Chamber of Commerce, the Canadian Manufacturers' Association, and the Business Council on National Issues all disagreed.

The Social Charter

It was Ontario premier Bob Rae who had proposed the social charter during the Canada Round. In doing so, he was motivated by the increasing withdrawal of the federal government from national social programs through reductions to the federal contribution to shared-cost programs such as medicare, the Canada Assistance Plan, and post-secondary education. Earlier the three wealthiest provinces — Ontario, Alberta, and British Columbia — had taken the federal government to court to try to enforce its earlier commitments on spending levels, but the Court had found that the federal government was not legally obliged to cough up. It was this ruling that led many to conclude that a constitutional amendment to "force" the federal government to "live up to" its financial obligations would be a good idea.

Supporters of the social charter believed that both levels of government would be bound to continue support for the extensive set of national social programs that Canadians cherish. Most experts believed this was doubtful. Unless actual levels of funding were proposed and entrenched in the text, the commitment to these programs would be only a commitment "in principle," which is not enforceable in financial terms. In addition, changing fiscal realities could lead to a situation in which either or both levels of government would simply not be able to live up to their constitutionally imposed financial obligations if actual spending levels were entrenched in the Constitution.

The final text of the Charlottetown Accord produced a non-binding statement of principles that could not be enforced by the courts. The social charter, in the end, ceased to be referred to as the social charter, but became part of the clause entitled "Economic and Social Union."

Since critics of the accord recognized the practical limitations on its effectiveness, they did not focus their attack on the lack of a real social charter until the federal government and other supporters of the deal began to refer to it as one of the positive accomplishments of the accord. Yes advertisements proclaimed, "If you vote yes, you will be voting for key social and economic objectives" such as "universal health care and a commitment to environmental protection." To many Canadians, the ads left the distinct impression that a binding social charter would indeed be entrenched in the Constitution. National polls throughout September and early October continued to indicate that the social charter provision was among the most popular and influential elements of the package for those who planned to vote in its favour.

This situation infuriated critics of the deal, who believed Canadians were being seriously and deliberately misled. Judy Rebick of the National Action Committee on the Status of Women (NAC) responded to the Yes ad campaign by declaring that "the social union is nothing more than a fig leaf to cover up what's happening in the rest of the document, which is really giving governments the instruments to dismantle national social programs."

Aboriginal Self-Government

Easily the most popular new issue raised in the Canada Round in light of the Oka crisis, the concept of aboriginal self-government and the entrenchment of the inherent right to self-government received broad-based support. Polls throughout the Canada Round process demonstrated significant support among Canadians across all regions and income levels.

The overwhelming preponderance of criticism regarding this aspect of the deal did not stem from philosophical concerns or differences of opinion on the merits of the concept, but rather from concerns about the wording and meaning of specific provisions. (Historian Michael Bliss, who questioned what he termed the "moral validity" of separate political systems based on race, was a noted exception to this prevailing view.)

Expert concerns centred on the potential extension of the powers of aboriginal governments to areas such as the environment, criminal law, and public education, as well as the implications for individual rights of the application of the notwithstanding clause, as outlined above in the discussion of the Canada clause. Concerns were also raised as to the implications of the agreement for natives and non-natives in urban areas, and as to the degree of financial commitment the federal government was offering, given that the funding of self-government was one of the many provisions left to a further round of political negotiation. (Ironically, it was concern over the funding issue that led many native communities to reject the agreement as well.)

Bryan Schwartz raised these concerns in a column in the *Globe and Mail* of October 4, 1992. Noting his support for existing self-government models such as Nunavut and for "the exercise of more authority by reserve-based governments," he nevertheless decried the lack of clear details and legal language surrounding the proposal. He attacked what he called a non-deal, in which no single concept of aboriginal self-government existed at the negotiating table, resulting in a decision to leave details to five years of political negotiations and then court decisions. In Schwartz's view, "The level of legal uncertainty here greatly exceeds anything associated with the distinct society clause in the Meech Lake Accord."

Schwartz then offered an example of the possible outcome of leaving such decisions on definitions to the courts in respect of urban native self-government. "The Clark deal does not reflect any real meeting of the minds.... The deal creates the possibility that the courts will declare that separate aboriginal schools are a constitutional right which cannot be denied by any local community with a substantial urban population."

Responding to these concerns Ron George, president of the Native Council of Canada, referred to the religion-based separate school system in many provinces and the use of military tribunals to counter the concern about separate political and legal systems in urban areas. "Doing things differently is both possible and normal," George argued. "Any new arrangement will be designed to work closely with other governments to ensure that order is maintained, the transition is smooth and there are no gaps or overlaps."

This non-legal response, focusing on practical application and the goodwill of the political actors to ensure implementation, was one that was echoed by representatives of the Indian and Inuit communities, as well as other proponents of the accord. Although it did not address the legal issues raised, it appeared to provide comfort to many Canadians.

Indeed, those opposed to the accord frequently raised the issue of aboriginal self-government as the one area of the deal that they supported, and one that they believed should be implemented regardless of the fate of the accord. Both Sharon Carstairs and Judy Rebick, for example, stressed this point in a final series of interviews in the CBC "Townhall Debate" series.

Transfer of Powers

Despite the obvious importance of institutional reform, the issue of the transfer of powers from Ottawa to the provinces could well be described as the most important addition of the Canada Round. Reinforcing the federal proposal outlined in September 1991, the Charlottetown Accord proposed to do three things: first, to give exclusive provincial jurisdiction to six areas in which both the federal and provincial governments have traditionally been active because these areas are not specifically mentioned in the original list of jurisdictional responsibilities. These "six sisters" include municipal and urban affairs, housing, mining, forestry, tourism, and recreation. Second, the accord proposed that the federal government cede labour market training programs and "cultural matters within the provinces" to those provinces that so chose. Third, it obliged the federal government to negotiate immigration agreements similar to the Cullen-Couture agreement (already in effect between the federal and provincial government of Quebec on immigration, which had been included in the Meech Lake Accord) with any province that so chose.

Proponents argued that these were reasonable measures to modernize the system and more adequately reflect regional diversity. Opponents argued that this massive "power grab" by the provinces would lead to an ungovernable country in which the federal government could do little except regulate postage and declare wars. As historian Michael Bliss put it, in this deal "Ottawa gives, gives, gives to the provinces.... the Charlottetown Accord represents the triumph of the doctrine that Canada is a league of provinces. That is not the Canada that the Fathers of Confederation created, not the Canada we have known, and not the Canada that every prime minister from John A. Macdonald through Pierre Elliott Trudeau strove to defend."[17]

McGill law professor Stephen Scott declared in an article appearing in the *Montreal Gazette* of October 22 that he would be voting no without hesitation. He argued that divesting the federal government of so many powers could not be tolerated in a country that is already among the most decentralized federations in the world. "The Charlottetown agreement gives too much power to the provinces," he wrote, and will lead to "the Balkanization of Canada." In Scott's view, "Canada after Charlottetown will look increasingly like a collection of provincial baronies."

For York University law professor Patrick Monahan, a former constitutional adviser to Premier David Peterson and a staunch supporter of Meech Lake, the transfer-of-powers issue was the straw that broke the camel's back. In his view, the Charlottetown Accord measures were a totally unnecessary complication to the negotiation process. "By trying to neatly compartmentalize responsibilities best left obscure," Professor Monahan noted, "the accord tinkered with an element of the current constitution that was functioning well." Moreover, in Monahan's view, "it is likely to create a whole new set of unintended and unforeseen problems of its own."[18]

Albert Breton, a former chairman of the Economic Council of Canada and professor of economy at the University of Toronto, argued that in general these issues were better left to federal-provincial negotiation rather than constitutional reform. Such negotiations permitted the greatest possible flexibility over time and prevented the entrenching of a "checkerboard" Canada in which citizens in different provinces would be faced with the prospect of very different levels of service, while interprovincial businesses would be confronted with a labyrinth of rules and regulations.

Other experts focused on particular powers affected by the deal. An article by Robert Jackson of Carleton University in the *Ottawa Citizen* of February 25, 1992, stressed that "tinkering with housing responsibility" would be potentially dangerous, leading to the elimination of such federal programs as low-income social housing, national standards, and mortgage guarantees through CMHC. Noting that guarantees on funding were vague or non-existent, Jackson pointed out that "if the provinces are left to find money for [social] housing programs they will not be able to...."

A number of experts pointed out the clear linkages between forestry and mining policy and the overall issue of environmental protection, a federal responsibility that could be seriously hampered by its proposed exclusion from these areas. Similarly, a coalition of cultural groups formed after the publication of the government's proposals in January 1991 declared that the accord's "proposed amendments on culture" were "unsatisfactory." Its reading of the legal text led the coalition to conclude that "federal power in cultural matters is subsidiary to provincial power," a situation that cultural groups across the country, including Quebec, considered to be unacceptable. A parallel complaint was issued by the tourism industry, whose association president, Debra

Ward, declared, "You can't sell bits of Canada overseas. You need a unified, national program."

In a similar vein, many economists, and particularly trade specialists, expressed astonishment that the federal government would consider vacating the field of labour market training at the very moment when it was initiating a second trade initiative (NAFTA), which would have serious employment consequences. As David Husband, a former finance and Bank of Canada mandarin put it, "Ottawa may be forced out of labour market development activities just when logic argues in favour of an even greater involvement."

Dr. Husband, an economist and president of Global Economics, was a supporter of Meech Lake, but found himself opposed to several provisions of the Charlottetown Accord, notably those relating to the transfer of powers. In an article published in the *Toronto Star* of September 4 he explained that the transfer of powers issue was for him a decisive factor. "North American free trade and the whole process of global restructuring necessitate more attention to the adjustment of workers, not less," he wrote. "Canada's labour force is its most important resource and the federal government has an important role to play in ensuring the proper policy framework for its best development and deployment."

While former Justice department deputy minister Roger Tassé, who advised the Beaudoin-Dobbie Committee, argued that the proposals on labour market adjustment simply "recognized that there are legitimate provincial interests ... but ensures at the same time a strong federal presence" in the field, most experts agreed with Husband that this was not likely to be the case. Robert Howse of the University of Toronto disagreed with several of Tassé's specific arguments as presented in an article for the *Network* journal of October 1992. He also maintained that "despite Tassé's repeated praise of co-ordination and cooperation, important values of transparency and democratic participation make it undesirable to continually recast the division of powers in Canada — as proposed in this agreement — through collusion among the same kind of policy élites that brought us the Meech Lake Accord."[18]

For critics of decentralization, the problems that the accord posed were perhaps best summed up by Professor J.F. Conway of the University of Regina, who wrote in an article in the *Montreal Gazette* of September 24, 1992, that "the only clear overriding power left to Ottawa is 'peace, order and good government', which is so vague that its practical meaning will require repeated Supreme Court interpretations."

A Good Deal for Canada?

The Charlottetown Accord contained many of the same provisions, with modifications, that were found in the Meech Lake Accord. It also contained some elements of the 1991 federal proposal, but it contained none of the elements that the federal government originally proposed as its own minimum set of demands. Very little of the additional input from the consultative process of the Canada Round was present in the final deal, and some measures directly contradicted the recommendations of those consultative forums.

Perhaps most important, the accord contained a number of elements that emerged for the first time in the final round of closed-door negotiations among first ministers and the native leadership. They enjoyed the benefit of neither detailed scrutiny by experts, nor public input in a consultative process such as a parliamentary committee, before they were presented to voters in the referendum.

In the final analysis, then, much of the last stage of the Canada Round clearly marked a return to the brokerage politics of Meech Lake. Deals were cut and concessions made in the interests of achieving a consensus, regardless of the overall effect of the final package on the constitutional framework. Lacking the delineation of a coherent national vision by the prime minister or any other players, the participants, despite the best of intentions, were reduced once again to the lowest common denominator, articulating narrow concerns and selfish interests, and the package provided graphic evidence of this flawed approach. Full of incomplete plans and vague promises, it essentially asked Canadians to hand the political élites a blank cheque.

On many of the key issues of the accord, a significant difference of opinion along philosophical lines emerged. Supporters of the accord favoured the protection of collective rights, the establishment of a form of aboriginal self-government in both reserve and urban settings, and a more decentralized federation in which the devolution of powers to the provinces and the limitation of the federal spending power were crucial elements.

Opponents maintained that the protection of individual rights must prevail, that aboriginal self-government, although desirable in theory, must be carefully considered and defined, and that the need for a strong central government outweighed provincial concerns for more authority over specific areas of constitutional responsibility.

It might also be said that supporters of the accord were in favour of change, while opponents supported the status quo. Proponents believed the existing constitutional arrangement either was unsatisfactory or could be significantly improved. Opponents, on the other hand, argued that the status quo was working reasonably well, that such minor changes as might be necessary should be accomplished in small steps rather than massive reorganizations, and that many of the issues being raised in the Charlottetown Accord could more properly be resolved through administrative arrangements between Ottawa and the provinces.

As the results on October 26 demonstrated, many Canadians believed the status quo was preferable to the huge leap of faith that the Charlottetown Accord required.

Setting the Stage:
The Politicians Turn to the People

Prime Minister Mulroney had learned this much from the Meech Lake débâcle: that public consultation was essential if constitutional reform were to be successful. He did not intend, however, that a referendum be a part of that consultation process. Through more than two years of public meetings and federal-provincial negotiation, the referendum option was kept on the back burner. To paraphrase former prime minister Mackenzie King, there would be a referendum if necessary, but not necessarily a referendum.

There were sound historical reasons for Mulroney's caution. Canada has no political tradition of direct consultation by referendum in the way that Switzerland and even Australia do. Provincial and municipal referendums have been held to settle minor issues — prohibition and property-tax reassessment, for example — but the federal government has consistently avoided the device. On the two exceptional occasions on which national referendums have been held in Canada, the results have been divisive. Neither vote had the effect of strengthening the government's position.

When, in 1898, Sir Wilfrid Laurier referred the question of prohibition to the country in a referendum, the result was inconclusive. A scant 51% of Canadians approved the proposal, while his home province of Quebec overwhelmingly rejected it. The legitimacy of the result was further complicated by the fact that fewer than 44% of eligible voters participated. Although technically the proposal was carried, Laurier dropped it.

The only other national referendum held in Canada was even more divisive. The topic was more significant and the stakes far higher. The conscription crisis of 1942 led Prime Minister King to hold a national vote in order to proceed with the draft, despite an earlier election promise not to do so. While the question received the support of 65% of voters, it was rejected by a massive margin (71%) in Quebec. King's decision to proceed anyway led to heightened English-French antagonism and Quebec resentment that persisted for decades. For many Quebeckers, and especially for many of the Quebec members of Mulroney's government, the very concept of a national referendum was anathema. In their view, it could serve only to re-create long-standing divisions and risk further alienation.

But historical precedent was not the only reason the federal government was exceedingly hesitant to pursue the avenue of direct consultation through a referendum. There were many other compelling reasons that they wished to avoid that option, most of them grounded in the nature of referendums themselves.

Problems with the Referendum Option

To begin with, referendums are best suited to the resolution of straightforward problems, since they essentially require a yes or no answer. The Constitution is not a simple matter. It is debatable whether the complex issues involved can or should be simplified to fit the simple format that a referendum requires.

The wording of a referendum question can be crucial to the outcome. If the question is too concise, it may fail to address the issue, so that the response is meaningless. If the question is too long, it may make the exercise hopelessly obscure. Although the federal government would be in charge of wording the question, this was cold comfort to officials familiar with examples elsewhere in the world in which the wording, although carefully chosen, had produced unintended consequences and cost supporters their victory. Some commentators felt that this was the case in the Quebec referendum of 1980 when René Lévesque's government tried to water down the question to appeal to a greater number of voters and ended up pleasing no one, asking Quebeckers if they would give the government a "mandate to negotiate" sovereignty-association with Ottawa. Such problems in the construction of questions can lead to lengthy debate and disagreement over what exactly the people have decided. According to many analysts, Australian referendums on constitutional matters have a history of failing *primarily* because the questions posed were too lengthy and complex.[1]

The problem of simplicity is compounded by the problem of neutrality. In theory a consultative referendum is unbiased; that is, the government is genuinely interested in determining the general will. This works reasonably well for moral questions — such as abortion, prohibition, or divorce — which tend to cut across party lines and for which the governing party may not wish to accept responsibility. And it may also work for issues on which the governing party is divided and seeks a neutral form of resolution, such as the British referendum on entry into the European Community.

In practice, however, governments often use a referendum to decide issues in which a particular outcome is desired. The British vote on devolution, the French votes on Algerian independence, and the more recent Danish and French votes on the Maastricht Treaty, all demonstrate the dangers of using a referendum to validate a position that the government has already assumed.

The problem is that referendums are not like general elections. There are no obvious cues for voters, or sources of allegiance, to help them in their decision. Political party affiliation — and the philosophy and leadership the parties espouse and represent — become irrelevant in a national referendum. Consequently, popular support for a particular question is almost impossible to predict in advance.

For the framers and supporters of the referendum question, the conduct of the campaign is very different from that of a general election campaign. In a general election, campaign managers for political parties know who their hard-core supporters are, and can make certain assumptions about voting behaviour based on age, gender, and income, developing a campaign strategy keyed to these variables. These assumptions may be entirely irrelevant in a referendum, where voting behaviour is determined by other factors and partisan affiliation counts for very little. Instead, the most important element in a referendum campaign can be geographic rather than demographic.

When voters are apt to divide along regional lines, the problem faced by a referendum's sponsors becomes still more complicated. It may not be enough simply to win a majority of votes. Instead, a *double* majority — that is, the support of both a majority of voters and a majority of regions — may be needed to assure the legitimacy of the outcome. This means, of course, that referendum supporters in a country like Canada must deal with either 5 regional or 11 provincial jurisdictions, and hence 11 separate campaigns, while opponents need focus only on one or two of the regional or provincial jurisdictions to ensure defeat.

In Canada, concerns were also raised in the past about the appropriateness of using a referendum in a parliamentary democracy, despite the fact that the British themselves have resorted to this method on several occasions. In 1980 the option had so little credibility that Pierre Trudeau's original proposal to include a referendum as part of the amending procedure in his constitutional reform package was roundly criticized by almost all observers. It was discarded. Apart from the historical context, criticism at that time ranged from the view that it was incompatible with the British parliamentary tradition of representative democracy, to the more extreme (and incorrect) view that it was actually "undemocratic."

Yet a decade later, the idea of a referendum was becoming increasingly popular with the general public. The decreasing credibility of the political actors and the political system itself were leading Canadians to a crisis of confidence that only a sense of personal intervention and control seemed likely to alleviate. At a minimum, some type of direct consultation would be required to legitimate future constitutional proposals.

The federal government created the Spicer Commission to respond to precisely this sense of widespread dissatisfaction. It appeared to many observers, however, that the commission served merely to open the floodgates of popular discontent. Public opinion polls in the wake of the Meech Lake débâcle consistently indicated strong public support for a national plebiscite to ratify any new deal that the first ministers might reach.

So the Mulroney government's throne speech of May 1991 announced that legislation would be introduced to enable the federal government to conduct a referendum if it wished. At the same time, aware of all the problems associated with the referendum option, the government continued to deploy a number of alternative mechanisms to satisfy the desire for consultation. The Spicer Commission was followed by the special parliamentary committee (Beaudoin-Dobbie) and the convocation of five consultative national forums under the auspices of Joe Clark as minister of constitutional affairs, in the hope that a potentially divisive and unsuccessful national referendum could be avoided.

The Spicer Commission, Joe Clark's five public forums, and the public hearings of the special parliamentary committee — all of these types of consultation were perfectly acceptable to Mulroney and his government and most of the premiers. What they had in common was the fact that the consultation was taking place *before* a final package was prepared. The referendum, however, would have to be held *after* the package was completed, when public involvement entailed much greater risk. Public criticism before the fact could be deflected or absorbed by the politicians. Public disavowal after the fact would lead to national divisions over which the politicians had no control.

The extent of the federal government's desire to avoid the referendum option can be most easily measured by the length of time it took to introduce the enabling legislation proposed in the throne speech.

First promised in May 1991, it was not until more than a year later that draft legislation was finally tabled in Parliament.

Joe Clark's public announcement in late April 1992 that the government had not ruled out a referendum option caused considerable consternation within the ranks of the national Conservative caucus. Left to his own devices by the prime minister, Clark was then forced to defend the idea before an extremely hostile Quebec Conservative caucus. He emerged bloodied and bowed from that meeting, announcing that he had just discovered there were serious historical grievances and objections to the referendum concept that required the government to proceed with caution.

Indeed, the federal government clearly would not have proceeded with the referendum if, first, its various consultative bodies had produced a consensus acceptable to Quebec, and, second, Quebec's agenda had not driven the federal government to take more precipitate action.

The disagreement over the referendum option that Joe Clark had discovered within the federal Conservative Party became more evident with each passing day. Other politicians also were wading into the debate with conflicting views. Ontario's former premier David Peterson, for example, urged the government not to proceed with the idea of a national referendum because it was potentially far too disruptive, while his successor, Bob Rae, declared it was an essential element of a democratic process.

The federal Liberal leader, Jean Chrétien, increased the pressure on the government by threatening to withdraw his support for the Beaudoin-Dobbie compromise unless referendum legislation was introduced.

Even after the decision to proceed with legislation was taken, the government's ambivalence was clearly revealed in statements by the prime minister and his House leader, Harvie Andre, when the legislation was brought before the House of Commons. As the federal government's lead speaker in favour of the legislation (entitled Bill C-81, An Act to Provide for Referendums on the Constitution of Canada),

Mr. Andre expressed enthusiasm for a referendum that could only be described as restrained.

"This legislation is a precautionary measure," he told the House on May 19, 1992. "It is no more and no less than that. This legislation would enable the federal government to hold a referendum on Canada's constitutional future *should such a step be required* [emphasis added]." In an apparent effort to reassure those antagonistic caucus and cabinet members from Quebec, he continued by stressing that "in saying that this measure is a precautionary one, it is important to underline that there is nothing in the legislation saying that there will be a referendum at all. No decision to hold a federal referendum has been made." In fact, Mr. Andre continued, "nor has there been any decision about what a referendum question would ask. There is no provision in the legislation saying what a so-called victory would be." Ramming home his message that the legislation was no more than a tentative last resort, Andre concluded, "Speculation on anyone's part on these issues is meaningless because the bill before us only provides that a referendum could be held — could be held, and nothing more."

In the parliamentary system, the opposition parties are accustomed, even expected, to speculate. In principle, their role is to oppose legislation as a matter of course on the theory that their criticisms and comments could both educate the general public as to its flaws and possibly improve the final product if the government is willing to listen. In the case of Bill C-81, the Liberal Official Opposition and the NDP found no end of problems on which to speculate.

Problems with the Government's Referendum Legislation

The federal government had not wanted a referendum and had avoided drafting a bill at an earlier stage. As a result, the legislation that was finally tabled was a hastily drawn-up measure in which the details were left to be resolved by bureaucrats without the benefit of parliamentary review. The lack of detail in the bill was compounded by the lack of time the government allowed for its consideration. The bill was tabled when only four weeks remained before the parliamentary recess in mid-June.

This timetable left the opposition parties with far more questions than answers and little opportunity to analyze the proposal properly and recommend changes. Both parties complained that the bill left far too much to the imagination. If there were no details to be found in the bill because it was simply a method of permitting Parliament to hold a referendum in case it ever wanted to, when would the details be worked out and by whom?

The Liberals in particular were extremely unhappy with the nebulous state of affairs. The Liberal House leader, David Dingwall (Cape Breton-East Richmond) and the national caucus chair, Sergio Marchi (York West) dissected the bill and identified what they considered to be six major problems. First, the legislation did not require that a national referendum be mandatory before any future constitutional reform was implemented. Mr. Marchi observed that the government House leader would likely prefer not to have a referendum at all and declared, "It should not be an option that Canadians only perhaps, or maybe, will be given a franchise."

A second problem identified by the Liberals was that the legislation did not stipulate that the referendum be conducted on a national basis. Instead it would permit a referendum to be conducted by the federal government in "one or more provinces." In light of the pressure tactics used by the federal government on Newfoundland and Manitoba during the Meech Lake debate, Mr. Dingwall speculated that the government might use the referendum option in future "not as an instrument for legitimizing a constitution, but as a tool to be used against a particular premier or premiers." (Revelations by officials after the fact confirmed that these fears were well-grounded. Using the referendum as a last-ditch weapon to blackmail recalcitrant provinces had indeed been the government's intention.)

The third complaint was the absence of a formula to determine if the referendum question had been approved or rejected. In the absence of such a formula, they concluded, there would be endless speculation both during and after a referendum campaign as to what in fact would constitute a victory for the government. This lack of certainty could only lead, in their view, to a lack of legitimacy for the process. What possible reason could the government have for not specifying the margin of victory required?

The Liberals supported the concept of a double majority — their idea was that a national majority vote would also need to be reinforced by a regional (not a provincial) majority vote. Referring to the amending formula suggested in the Victoria Charter as a suitable model, Mr. Dingwall argued that "a national referendum on constitutional change should require the approval of the majority of voters nationally as well as the majority of voters in each of the four regions of this country." In this way, he concluded, "no one region would ever be made to feel that the other regions had forced it to accept an arrangement with which it was not comfortable."

The fourth and fifth problems identified by Liberal spokespersons related to the actual operation of the referendum campaign. Not only were there to be no limitations on spending by groups or individuals, but also there would be no overall limitation on the total amount spent by the Yes and No sides. The Liberal House leader argued that this state of affairs was totally unacceptable. He argued that "if the results of the referendum are to be considered credible it is essential that the process be transparently fair."

He recalled that in the 1988 federal election campaign, the business community was able to expend massive amounts of money in support of free trade, while opponents of the free trade agreement had no comparable resources to draw on. "We must never allow the losing side to be in a position to claim that the victory was bought," he argued.

Sergio Marchi concurred with Mr. Dingwall's arguments on the financing of the campaign and suggested another option to ensure greater fairness and balance between opposing sides, namely that "there be a component of public financing through the tax credit." In the same vein, the Toronto-area member also argued in favour of limitations on government spending and possibly the exclusion of government finances from a campaign.

A sixth and final point raised by the Liberals related to the formulation of the referendum question. Outraged that the legislation provided for only three days of debate on a question that the government would have formulated in advance, both Liberal spokespersons called for interparty consultations before any question was tabled for consideration by Parliament.

Lorne Nystrom (Yorkton-Melville), speaking for the NDP, noted that in the legislation the referendum result would be taken into account by the government, but that it would not be binding. He argued that "if the federal government decides to go ahead it should, at the same time, say that even though it is not legally binding, it would be politically and morally binding on the government of the day."

The NDP House leader echoed Liberal concerns on the issue of the referendum question. "If this is to be a non-partisan issue," he asked, "why should we not have a non-partisan committee involving members from all sides of this House that drafts the question?" He also suggested that, given the extreme importance of the question to the outcome of any referendum, a special majority of 60% or even two-thirds should be required for approval of the draft question by the House of Commons.

Mr. Nystrom also supported the Liberal call for a double majority to determine if a plebiscite result was successful. "A double majority is necessary because without it," he argued, "it would be easy to isolate not only Quebeckers but also western Canada, the Atlantic provinces or Ontario.... It should not be possible to change the Constitution of Canada without the massive support of Canadians." Like the Liberals, then, the NDP advocated a regional, not a provincial, majority.

The most important problem raised by the NDP spokesperson dealt with the lack of funding limits for groups during a campaign, a problem that proved to be insurmountable for his party and leader.

Both opposition parties introduced a number of amendments to the bill, but the government, with its vast majority, rejected most of them, and the legislation reached the third and final stage largely intact. At this point both parties were obliged to decide whether to support the proposed legislation despite their misgivings. When he addressed the House on June 4, the Liberal leader, Jean Chrétien, concluded that the bill, though flawed, deserved his party's support. "We are disappointed with some elements of the bill," he said, but "whatever the results of these negotiations, we have to go to the people."

NDP leader Audrey McLaughlin came to a different conclusion. She stressed that "what we are speaking about today is not whether Canada should have a referendum. It is not whether Canadians should have a voice. We are debating Bill C-81 which would set out the details of how that voice would be heard and how that voice would be interpreted." Objecting above all to the government's refusal to accept amendments that would have put a limit on overall spending by both sides, and to provide for non-partisan consultation on the eventual referendum question, the NDP leader concluded that "this referendum bill fails the test of fairness at every step." She indicated that her party would not support it.

Bill C-81 was nevertheless passed by the House of Commons later that day, with the Liberal and government members supporting it and the NDP opposed. Shortly thereafter it was passed by the Senate and received royal assent. This left the government in the position of being able to call a referendum if it chose but in no way obliged to do so.

Although a great deal was left to be determined by regulation, the bill did outline the basic procedure to be followed during a federal referendum. The chief electoral officer and his staff would be responsible for administering the referendum wherever it was held. There was still no requirement for a *national* referendum. The federal government remained free to hold the plebiscite in as many or few provinces as it chose. There would be a writ issued by the chief electoral officer, as in a general election, but the campaign period would be only 36 days, much shorter than the regular 51-day federal election campaign. Quebec would hold its own referendum under its own rules, while the campaign in other provinces would be guided by this federal legislation.

Although there were still no limits on total spending, any groups planning to spend more than $5,000 would be required to register as a referendum committee and would be limited to spending 54.6 cents per voter. Ignoring the concerns of the opposition, the government left the legislation as it was on many more key points, a decision that would prove crucial during the campaign. There would, for example, be no limit on the number of committees that could register on either side of the issue. As in election campaigns, groups would be entitled to proportional free-time telecasting and advertising.

In addition the bill contained a provision that required that, if a referendum were to be called, Parliament would be summoned to debate the specific question that would be put to Canadians. That question would be drafted by the government.

And so it turned out. While Parliament was debating the referendum bill in June, the federal minister responsible for constitutional affairs, Joe Clark, was in the midst of discussions with provincial officials and the premiers, but they were unable to arrive at a consensus. Two months later, at the end of August, a package had been agreed upon, but the process by which it was achieved had taken a toll on all participants.

Clark and Mulroney ended up working at cross purposes. The result was that Mulroney and eventually Quebec premier Robert Bourassa found themselves negotiating with the other premiers on the basis of a proposal they otherwise would never have considered. Neither had wanted a national referendum. Mr. Bourassa, however, had to put some kind of question to his electors by October 26 — his own Bill 150 required it. To them the obvious and perhaps the only solution was to convert the Quebec referendum into a national referendum, in which the citizens of all provinces were asked the same question.

This is eventually what the prime minister and the premiers agreed to do, although not without considerable backroom bargaining. Both Alberta and British Columbia had their own referendum legislation on the books, and their premiers feared yielding to the federal government might be politically unacceptable to their citizens. But the cost of administering the referendum campaign would be considerable. It would be far cheaper, as well as simpler, to allow the federal government to assume responsibility. In addition, every province had a vested interest in pre-approving, behind the scenes, the actual wording of the question to ensure that there were no unpleasant and potentially costly political surprises.

As a result, every province except Quebec agreed to have the federal government administer a federal referendum campaign. The referendum option, which originally had been viewed as a last resort for sound reasons, was adopted in the end for the worst of reasons — the lack of credibility of the political élites nationally and provincially, and their desire to limit debate by moving quickly. Recognition of their low standing led them to conclude (correctly) that some type of public endorsement was now necessary to provide legitimacy to their solution, but their failure to appreciate the public's real concerns and core values led them to attempt a simplistic and speedy short cut rather than the more rigorous route of parliamentary committee and public hearings *before* putting the package to a national vote. Just as they did not consider postponing the Quebec vote to a later date, they did not realize that public consultation *after* the accord was reached, and before a referendum was held, would improve their chances considerably. Nor did they consider the consequences of two separate campaigns.

Although the question asked in Quebec would be identical, the fact remained that an entirely different set of rules would be used in Quebec, administered by provincial rather than federal officials. At the time this appeared to cause neither the prime minister nor the other premiers much concern. Later, the rather bizarre arrangement caused large problems for the Yes campaign.

So did several other provisions the Opposition had identified as potential problems, and which the government in its wisdom had refused to modify. Among these was the fact that an unexpectedly large number of No committees were formed. Having refused to limit the number of committees, the Yes forces stood by helplessly and watched as these many groups were then entitled under the legislation to take advantage of free broadcast advertising time. This provision alone was a highly detrimental blow to the Yes forces. As the chapters on the campaign itself demonstrate, the use of television by the No forces was extremely effective in reaching a large and impressionable audience. With almost no funds, such a campaign would not have been possible for the No side without this free time.

Similarly, the government's refusal to define a victory in the campaign as a double majority of national plus *regional* votes, as both the Liberals and the NDP had suggested, meant that the victory was defined for them during the campaign, forcing them to win in 11 jurisdictions instead of five or six.

Problems with the Referendum Question

On September 8, 1992, the House began consideration of the actual question that would be put to Canadians on October 26.

That question read, "Do you agree that the constitution of Canada should be renewed on the basis of the agreement reached on August 28, 1992? Yes or No?"

Almost immediately a number of social scientists and pollsters pointed out that in their view it contained biased wording favouring a positive response. They noted in particular the use of the phrases "Do you agree" and "should be renewed" as wording that would send a subconscious message to the voter to respond positively. Most critics tempered their criticism, however, agreeing that the effect of the wording would be marginal.

In the event, critics in the House of Commons devoted little time to the actual wording of the question. The tone was set by Joe Clark for the Conservatives, Liberal constitutional spokesperson André Ouellet, and NDP constitutional critic Lorne Nystrom, all of whom focused not on the wording of the question but on the provisions of the Charlottetown Accord. It was left to one of the few members who was unsympathetic to the package to outline the problems with the question and the referendum process.

Liberal MP Charles Caccia zeroed in on a number of the problems that were to become procedural issues and headaches for the Yes forces during the course of the campaign. "What does the term 'on the basis of' mean?" asked Mr. Caccia. "Does it mean subject to the legal text? ... When will the legal text be made available? Will the legal text subsequently be changed? Will there be a parliamentary committee to examine such text? Will there be amendments permitted?"

Caccia accused the government of accelerating the referendum process in order to avoid what it viewed as the mistakes of Meech Lake. Canadians were to be denied both time and the legal text in order to make constructive opposition as difficult as possible. "When it comes to such a profound change in our system, Canadians have to be given all the means and time to understand how the proposed changes will work," he argued. "Not just a six-week wonder with no legal text, no public hearings and no expert analysis." The former Trudeau-era minister of the environment concluded that Canadians had not missed the significance of the fact that all consultation had taken place before, not after, the premiers reached a consensus on the accord. "It is worthwhile noting," he said, "that to the question 'Do you think there has been enough consultation about changes to the constitution' some 60% of Canadians answered No in a poll just published by the *Toronto Star*."

Although Mr. Caccia was not alone in his criticism of the question and the process, he was one of the few members of the three major parties to bring his concerns to the House. Apart from the predictable rejection of both the package and the question by the Bloc Québécois spokespersons, only two independents, Alex Kindy and Pat Nowlan, and lone Reform Party member Deborah Grey, spoke critically in the debate. (Tory M.P. Chuck Cook also voted against the bill, but did not speak in the debate.)

Like Mr. Caccia, Ms. Grey focused on the lack of final text and the ambiguous nature of the question. "The most frightening aspect of this question," she stated, "is that it does not actually ask voters whether they accept the package or not. Rather it asks whether the Constitution should be changed on the *basis* of the agreement, not on the agreement itself. Why? The answer is because there is no agreement at this point, at least no legal text." Taking the argument to its logical conclusion, she charged that "such an open-ended question will allow the first ministers to alter the agreement after the referendum if they find it expedient to do so and perhaps even go ahead with ratification despite a No vote in one or more provinces."

Problems with Partisan Politics

If there was little evidence of dissent inside the House, arguments raged within all three parties behind the scenes. The Conservative caucus remained deeply split over the question of whether a referendum should be held. Both NDP and Liberal members harboured deep misgivings about the process and the question and fretted anxiously about the political ramifications of their close association on this issue with the deeply unpopular federal Tories. Their dilemma was having to choose between support for the accord, which reduced their role to that of largely irrelevant cheerleaders, or opposition, which might be interpreted as the triumph of partisanship over the national interest.

In the end the Liberals decided to maintain a united front for two reasons — the apparently sincere belief that approval of the package, whatever its merits, was necessary for national unity, and a degree of political expediency. Rightly or wrongly, they believed that internal dissent over Meech Lake had cost them the 1988 election, and they were determined to avoid the same mistake. Caucus unity was seen as the overriding imperative in this round of constitutional negotiation, and the vast majority of members were prepared to follow the leader's position without question to achieve that objective, even if they personally were not comfortable with the package.

A different debate developed in the NDP caucus. The party's only Quebec MP, Phil Edmonston, indicated that he would probably vote no and campaign in the referendum. Apart from this potentially disastrous piece of news, the main concern in the meetings of Audrey McLaughlin's team was how to avoid losing partisan momentum on non-constitutional issues such as the North American Free Trade Agreement (NAFTA). Like the Liberals, the NDP was determined to appear non-partisan in the referendum campaign, but worried that this would neutralize their effectiveness on other matters.

The government, however, had no such qualms. Having accused the Reform Party of being "the only party which is playing politics with the Constitution," the Conservative government proceeded to exploit the self-imposed restraint of both opposition parties. Having achieved all-party consent on the question, the bill passed quickly through the House and Senate, coming into effect in less than two weeks. The prime minister then announced that the House would continue to sit for another two or three days in order to push through the highly contentious changes to the pharmaceutical legislation and the elimination of the baby bonus.

Undeterred by opposition charges that this approach was making it hard for them to maintain their non-partisan solidarity on the constitutional front, the government then announced that it was planning to recess immediately after the legislation was passed, in order to allow MPs to campaign in support of the referendum package in their ridings.

While the NDP responded positively to this suggestion (due in large measure to the low ratings of their leader, whom many supporters believed needed the opportunity to campaign and raise her profile in the public eye), the Liberals expressed disbelief that the Parliament of Canada, having been adjourned for more than two months for the summer recess, would now be silent for another two months, leaving only a few weeks at the end of the year to debate the crucial economic issues of the day, including the government's intended signing of the NAFTA agreement. Despite heated interventions by Liberal House leader David Dingwall and others, the government's view prevailed, supported by the NDP.

Parliament adjourned and the referendum campaign moved into the real world. The politicians had put their fate and the fate of the Charlottetown Accord into the hands of the people.

5

Saying Yes to Canada:
The Establishment Organizes Its Troops

In early September 1992, long-time Tory backroom strategist Harry Near boasted about the organizational strength of the national Yes committee, known as the Canada Committee. "It's one thing to fight the referendum by popping up and making an announcement.... It's another to make an announcement and follow that up with organization at the national, provincial and grassroots levels," Near declared. "That's the difference people will see in our campaign. The organization is there." To the political insiders in Ottawa it seemed that truer words had never been spoken. All the evidence was there in black and white — on the complex organizational charts that had already been drawn up and distributed, in the $7 million budget, in the luxurious and technologically state-of-the-art campaign office that was being set up. They were already planning a comprehensive leaders' tour, weekly and daily polling, elaborate media events across the country, and more...

The Yes side had money, personnel, and election campaign expertise. With the combined efforts of the best politicians and staff each of the three federal parties had to offer, it was going to be a "Dream Team" operation. According to one account of the Yes team's plans, "It will have the best organizational, strategic and communications brains the federal backrooms have to offer. And it will be a synchronized formation of some 900 local organizations, armed by a cadre of more than 20,000 experienced political volunteers."[1]

To Canadians as well, it seemed obvious that the Yes side had the overwhelming advantage. In the first few weeks after the announcement of the Charlottetown Accord on August 28, it was almost impossible to find anyone of any significance among the country's élites who was prepared to dissent from the solid front being presented to the public. Those few who did were dismissed as marginal players, malcontents, or "enemies of Canada."

Everybody who was anybody was vying to be associated with the Yes team. As their campaign literature reminded voters, the supporters of the Charlottetown Accord represented the most massive coalition of diverse interests ever assembled. As it turned out, its very diversity would prove to be its undoing.

The Yes campaign was never a monolithic structure in organizational terms. Although it appeared that the élites were presenting a unified front, behind the scenes there were many distinct organizational entities, several of which were at odds with one another. Harry Near himself acknowledged that "complexity is a problem — take a campaign and multiply it by nine." The various entities took on a life of their own, often operating in sublime isolation from, and ignorance of, any overall strategy that the national Canada Committee operations unit devised.

In reality, the organization *wasn't* there on the Yes side. Or rather, there was a great deal of structural organization in place, but it had no effect, or even a negative effect, on the campaign. The very items that had been seen as evidence of strength in the beginning began to be viewed as handicaps. There was too much money, too much personnel, and too many activities to co-ordinate.

From the beginning the chances of developing a harmonious working relationship among all the various groups was slim. As it happened, the full-time national staff gave up on unity at an early stage. What they did attempt was to run a professional, election-style campaign. Since many of them were recognized by their peers as the best in the business, this should not have been difficult, particularly given the resources at their disposal, yet the attempt failed.

As poll after poll demonstrated throughout the campaign, the Yes organizers were consistently outmanoeuvred and outclassed by the ragtag collection of diverse No groups, who lacked not only money but any real organization at all. Worse still, the Yes side's money and slick campaign cast the No forces, with their total lack of logistical support and their one-room office, in the role of the underdog that people love to support.

The reasons the Yes side failed to capitalize on its advantages — its superior numbers, finances, and human resources — to create an unbeatable campaign "machine" are as varied and unexpected as the coalition it forged. This should hardly be surprising, given the nature of the coalition. The Yes supporters consisted of the leadership of all three major federal parties and almost all of their provincial counterparts, as well as 191 local or community-based non-partisan organizations, "prominent" Canadians recruited as voluntary "national chairs," and the leadership of the native, labour, corporate, media, and cultural élite. Many of these players had little in common. Others were natural enemies.

The professional organizers tried to impose some order on their campaign. But they themselves fell victim to the problems of diversity of interest and partisanship in the early days of the campaign — to say nothing of the sin of overconfidence.

The Professionals Try to Organize

Working on the mistaken assumption that a referendum campaign would resemble an election campaign, the leadership of the three federal parties, having agreed to work together in support of the accord, also agreed on a shared campaign organization structure that would benefit from the best professional staff each had to offer.

The all-party agreement posed delicate problems, since both opposition parties insisted on equal representation. This meant a tripartite leadership to the committee, which in itself was not the most efficient structure from a managerial perspective. The diplomatic need to achieve a consensus when firm decision making might be required on short notice was a problem from the beginning.

The Conservatives appointed long-time Tory strategist and Ottawa lobbyist Harry Near to head their side of the operation. The Liberals selected Gordon Ashworth, who was their campaign director in 1984 and will be again in the upcoming election. The NDP appointed Les Campbell, Audrey McLaughlin's chief of staff. These three were joined by the political aides of the Conservative and Liberal leaders, Hugh Segal and Eddie Goldenberg, which made for a crowded table at daily tactics meetings.

To these five were added a number of high-level organizers from all parties. Michael Robinson, former Liberal finance officer and Ottawa lobbyist (and partner of Harry Near in the Earnscliffe Strategy Group), and the NDP's Gerry Caplan, a former national director of the party and Toronto-based consultant, were in charge of their parties' responses. John Tory, a close friend of Brian Mulroney and the Conservatives' 1988 and 1993 campaign chair, was put in charge of organizing the grassroots campaign for the Conservatives. He too found himself working alongside his Liberal and NDP counterparts. As one senior aide remarked, "This is one of the hardest things I've ever had to do."

Internal dissension was never far from the surface, not only along party lines but also *within* them. More than one heated exchange occurred between Hugh Segal, the prime minister's chief of staff, and Harry Near of the Canada Committee over the prime minister's behaviour on the campaign trail. Segal's meetings in the Langevin Block (where the PMO is located) at 7:00 each morning to discuss the prime minister's agenda were separate from the Canada Committee's strategy sessions, and Segal was held responsible, rightly or wrongly, for many of the prime minister's blunders. In the end there was no resolution of the problem. It became obvious that the prime minister could not or would not be contained. With the chief spokesperson for the Yes side determined to pursue his own agenda despite the recommendations of the experts and pollsters, the organizers had only one option: to work around him.

The partisan squabbling was focused not only on tactics. A great deal of money was being made available by the federal government through the Federal-Provincial Relations Office (FPRO), and private funding was pouring in from the business community as well. (One source at the time indicated that the "suggested contribution" for corporations was $25,000.) With an overall budget of at least $5 million, advertising contracts were a source of rising conflict between the party activists of the three parties.

Already evident to many Ottawa insiders, the conflict was becoming a matter of public knowledge because of "their inability to mould a co-ordinated advertising program," as Ross Howard reported in the *Globe and Mail* of October 1. Instead, contracts for television and radio advertising and print materials were given to three different firms selected by each of the parties. These firms were Supercorp (Tory Jim Red) and Vickers and Benson (Liberal Terry O'Malley), and Jim Ryan (an independent agent who had worked for NDP premier Bob Rae).

Polling was supposed to be divided among the three federal parties. This was no minor matter: an estimated $3 million was invested in polling over the course of the campaign, an amount exceeding that spent by all three federal parties during the 1988 federal election. In the end, the lion's share went to firms with impeccable Tory connections, while Liberal and NDP appointees picked up the crumbs. Two firms in particular, Anderson Strategic Research (owned by Bruce Anderson, another Earnscliffe partner) and Decima Research (Conservative pollster Allan Gregg's original firm), were awarded sizeable contracts to conduct weekly national and provincial polling and focus groups.

The Liberals' new pollster, Michael Marzolini of Toronto, was reduced to conducting focus groups in the three Prairie provinces while the NDP's Viewpoint Research was given a minor contract to conduct polling in British Columbia. The unequal allocation of resources in this area was particularly galling to the pollsters because they knew, as one bureaucrat from FPRO remarked confidentially, "there is no budget here. The sky is the limit." As Canadians learned after the fact, the firms of several Yes organizers benefited handsomely from this fact, receiving substantial government contracts without tenders being called. Anderson and Decima alone received contracts of $1 million and $500,000, respectively.

The unrestrained polling was to a large extent pointless. The finding that Canadians disliked the prime minister and generally mistrusted all politicians was already evident to most observers. Other findings tended to reveal information that the organizers were unable to act upon. Polls showed, for example, that the referendum campaign was unlike any election, that party affiliation was irrelevant, and that the undecideds were a huge group that was difficult to categorize.

When it became obvious that the Yes campaign was in trouble, the carefully constructed tri-partisan organizational structure gave way to acknowledged expertise or the most impressive reputation. In British Columbia, former Conservative national director Jerry Lampert was increasingly prominent as a co-chair of the Yes campaign. David Morton of Quaker Oats, the Liberal advertising guru who ran what virtually all the experts described as an outstanding campaign for that party in the 1988 election, was named chair of the national advertising committee, put in charge of the three companies and the three pollsters.

On October 1, in another dramatic move that demonstrated the depth of the Yes campaign's concern, veteran Liberal strategist and Ottawa lobbyist Torrance Wylie was brought in to run the entire Yes campaign as "chief strategist and spokesman for the campaign office." This meant Liberal professionals were now entrenched in most of the senior and influential positions of the campaign structure, a situation that gave Liberals great satisfaction but proved increasingly irksome to both the Conservatives and the NDP.

None of the political parties was above using the referendum as a vehicle to enhance its organizational and public relations efforts in preparation for the next election. Quite apart from the daily communiqués and reams of other material emanating from the Canada

Committee headquarters, each party took the opportunity presented by the referendum to get its own message out to its own grassroots — putting the party "spin" on the events of the day and the week.

The Liberal Party's professionals in Ottawa were particularly adept in this game. The Liberal Faxletter, for example, was sent three times a week to nearly 600 "key" people. In it, Liberal insiders were given such vital information as "Jean Chrétien was the first national party leader to speak out on the Charlottetown Accord in Quebec." A similar referendum Infoline was being run from the leader's office to explain recent developments and highlight the leader's activities to party activists.

If both NDP and Liberal organizers were involved in promoting the interests of their respective parties under the guise of nonpartisan support for the accord, they were motivated in part by a perception that the Conservatives were attempting to steal the show. It was noted, for example, that neither Chrétien nor McLaughlin was offered a starring role in promoting the Yes cause by Canada Committee organizers. The Liberals were particularly unhappy with Conservative efforts to keep Mr. Chrétien out of Quebec. Considering Mulroney's less than stellar performance in that province, to say nothing of his unpopular appearances in British Columbia and Alberta, the Liberals felt their leader could hardly do worse.

Ironically, as the Yes campaign unravelled, the Conservative campaign organizers attempted to hold more than one massive rally at which all three political leaders would appear on the same stage, but neither Chrétien nor McLaughlin was "available."

The National Politicians Set the Tone

It is difficult if not impossible to "organize" politicians. When the stakes involve the future of the country and the possible future of political parties, the task becomes even more difficult. Asking the leadership and rank-and-file politicians of three political parties to suddenly abandon longstanding enmity and work together, sharing campaign supporters' lists and resources in a non-partisan effort to "elect" a written document, rather than a political leader, is asking a great deal.

For most of the political élite involved in this exercise, the referendum was a first. Only those few who had been through the 1980 referendum in Quebec could have any idea of the difficulties that would be faced. It was perhaps for this reason that Liberal leader Jean Chrétien, who alone had campaigned in that earlier plebiscite, was apparently the least unhappy of the three federal leaders to find himself on the same podium with his erstwhile opponents. Chrétien had appeared in public with former prime minister Joe Clark in the earlier Quebec referendum, and he told his caucus and advisers on more than one occasion that he would be willing to appear with Clark in this one. Appearing with Brian Mulroney, he said privately, was another matter entirely.

Although all three leaders had agreed to handle the referendum issue in a non-partisan fashion, it soon became apparent that old habits die hard. The temptation to turn a lecture on the referendum into a referendum on the partisan issues of the day is sometimes irresistible. Audrey McLaughlin had been moved to comment more than once that she would much rather be debating the prime minister on NAFTA than siding with him in a referendum campaign. Jean Chrétien, meanwhile, became the master of backhanded diplomacy, frequently declining to criticize the prime minister or his handling of the campaign, but immediately adding that on October 27 all bets were off. "Say yes in the referendum," he would say, and there will be "plenty of opportunity to say no" shortly thereafter in a federal election.....

As for the prime minister, the problems with his performance were for once not related so much to partisanship as to a refusal to be programmed by a campaign game plan or "line" of approach. Although it later became evident that he was receiving advice from several different sources, the unpredictability of his interventions (including the ripping up of a document during a speech in Sherbrooke) left some

NDP and Liberal members of the national campaign committee furious. Eventually, as one adviser confided, "We simply agreed not to talk about that any more. It's not productive."

Other high-profile Conservative politicians were brought in to counter Mulroney's negative image. Increasingly, Joe Clark was required to sell the accord everywhere except Quebec. Justice Minister Kim Campbell, who had proven one of the very few ministers able to deal articulately and cogently with the details of the package, was increasingly in demand to defend the package on nationally televised debates and in formal interviews. The Liberals usually chose on these occasions to be represented by deputy leader Sheila Copps, apparently on the theory that her aggressive debating style would overcome a shaky grasp of constitutional matters. The NDP increasingly relied on B.C. member and House leader Lorne Nystrom, an articulate veteran of every constitutional debate since 1982.

Several other ministers and opposition party members felt free to speak out on the deal as well, sometimes with unanticipated or negative consequences. Several Tory staffers spent two precious days of the campaign explaining that the Conservatives' Quebec lieutenant, Benoît Bouchard, had not predicted the accord would be defeated, nor (they said) had he stated that he would resign if it were.

The problems that the Canada Committee encountered with members of Parliament were in some ways more acute than those of their leaders, because members were expected to organize or even "co-chair" local all-party Yes committees in their ridings. As an impressive 19-page document entitled "The Registered Yes Committee Campaign Team" made clear, this meant sitting members of one party were expected to contact riding association presidents of the two other parties and meet to share lists, plan strategies, and organize events.

They were also expected to put in place a complex organization in very little time. The organization chart at the beginning of the manual recommended that some 22 positions should be filled to cover such items as budget, fund raising, door-to-door canvass, advertising, and

media relations. An auditor and legal counsel also were seriously recommended. What was being suggested, as the manual itself admitted,
was the equivalent of an election campaign committee. As for fund
raising, it was made clear that members would be left to their own
devices. The publication of this manual provoked consternation on all
sides of the House.

The manual was distributed in mid-September, but far fewer than
half of all MPs had acted on its proposals by early October. One Liberal
backbencher admitted frankly his decision to sit on the sidelines. "I
just can't do it. How can they expect me to sit down with the Tory and
NDP presidents in my riding knowing they'll use everything I give
them and everything they learn about my organization against me in
the next election? It's crazy!"

Indeed the next election was never very far away from the minds
of many members. Some actually decided to use the campaign as an
election dry run, organizing their own troops and practising canvassing and other techniques they would need in the next federal show-
down. In such cases, however, there was no effort made to form a
non-partisan committee or to play ball with the opposition.

This left the national organizing committee up in the air. Instead
of some 295 registered committees set up in standard format as suggested by the guide and shepherded by the local member, who could
be the contact person for campaign literature and directives, the national organization was faced with the prospect of committees that were
totally independent of party organizations and several that were within the same riding. At the final day of official notification, some 191
local Yes committees had been registered, but fewer than half were of
the kind the committee had envisaged.

The Provincial Political Élites Join In

If the national committee thought it had difficulties with federal leaders and politicians, however, its problems with provincial politicians

were even greater. Apart from the obvious problems of distance and differing party affiliations, the difficulties of organizing these supporters, despite their presumed goodwill and vested interest in selling the deal, were amplified by regional enmities and conflicting expectations.

The Yes advertising committee set out to devise a campaign message that would suit all regions of the country. They couldn't do it. Even if they had succeeded, making all provincial politicians adhere to the common line was clearly impossible. No sooner had B.C. Intergovernmental Affairs Minister Moe Sihota joined the fray to bail out his beleaguered boss, Mike Harcourt, than he found himself in difficulty for having told an audience in his province that Premier Bourassa of Quebec had faced a "brick wall" of opposition to several of his demands and got virtually nothing in the deal. This claim, replayed over and over in Quebec, did immeasurable damage to the credibility of the Yes campaign in that province.

Similarly, Ontario premier Bob Rae refused to pay attention to a daily briefing note from the national committee in Ottawa, which recommended against criticizing former prime minister Pierre Trudeau for his comments in his Maison Eggroll speech in Montreal on October 1. Rae's public comments the next day became increasingly vitriolic with every interview. Referring to the "petty" attacks of the former prime minister, whom he described as an "egotistical has-been" intent on destroying the country, Rae denounced Trudeau in an hour-long CBC open-line radio talk show as someone who "appeals to the least generous, the most mean-spirited and, in my view, the most destructive forces at work in Canada today." Needless to say, these unscripted remarks once again proved to have serious negative ramifications for the Yes vote, this time in Rae's own province.

A few provincial premiers posed a problem by their *lack* of participation. Clyde Wells of Newfoundland, considered one of the more "useful" spokespersons for the Yes side, was extremely reluctant to join the debate outside his home province. Worse, he made public a number of his concerns with respect to the legal text. Premier Gary Filmon of Manitoba left the country on business and abandoned the Manitoba Yes campaign to its fate for the first several weeks of the campaign. Premier Cameron of Nova Scotia indicated that he believed his role was essentially over and others should take up the fight during the actual referendum campaign.

Several premiers, furious with the prime minister because of the scare tactics and "fear-mongering" that he employed in some of his speeches, began to speak about it publicly.

The provincial Canada Committees, meanwhile, were also headed by partisan professionals. They generally assigned the lead role to someone of the same political stripe as the provincial government. In Ontario, the Canada Committee was headed by the NDP's Gordon Cressy, for example. The problem of using partisan professionals was highlighted in those cases where the provincial government did not enjoy vast popular support to begin with. In Ontario, where the Rae government was embroiled in a number of high-profile controversies, including a battle to introduce labour legislation that the business community violently opposed, the credibility of an NDP campaign spokesperson was limited. It may not have mattered, however: the eight-person Ontario Yes Committee was not very visible at the best of times and, like the other provincial committees, was largely dependent on the national committee.

"Prominent Canadians" Lend a Hand

When polls indicated that the Yes side was losing its early lead and that politicians of every stripe had lost their credibility, the national organizing committee came up with another strategy. In a matter of weeks, the idea of appointing seven non-partisan chairs (they later came to be known as the "Seven Angels") of the National Canada Committee was devised and implemented. Such was the speed with which the ploy was put into effect that some of the chairs were approached only a day or two before their names were announced to the public.

The appointees came from all political persuasions and backgrounds. They included journalist June Callwood; consultant Iona Campagnola; former U.N. ambassador Yves Fortier; Ontario physician and community worker Dr. Joseph Wong; businessman Michel Bastarache of New Brunswick; aboriginal leader Mary Simon; and Alberta businessman Ted Newall. Another 32 "eminent Canadians" were appointed members of the national committee. These members' backgrounds ranged from participation in arts and church organizations, to sports, business, and legal communities. Several retired politicians and judges were also listed, including Bill Davis, Robert Stanfield, Jean-Luc Pepin, and Ed Broadbent.

Although the concept was really to demonstrate that prominent, successful Canadians from all walks of life supported the accord, it was difficult to overlook the fact that these were no ordinary Canadians but members of the ruling élite. Many of the appointees had obvious political connections. Several were former premiers or cabinet ministers.

The launch in an Ottawa high school gymnasium of the national Canada Committee was a media flop. The attempt to portray the event as a grassroots effort failed to convince anyone who was there to see the considerable evidence of financing and advance planning. Far more important, however, was the inattention to detail that results when authority is too diluted and too many individuals are involved. In this case, the absence of print material in French, or a translated version of the large Yes banner, focused media attention on the event as a negative issue for several days in Quebec and elsewhere. (Of course, this error could also be attributed to the organizational structure of the committee itself. Since the Yes forces in Quebec were operating an entirely separate campaign, the "national" committee was in fact one that operated in only nine provinces.)

Left to their own devices after the launch, many chairs and members disappeared from the public eye for weeks. Only after a concerted effort was made by the national committee to schedule events, arrange tours for those who were available, and provide promotional materials did the "seven angels" begin to receive any real media attention. By then, the campaign was nearly two-thirds over.

In a bizarre footnote to these activities, the allegedly neutral office of the Governor General was brought into the debate through a letter sent to recipients of the Order of Canada. Written by author Peter Newman, a Companion of the Order and authorized biographer of Brian Mulroney, the letter requested donations for pro-Canada ads that would appear before October 26 across the country. It was accompanied by a letter on the Governor General's letterhead from his secretary, Judith LaRocque, a former aide to several Conservative ministers. Although LaRocque subsequently indicated that the idea had been approved by the Order of Canada advisory committee, this did little to reassure Canadians that the constitutional debate was not becoming an overmanaged propaganda campaign by The Establishment, particularly when it was learned that any contributions would be tax-deductible, a benefit not available to the formal Yes and No committees.

Professor Michael Behiels of the University of Ottawa, a co-founder of the national No campaign's Canada For All Canadians, said of the Newman letter: "This is obscene in the extreme. This campaign is a travesty of democracy." "Apparently," said Professor Behiels, "if you wrap yourself in the flag, anything goes."[2]

The Interest Group Élites Volunteer Their Support

There was no way the professionals could organize or co-ordinate the activities of the various élites that supported the accord. The business community and organized labour, the media and cultural élites, and the leadership of native peoples, all came together to support the Charlottetown Accord, but no one knew what to do with them. Indeed, no one was entirely sure who all these supporters were.

As the campaign wore on, more and more members of the country's Establishment intervened on the Yes side, but these interventions were scarcely controlled or co-ordinated.

The corporate élite was at first extremely reluctant to be seen to participate in the debate at all because of the widespread criticism of their interventions in the 1988 federal election campaign over the free trade issue. At the beginning of the campaign, Business Council on National Issues chair Tom d'Aquino stated categorically that the business community would not be active in the debate, either as spokespersons or financially. By the middle of the campaign, with panic starting to set in at Canada Committee headquarters, this attitude changed dramatically.

In fact, the banking sector of the corporate élite was involved almost from the beginning. Royal Bank chairman Allan Taylor began the interventions with the release of a detailed report prepared by the bank's economists on the presumed financial costs of Quebec separation. In a production remarkably similar to that enacted in the 1980 referendum debate, it appeared the Yes forces would again hold the threat of financial disaster over the heads of opponents. The ploy failed to have the desired effect.

In Quebec, Jacques Parizeau and his associates made fun of the Royal Bank report. In the rest of Canada, opponents of the accord were joined by undecided Canadians and even a number of Yes activists in their condemnation of alarmist tactics. For many Canadians, the No message that the debate was about the constitutional amendment package, not about Quebec separation, began to take shape as a result of this intervention. When the report was subsequently defended and reinforced by statements from the lead bankers at the CIBC and the Toronto Dominion, it only made matters worse. The Canadian public was now beginning to form a clear picture of the campaign as a battle between the "little people" referred to by Pierre Trudeau, and the Establishment. If Canadian bankers liked the deal, it could hardly be good for ordinary citizens.

The bankers appeared to be unaware that they had an image problem. In the days after the Royal Bank report, a series of economists and financial experts waded into the debate, followed in turn by a number of high-profile business executives. Many of the business people resorted to the tactics that were employed during the free trade debate, distributing letters with employees' paycheques and making speeches at employee gatherings. In many cases, the tactics had a negative effect on those at whom they were directed. In addition, the image of corporate Canada united in support of the deal proved not to be advantageous to the accord's sponsors among the wider population.

This did not stop the umbrella organizations of the business community from leaping into the fray in the last third of the campaign. Spokespersons for the Canadian Chamber of Commerce (Tim Reid), the Canadian Manufacturers' Association, and the Business Council on National Issues (Tom d'Aquino) abandoned their earlier stated intention not to become involved and began to campaign aggressively, distributing materials, giving speeches, and holding special meetings of their membership.

In what many Canadians viewed as the ultimate irony, the majority of the labour élite was on side with the corporate sector in defence of the accord. Bob White of the Canadian Labour Congress participated aggressively and directly in many activities of the Yes committee. With only one notable exception, the unions under his control followed suit.

Similarly, the leadership of the aboriginal community — Ovide Mercredi of the AFN (status Indians), Rosemarie Kuptana of the Inuit Tapirisat, and Ron George of the National Council of Natives (non-status Indians and Métis) — somewhat surprisingly found itself on the same side as the political élite. While some of Mercredi's membership began to question the wisdom of a Yes vote, embarrassing him on more than one occasion in Manitoba and British Columbia, the "middle management" of the other organizations held firm. To some Indian chiefs, however, what Mercredi and his colleagues viewed as a successful negotiating process was interpreted as a co-option by the political élite.

Representatives of the multicultural élite also participated on the Yes committee, despite several earlier stated misgivings about provisions of the Canada clause and the "categorization" of citizens, as well as the protection of minority language rights. One by one the Canadian Ethnocultural Council, the Canadian Jewish Congress, Alliance Quebec (the representative of English-speaking Quebeckers), the Federation of Francophones Outside Quebec, and a variety of specific ethnocultural community leaders all announced that they supported the Charlottetown Accord.

Virtually all the influential print media élite across the country mounted Yes campaigns. Although the coverage of news events was generally balanced, the editorial boards were clearly tilted in favour of the accord. This striking homogeneity (which even more surprisingly included the *Toronto Star*, a paper that had long supported the "Trudeau vision" of federalism and opposed the Meech Lake Accord) culminated in the simultaneous publication of Yes editorials on Saturday, October 17, in the *Globe and Mail*, *Ottawa Citizen*, *Montreal Gazette*, *Toronto Star*, and several other dailies across the country.

Although the Yes organizers' attempts to recruit Guy Lafleur, Wayne Gretzky, and a number of Olympic athletes to the cause had been conspicuously unsuccessful, there were other, genuinely spontaneous demonstrations in support of the accord across the country. But after so much manipulation, it was difficult for Canadians to separate out these activities from those that were artificially contrived. Put another way, it began to appear to ordinary Canadians that "the fix was in." For any event that was significant enough to receive media coverage, Canadians were immediately inclined to ask who was pulling the strings behind the scenes.

The Yes Strategy at the Start of the Campaign

Apart from attempting to organize and co-ordinate the many disparate supporters of the Yes campaign and provide daily tactical advice to key players in response to polling data and other developments, the professional organizers were also responsible for mapping out an overall campaign strategy, much as they would do for an election campaign. They helpfully outlined this strategy to a number of observers after the first week of the campaign.

An overall strategy of the campaign team called for the "non-partisan prominent Canadians" chairing the Canada Committee (June Callwood and the other six "angels") and the elder statesmen (Lougheed, Davis, Broadbent, and the others) to address the details of the accord and the issues that were raised about it in a positive, educational fashion. "Look, no politics" was to be the theme of this approach.

Meanwhile the political élites at the federal and provincial levels would counter the arguments of the No supporters and hammer out the message about the consequences of the deal. As the following chapters demonstrate, this was a strategy that was successful in its execution but a failure in reaching its objective.

The campaign strategy was to have three stages. In the first half of the campaign, from roughly September 20 to October 7, the objective was to "get the message out." This meant distributing millions of copies of the Consensus Document to households across the country. (No sooner was this accomplished, a remarkable logistical feat in the time permitted, than public anxiety over the absence of a legal text made the exercise redundant. A second educational effort to produce and distribute copies of that text kept the Yes side constantly on the defensive and behind schedule...)

The second stage of the campaign, from roughly October 7 to October 18, was supposed to "make the message local." Here the provincial and local committees were supposed to carry the ball. As outlined above, these local committees simply did not materialize in many areas of the country. Alberta was exceptional in this regard. The provincial government took control of the situation early on, distributing "personalized letters" to hundreds of "opinion leaders" in each community.

In the third and final stage — the last week of the campaign — all the stops were pulled out in an effort to "get out the vote." The plan called for door-to-door canvassers to blitz communities and distribute promotional material. In Toronto, for example, over the final weekend, volunteers distributed hundreds of thousands of flyers. These flyers were remarkable for what they revealed about the Yes forces. They addressed accurately voters' key concerns as defined by the No side, and answered each one in highly persuasive, but misleading, language. It was clear that the Yes side's strategists had access to sophisticated polling reports, which, at this stage, revealed a large and volatile undecided faction among voters. The flyers constituted a brilliant stroke on the part of the Yes campaigners in that there was no way the No forces, lacking an organization on the ground, could respond to them.

But no single last-minute stroke of genius by the Yes side was going to carry the day.

6

Saying No to the Deal:
The Outsiders Take On the Establishment

O n August 28, 1992, Prime Minister Mulroney described opponents of the Charlottetown Accord as the "enemies of Canada." At the time, he had no idea what powerful forces he was unleashing. Across the country, ordinary Canadians, more than 70% of them inclined to view the accord favourably on that sunny day, were filled with rage and indignation at his apparent view that opponents of the "historic compromise" he and the premiers had just achieved were unpatriotic. Indeed, countless writers of letters to the editor and political columnists concluded it wasn't patriotism that was at issue, but democracy, and it was the prime minister who was undemocratic.

Although Mr. Mulroney subsequently hastened to distance himself from those remarks, for several weeks they remained what Graham Fraser of the *Globe and Mail* termed on September 19 "the three little words that just won't go away." Because of the backlash Mulroney's statement inspired, many supporters of the Yes side believed throughout the campaign that opposition to the deal was primarily based on anger or mean-spirited vengeance rather than principled disagreement. The continued exhortations by the Yes élites for Canadians to be more "generous," "tolerant," and "open-minded," to "care enough" about their country and to put aside their personal dislike of Brian Mulroney or the GST, came from even the more level-headed members of the Yes leadership.

The Yes team was certainly correct in its second contention, namely that the No forces constituted a highly disparate set of individuals and groups. (The Yes forces found themselves in some unusual alliances as well.) But it was wrong about the motivation of these groups and individuals if it truly believed that ill will determined their opposition to the accord.

The exhaustive polling conducted publicly by the media and privately by the Canada Committee undoubtedly revealed massive voter dissatisfaction with politicians and the Establishment in general. But by focusing on this discontent alone, the national Yes campaign demonstrated surprising ignorance of the factors motivating the vast majority of No supporters outside Quebec.

True, ordinary Canadians were furious with the current political élite who had given them free trade, the GST, and the Meech Lake débâcle. They were also furious at being treated like recalcitrant children by a Yes campaign based on what many considered to be fearmongering and blackmail. But behind these feelings of anger and discontent lay a reasonably coherent set of beliefs about the nature of the country. This alternative vision was clearly reflected in the arguments of the No leadership outside Quebec, from the Trudeau federalists and the special interest groups to the Reformers.

The political élite refused to acknowledge the substantive differences of opinion between themselves and those Canadians who opposed the deal on a number of fundamental issues: individual versus collective rights, equality of provinces and individuals versus special status, and the appropriate degree of centralization or decentralization of federal powers. Because the Yes side refused to recognize these differences, they conducted a campaign that did not even attempt to make the case for their view, or to justify the compromises they believed were necessary to achieve their much-vaunted consensus. This was ironic, in a way, because the spokespeople for the élite could correctly identify the three different categories of opponents to the deal. But their purpose in identifying them was to marvel at the strange or "unholy" alliance that had been formed against them. They missed entirely the common values and principles that had drawn their opponents together.

The Grassroots No Campaign

Choosing the No option did not come easily for most Canadians and gave them no pleasure. It was a traumatic experience that, by the end of the campaign, was leading psychiatrists to conclude that many voters were suffering from "referendum stress."

Citizens across the country took the referendum seriously, as the turnout of more than 75% of eligible voters on October 26 demonstrated. They considered the issues seriously, deliberated long and hard, struggled with their conscience, and arrived at their decision based on the issues raised in the deal itself. For many voters, the leading opponents of the deal were a source of information and inspiration. For all those Canadians who were trying to "do the right thing" and decided that No was the answer, the accusations that they were unpatriotic, self-centred, or irresponsible touched a raw nerve.

For some, these accusations were the factor that spurred them to participate actively in the campaign. Many became involved in political activity for the first time in their lives. As countless polls and television coverage demonstrated, the No forces were everyday Canadians, marching with home-made signs and setting up information booths in shopping malls. Lacking the resources of the Yes team's veritable army of foot-soldiers, they resorted to hit-and-run tactics in small, uncoordinated efforts.

In reality, the grassroots elements of the No forces were not organized or co-ordinated at all. Operating in cell-like units, they had little or no contact with other Canadians who opposed the deal. The No campaign at the local level resembled nothing so much as guerrilla warfare. As other regular armies have found at other times in other places, guerrilla tactics can be damnably effective.

Where the supporters of the accord established 191 local Yes committees formally registered with Elections Canada, the opponents of the deal managed to set up only 34. Instead of formal and officially recognized committees, the No forces consisted of innumerable smaller grassroots operations "headquartered" in kitchens, neighbourhoods, and hockey arenas, run by retired couples and working men and women who designed their own materials and paid with their own money to have buttons, posters, and signs made up.

Their identities and efforts were largely unknown to those waging the battle at the national level, a battle in which the odds were equally bad.

The "National" No Campaign

At the national level, the Yes side's Canada Committee organization with its elegant uptown offices on Ottawa's Metcalfe Street near Parliament Hill, its official budget of $7 million, and its endless supply of professional staff and volunteers, was countered by the "Canada for All Canadians" No committee — a one-room office in an old building on Montreal Road, miles from the action, manned by two or three tireless volunteers with a shoe-string budget and no technology to speak of.

No one decided to participate in the national No campaign because of a desire to be part of the "in" crowd. For virtually all the opinion "leaders" of the No campaign outside Quebec, the realization that they would be outsiders in the debate came the day the accord was announced.

Many of the deal's opponents had been fighting the Establishment's approach to the Constitution for years, throughout the Quebec Round and the Meech Lake approval process. They had seen many of their colleagues and comrades-in-arms fall by the wayside in recent times, too disheartened, discouraged, or tired to continue. While virtually everyone who had opposed the Meech Lake agreement could be heard describing this deal as "Meech Plus" or worse, most also said that, this time, nothing could be done to stop it. How had this amazing demoralization come about?

To begin with, the speed with which the political élite rebounded from the Meech Lake débâcle and launched another constitutional initiative surprised almost everyone. No one was more surprised than ordinary Canadians, who after nearly five years were suffering from what both pollsters and psychologists labelled "constitutional fatigue."

Despite earlier misgivings, the political leaders who signed the Charlottetown Accord in August were confident of victory in the proposed referendum campaign. This was not only because some 70% of Canadians, in every region of the country, indicated they were inclined to support the deal. As the polls also made clear, the public was obsessed with the downward-spiralling economy. The élites wrongly concluded that this meant Canadians would be willing to support almost any deal to "get the Constitution out of the way."

This was hardly good news for the deal's opponents. They joined the battle reluctantly, with full knowledge that their opposition would be unpopular at best and, at worst, a self-destructive career move.

For all the advantages they enjoyed, the Yes side took no chances. They targeted people they knew had opposed Meech Lake and, with a zeal that struck some observers as ridiculous, launched a campaign designed to intimidate and scare. Lobbyists, contract personnel, and political staff who had been involved in the fight against Meech Lake received phone calls and visits from people who told them they would never work again with whichever party they were associated if they took up with the No cause. Several members of Parliament known to be unhappy with the deal received phone calls threatening them with expulsion from their caucus if they broke ranks with their party. In Toronto, rookie MP and Trudeau acolyte Dennis Mills was ordered to tone down his opposition to the deal or face the consequences. In Montreal, MP David Berger, a Trudeau-era veteran who had also publicly indicated his unhappiness with the deal, suddenly announced on October 1 that he had reconsidered and would be supporting the accord in the interests of national unity, despite his reservations.

In Ottawa, several prominent party organizers and consultants who considered opposing the deal were known to have reversed their position as a result of such threats and ended up working actively for the

Yes campaign. Richard Anderson, a lobbyist and former Liberal organizer who had joined the Reform Party enthusiastically only a year
earlier, surprised many observers when he publicly announced his support for the accord and began working actively with the Yes campaign.

In Toronto, lawyer Mary Eberts, a partner in the prestigious (and
Conservative-dominated) law firm of Tory, Tory, DesLauriers and
Binnington, was forced to take a leave of absence when her colleagues
found she had taken the case of native women trying to block the referendum vote by challenging its legitimacy in the courts. Even many
academics, in whose work environment freedom of expression is supposedly sacred, began to perceive subtle threats and enticements to
either support the accord or at least remain above the fray.

The No supporters certainly knew they were the underdog. Few
among them believed at the start of the campaign that they had any
chance of "winning." They had no organization, no money, and no
volunteers or membership lists to call upon. With only six weeks in
which to make an impact, rather than the three years of Meech Lake,
their situation looked bleak indeed. Seen in this light, their eventual
decision to participate publicly and actively was understandably taken
with more reluctance than enthusiasm. As they prepared to mentally
gird their loins for the upcoming battles, one national No leader commented it felt "a lot like David heading into the ring with Goliath."
As even tireless No leader Deborah Coyne remarked in early September, "I don't think we have a hope of winning but, what can you
do, at least we've got to try."

The task of the deal's opponents was further complicated by the
absence of a natural leader for the national No campaign. They had
no spokespersons who were household names and no network. What
they had were a few individuals with a great deal of knowledge of the
issues but little experience in political debate.

As the Yes side pointed out at every opportunity during the six-
week campaign, the various opponents of the Charlottetown Accord
outside Quebec also appeared to have little in common. Not only was

collaboration impossible between the separatist No forces in Quebec and the federalist No forces elsewhere, but the federalist opponents themselves were divided into three distinct philosophical camps and all three of them had every intention of maintaining their separateness. This "strange bedfellows" phenomenon of the No team was, of course, no greater than that reflected by the disparate groups of the Yes campaign, but it was more obvious because no attempts were made to paper over the differences.

Yet by the end of the campaign, each of the three groups opposing the deal had made a major impact on some element of the population. Although the influence of the Reform Party in western Canada is easiest to identify because of its geographic base, the influence of the Trudeau federalists and special interest groups on the decisions of individual Canadians cannot be overestimated; this is particularly true in Ontario, where half the population rejected the deal despite initially strong support.

The Trudeau Federalists

Many of the accord's supporters could not resist telling the world the morning after Pierre Trudeau's Maison Eggroll speech in Montreal that the former prime minister was "yesterday's man." From prominent Liberals such as Sheila Copps, Herb Gray, and Robert Bourassa to Prime Minister Mulroney, Canada Committee "angel" Yves Fortier, and NDP premier Bob Rae of Ontario, the Yes response was unanimous and often personally vicious. To a man and woman, they had two ideas they wished to communicate to Canadians: first, the vision of federalism that Mr. Trudeau had espoused for nearly 40 years was passé and, second, Trudeau himself was a bitter old man who could not bear to let go of the reins of power.

On the first point, the Yes side might well have been right, or so it seemed to a small group of Trudeau loyalists as they met in a small room in the University of Ottawa's history department, one night shortly after the accord was announced. They had expected to find many of their comrades-in-arms from the Meech Lake battle ready to oppose the accord, particularly those who held elected office, but they were disappointed. The strict application of caucus solidarity had thinned their ranks dramatically.

As one resigned backbencher put it, "I didn't enter politics to become a champion of lost causes." Another, depressed about the critical response he had received from his caucus colleagues whenever he raised the issue of possible opposition to the deal, finally concluded that "it's too much — I can't handle this all by myself this time." Yet another from within the Liberal ranks stated, "Look where opposition got us last time. The public decided if we were split as a party on the deal, we couldn't possibly be united in running the country. Our opposition to Meech Lake cost us the last election, and we're not going to let that happen again, no matter what any of us thinks about the deal."

It was in this atmosphere that the few surviving advocates of the Trudeau vision met at the university in early September to determine the best course of action among their limited options. They came almost entirely from one of two backgrounds — non-elected party activists (some of whom were risking their jobs as paid staff of members of Parliament or contract consultants of the parties), and a small but impressive group of constitutional experts, primarily lawyers and academics. Alone, it seemed, this small band of warriors was left to carry the torch.

For them, the Charlottetown Accord represented a direct threat to that vision, in which a strong central government was essential for the effective functioning of the federal system and the maintenance of national unity. The role of the federal government in setting minimum national standards was viewed as the key to maintaining the Confederation bargain in which all Canadians, regardless of where they lived, would be assured equal access to health care, education, and other government services as a right of citizenship. Support for a degree of state intervention in the economy and the maintenance of the welfare state were viewed by Trudeau federalists not merely as policies but as common values that provided Canadians with a sense of national identity.

The federal government's active promotion of official bilingualism was seen as vital for assuring that English- and French-speaking Canadians would feel equally at home in their dealings with their government, and that a pan-Canadian identity would emerge based on a bilingual, multicultural society. The Charter and especially its equality provisions were seen as fundamental to the promotion of individual rights and freedoms and equality of opportunity for all citizens. Federalism itself was seen as the ideal system to counteract the negative and inward-looking aspects of nationalism, moderating the influence of the majority and allowing a wide degree of cultural autonomy for regional-based minorities within a larger, pluralistic political unit. As Pierre Trudeau had often said, it was *Canada* that was the distinct society, and a role model for the world.

But in the fall of 1992, these views appeared to be outdated. The provisions of the Charlottetown Accord argued for a watering down of national standards, even greater provincial autonomy at the expense of the national government, and changes to the Charter that would have the effect of promoting collective powers at the expense of individual rights, so that the common values of a pan-Canadian national identity appeared to be severely threatened.

The national No committee that emerged from the deliberations at the University of Ottawa was aptly named the "Canada for All Canadians Committee," in response to Brian Mulroney's "three little words." The Committee's co-founders were two of the most prominent non-elected opponents of the Meech Lake Accord. Deborah Coyne is a constitutional lawyer who had advised Premier Clyde Wells of Newfoundland during the Quebec Round and who took a leave of absence from her job with Ottawa-based Infometrica to fight this perceived new threat to the Trudeau legacy. Her collaborator and host of the Ottawa University meeting was Professor Michael Behiels, a historian and author of the *Meech Lake Primer*, an edited collection of articles highly critical of that previous deal.

Working with them from the beginning were Professor Robert Jackson of Carleton University in Ottawa, a prominent political scientist and co-author with Doreen Jackson (also a member of the No team) of the standard textbook on the Canadian political system, and Professor Robert Howse of the Centre for Public Law at York University, Toronto, a lawyer and author of *Economic Union, Social Justice and Constitutional Reform*.

In Toronto, historian Michael Bliss of the University of Toronto, another tireless opponent of Meech Lake, was a potent advocate of the No option, authoring several major columns in the *Toronto Star* on the disadvantages of the deal and the reasons that he himself was voting no. Like Coyne and Behiels, he represented the No side in numerous interviews and televised debates and "starred" in free televised ads provided to the No side under the referendum laws.

Recognizing their logistical disadvantages, it was decided the committee would limit its efforts to the manning of a telephone hotline, the production and distribution of educational pamphlets, and participation in the free advertising for which they would be eligible under the legislation. Although each member would do what he or she could to assist in their small office, it was obvious to the No leadership that travel would be limited and outreach to local groups next to impossible. Their ultimate objective was modest but still likely unachievable — to defeat the accord in at least one province.

Among the party activists in Ottawa were local councillor Alex Cullen and Ottawa University lecturer Louis-Philippe Rochon; in Montreal two former Liberal aides, Michel Simard and Guy Sarault, a lawyer with the firm of Heenan Blaikie, were also heavily active in the No campaign. To this core group of opponents were added over the next few weeks the names of many of the most eminent constitutional scholars in the country, who publicly denounced the deal and/or wrote extensively on its implications. Among them were Professor Anne Bayevsky of the law faculty at the University of Ottawa, author of several definitive works on the Charter; Professors Stephen Scott and John Humphreys of the McGill Law Faculty, both noted constitutional scholars and the latter a former chair of the United Nations Human Rights Committee; Professors Loraine Weinrib and Ron St. John MacDonald of the University of Toronto, experts on the Charter and human rights issues; Professor Bryan Schwartz of the University of Manitoba, a constitutional scholar, expert on aboriginal issues, and well-known author of the highly critical *Fathoming Meech Lake*.

In addition, two of the country's most prominent civil rights lawyers and activists, Clayton Ruby of Toronto and Julius Grey of Montreal, were outspoken critics of the deal, as was communications mogul Izzy Asper of Winnipeg, a longstanding advocate of the Trudeau vision who was known to have provided the No leadership with much of their limited financial assistance.

Opposition to the Charlottetown Accord on the basis of the Trudeau vision of federalism was not limited to the academic community. Although federal politicians had almost entirely turned their backs on his approach, there remained a number of provincial (and primarily Liberal) politicians who continued to espouse the overriding principles of strong central federalism and individual rights.

Of these, two of the most visible and effective were Gordon Wilson and Sharon Carstairs. Wilson, the Liberal leader and leader of the Official Opposition in British Columbia, was an articulate spokesperson for a message that found surprisingly strong resonance in a province that had once solidly rejected the policies of the former prime minister. Carstairs, the Liberal leader in Manitoba, had fought strenuously against Meech Lake as well, and was among the first in the country to breach the solid wall of unanimity of the political élites with her categoric rejection of the accord.

Both Mr. Wilson and Ms. Carstairs rejected claims that they represented an "anti-Quebec, racist or bigoted" element of the population.

For Mr. Wilson, who opposed the distinct society clause in Meech Lake and objected to the deterioration of a strong central government in the Charlottetown Accord, it was "perfectly legitimate to take a No stand.... We're talking about the way Canada is administered and governed and, in my view, the deal does not do us any favours."[1]

Among those who joined the two party "mavericks" was a former candidate for the leadership of the provincial Liberal Party in Ontario the previous year. Breaking ranks with his party for the stated reason that the accord was a dramatic deviation from the Liberal/Trudeau vision of the Canadian federal system, Toronto MLA Greg Sorbara became one of the few political voices added to the growing chorus of dissent in Canada's largest province. Speaking to an audience in Toronto on October 2, Sorbara decried the fact that "the accord represents far less than what we are, and can be, as a nation." As for the Yes strategy, he argued "the referendum campaign has taken on the trappings of politics in a one-party state. As an alternative to rational debate, the Yes side has launched a campaign based on fear and intimidation."

In Nova Scotia, the dissenting voice of Eric Kierans, a former federal and provincial Quebec Liberal who had recently chaired a task force on the Constitution in that province, may well have had a significant impact on the dramatic and unexpected outcome. Kierans's announcement that he had voted No in the advance polls shocked the Yes forces, since he had earlier said on a CBC "Morningside" program that he would support the accord to keep Quebec in Canada. He explained his reversal as a final realization that he just couldn't support enough provisions in the accord to defend a Yes vote.

Last but not least, a few dissenting voices were heard among the country's media élite. That there were not more, given the stated positions of many during the Meech Lake debate, is odd. The degree to which political columnists and editorial boards in the print media across the country formed an enthusiastic chorus of support for the accord, especially in the latter days when the battle seemed to be lost, is perhaps one of the most disturbing phenomena of the six-week campaign.

Although it is unlikely that the reality of increased corporate concentration of ownership or fear of government retribution could have played a part in this matter, such universal consensus emerging among the media élites is equally unlikely. Nowhere was this more obvious than in the case of the *Toronto Star*, in which editorials opposing Meech Lake had been commonplace only two years earlier. Yet in the face of an agreement that they could only describe as Meech Plus, the *Star*'s editorials not only called for support of the deal but vehemently criticized its chief opponent and former *Star* icon, Pierre Trudeau.

Rising above this chorus to support the No side was a most unlikely figure, a popular Vancouver talk-show host known throughout British Columbia but, until word of his virulent opposition to the accord filtered through to the rest of the country, virtually unknown to Canadians east of the Rockies. Rafe Mair, a lawyer and former provincial cabinet minister who sat at the constitutional negotiating table with Pierre Trudeau in the 1980-81 round that led to the 1982 amendment, was arguably one of the most improbable candidates to lead the No forces in British Columbia.

By his own admission, the colourful and outspoken Mair had attacked Pierre Trudeau "with enthusiasm" on many occasions over the years for his policies in other areas. Nevertheless, as Mair explained in early October, "Mr. Trudeau should be listened to because he is a man of enormous intellect... and because he was prime minister for 16 years. He has credentials possessed by no others on the scene today." Referring to the insults hurled at Trudeau by several politicians after his intervention at La Maison Eggroll, Mair declared, "His arguments demand answers, not personal abuse."

Having outlined daily for his viewers the reasons he so disliked the accord — the unanimity of the amending formula, the guaranteed provision for seats in the House for Quebec, the flawed process by which the document was arrived at — Mair then concluded the document was too flawed to accept. When accused of providing one-sided coverage of the accord on his program, possibly in violation of CRTC regulations calling for balanced reporting, he retorted in a *Globe and Mail* interview of October 3 that the print media were all biased in favour of the Yes side. "If anything," he said, "the CRTC might want to talk to people on the Yes side... one lonely little voice out of Vancouver surely should not be discouraged."

William Johnson of the *Montreal Gazette* was virtually the only English-language print media columnist of note to repudiate the deal. Johnson had earlier led his readers to believe that he had abandoned the Trudeau vision of federalism, but after attending Trudeau's speech on October 1, he returned to that vision with a passion. In his column the next day he argued that "the agreement is one in which individuals are not equal, rights are not equal and freedoms are subordinated to governments." In another column on October 24 he went much further, declaring that the accord "introduces into the Constitution of Canada a principle of authoritarianism, of social engineering, of coercion of citizens in the name of ideological objectives...."

The Reformers

If ever a politician could be described as a maverick or an outsider, it would surely be Preston Manning, leader of a grassroots evangelical fringe party grounded in western alienation and supported, in considerable measure, by individuals whose view of Canada deviates in several important respects from the mainstream of the political culture. Manning himself, son of a former minister and long-time Social Credit premier of Alberta, has expressed views on immigration, feminism, and social policy that leave even the right wing of the Conservative party miles behind.

For Trudeau federalists, many of them leaning towards the left wing of the political spectrum, most of Manning's views and those of his party are anathema. Yet in the case of constitutional policy and the

Charlottetown Accord, it appeared the two groups found common ground, although neither would care to admit it, and no members of either group were seen together during the campaign.

Manning waited several days to announce his position on the accord. Joe Clark and others later criticized him for this delay. They claimed it was evidence that Manning was an opportunist who joined the No side only after assessing the political gains to be made. Manning, however, never appeared to be on the defensive. He consistently maintained that Reform was a grassroots party and that he, the leader, was obliged to consult with the rank and file to hear their views. There were leaks from disgruntled supporters at the party's convention in Winnipeg only days before the vote that Manning had initially been planning to support the deal and changed his mind at the urging of key strategists. Despite the rumour, these accusations appeared to have no effect on his influence or credibility with the general public.

Assisted by party policy adviser Stephen Harper and political scientist Tom Flanagan of the University of Calgary, Manning, like the Trudeau federalists, made clear that his opposition was to the contents of the deal. He emphasized the infringement on individual rights as found in the Charter, the lack of equality of individuals and provinces, symbolized by the provisions on the House of Commons, and the difficulties of setting national standards under the new provisions. He also criticized the large number of incomplete sections and the lack of a legal text.

It was Manning who first identified some of the concerns later expressed by Trudeau and his followers concerning the aboriginal government proposals and their exemption from certain Charter provisions. Attacked by native representatives as a bigot and racist, Manning declared, "The Reform Party's referendum campaign will have no room for extremists, bigots, demagogues or separatists." Flanagan also responded that, although some of the party's supporters may act out of such sentiments, it was not the motivation behind the party's position. Having received several legal opinions that came to the same conclusion, Flanagan argued that his party was raising the issue as a "moral imperative." He continued, "We really have no strategic reason to pick a fight with Ovide Mercredi...."

There can be little doubt that Manning's anti-accord speeches, which also emphasized the "kitchen table" economic concerns of ordinary Canadians, played to a different audience than that which the Trudeau federalists were courting. Appealing to less economically secure Canadians more naturally attached to the status quo, Manning also argued persuasively that "Canada is worth too much to gamble its future by trading a flawed constitution we know for one that is largely undefined, unfinished and completely uncertain."

The fact that Manning's audience shared many fundamental values in common with the Trudeau federalists were reflected in polls demonstrating increasing concern in all western provinces with the lack of definition of aboriginal self-government, and with the failure to obtain equality of provinces through the triple-E Senate model, to say nothing of the 25% provision for Quebec in the House of Commons.

Manning himself proved to be an extremely effective spokesperson for his party, which was fortunate for the party really had no other alternatives. The locally nominated Reform candidates were neither well-known outside their immediate area nor experts on the issues. Manning, on the other hand, combined an extensive knowledge of Canadian history and constitutional matters with a convincing public persona. In an age of great distrust of politicians, he was successful at presenting himself as a non-political politician — a man for whom an innate lack of rhetoric and straightforward talk on the issues became political pluses.

The Reform Party's organization during the campaign was dependent on the grassroots constituency operation already in place, although there were initial thoughts of expanding into the big leagues with a major national campaign. Reality quickly intervened to remind the Reformers that they were still outsiders. Having announced his intention to campaign on the No side, Manning first outlined ambitious plans for a national advertising campaign on the expectation of a substantial fund-raising campaign. This did not come to pass.

Instead, the corporate contributions that the party had begun to receive as its legitimacy had increased in the last few years suddenly dried up. Influential and well-known business supporters such as Jim Grey of Calgary resigned their membership over the party's position in the referendum. As Don Leier, a Saskatoon businessman and chair of the party's fund-raising committee indicated in an interview, "When we came down on the No side, basically what happened was that corporate Canada said, 'We don't want to be perceived as supporting the No campaign'." Instead of an expected $2 million, Leier estimated the party's revenue from business for the year would be only $200,000.[2]

In the end, the party was obliged to draw on its existing war chest to fund the little advertising it initiated outside the free-time televised messages. Manning's televised free-time ads were simple and even austere. The Reform campaign theme — "For the love of Canada, vote No" — was conveyed by Manning with a devastating effectiveness that dismayed the experts orchestrating the advertising of the Yes campaign. For many, Preston Manning became Canada's version of the American maverick billionaire Ross Perot.

For Preston Manning, the campaign was a great personal success. For the Reform Party, barely one year away from an election campaign and unwilling to incur a deficit for ideological reasons, the cost of the referendum was disastrous. They had won the battle but, the day after, many of its members wondered if they had not reduced their chances of triumphing in the war, that is, the general election to follow.

The Special Interest Groups

Contrary to the claims of the Yes supporters after the defeat of the accord, very few special interest groups opposed the deal. And unlike either the Trudeau federalists or the Reformers, the special interest groups who opposed the accord did not do so from the perspective of an opposing overall vision or set of principles related to Canadian federalism and the Constitution. Instead, the National Action Committee on the Status of Women (NAC) and a variety of native women's groups, for example, objected to particular elements of the deal that seemed either to restrict their existing rights or to present new problems for the individual Canadians they represented.

These groups did not address the issues of centralization of powers or equality of provinces, but almost exclusively the issues of individual and group rights. For them, Pierre Trudeau's argument at La Maison Eggroll that the proposed new Canada clause would create different categories of citizens was compelling. They had argued against tampering with the Charter on a number of occasions when their opinions were sought. And they particularly opposed adding restrictive language in other sections of the proposed new accord that would affect Charter rights.

Having failed to prevent the insertion of add-ons such as the Canada clause in the new deal, and worried about the legal effect of such add-ons, they felt obliged to make sure that the people they represented were included, too. As one spokesperson put it, many of the disabled people she represented "would happily head to polling stations to vote Yes in the October referendum" if only a sentence were added to include them in the Canada clause, or its language were otherwise changed or modified.

The reluctance of the Yes élites to respond to the concerns of excluded categories of citizens in the first few days of the campaign was a source of frustration that ultimately led to the suspicion that their exclusion had been deliberate. Previous experiences with the political élite had given many of these groups ample cause to fear the worst and to disbelieve vague promises of future improvements and reform. This was nowhere more true than in the case of women's rights activists.

In the mid-1980s, the National Action Committee on the Status of

Women (NAC) had achieved an almost mainstream air of respectability. But their influence with the federal government had steadily declined in recent years, causing the organization to adopt an increasingly hard line. This in turn had caused the government to view the group as unrepresentative and extremist. Government funding had been given to the arch-enemy of the NAC — an organization called REAL Women — and many projects that NAC supported had been cut or had seen their funding reduced. In 1987, the women's movement had publicly and vocally opposed the Meech Lake Accord, and their opposition had hurt the government. To describe them now as outsiders in the political process would be an understatement.

The organization was deliberately excluded from the closed-door negotiations in the summer of 1992, just as they had been excluded from the Meech Lake talks. Their exclusion was harder to bear this time because the aboriginal leadership was now on the inside. When the NAC's executive met to discuss their response to the Charlottetown Accord, they were torn between their instinctive dislike of the package and their fear that outright rejection would damage their cause. This fear was made more acute as their allies and benefactors in the labour unions and the NDP were both on the side of the government.

At first the NAC decided to attack specific aspects of the deal, or omissions from it, rather than oppose it in its entirety. Among their preliminary attacks, the case they made for seats in the elected Senate to be assigned on the basis of gender received the most public attention.

The NAC had called for a form of proportional representation in the election procedures for the proposed new Senate as part of its input during the policy sessions of early 1992. Electing senators by this method, which has proven in Europe to result in the election of a more representative sample of the population, was seen to be a less direct or arbitrary way of ensuring more equitable representation of women and minorities, rather than resorting to assigned seats or quotas. The package that was presented to the Canadian people on August 28 ignored their recommendations and contained no such provision for election by proportional representation.

The NAC executive then lobbied to obtain the informal agreement of the premiers that they would take steps to ensure gender parity in the Senate election process in their respective provinces through assigned seats. The issue soon became a national cause célèbre, in which Premier Harcourt reversed himself regarding his support for the idea several times, the national media had a field day, and public reaction to the proposal was almost universally negative.

The NAC's spokesperson, Judy Rebick, continued to make the case for allocated seats in the Senate, but it was a tough sell, and she knew it. The government's failure to accept the more moderate proportional representation model had, she said, driven her organization to the more drastic position. In a debate on the proposals in late September on the CBC's Montreal noon-hour talk show, she privately agreed with her opponent's suggestion that there were other, more serious problems with the accord with respect to women's rights, but she said that the NAC was refraining from outright opposition to the deal because they still hoped for changes that would make an open confrontation with the government unnecessary.

When no olive branch was offered by the Yes side, the NAC executive felt it had no choice but to reconsider its position. Rebuffed by the political élites, the media, and even the labour union élite under the stewardship of Bob White, and then urged by Joe Clark in a late-night phone call to maintain their tacit acceptance of the deal or remain silent, the NAC held an executive meeting the next morning at which, according to Ms. Rebick, they decided they "simply could not hold their noses" and support the accord. Although subsequent rumours of internal dissent surfaced, none of the senior NAC hierarchy publicly voiced disagreement with the decision. (As with the aboriginal organizations headed by Ovide Mercredi, it was at the "middle-management" level that expressions of disagreement were encountered. In the case of the women's organizations, it was the heads of some organizations brought together under the NAC umbrella who could later be heard to express reservations.)

Despite the early opposition of NAC to some measures in the accord, their formal decision to join the No camp came as a surprise to the federal government and supporters of the deal. Female spokespersons for all three political parties were immediately dispatched to spread the message that "NAC does not speak for all women." Kim Campbell, Sheila Copps, and Audrey McLaughlin all sang from the sang hymn book on this occasion, one of the few in which the Yes campaign succeeded in "getting out its message."

The Native Women's Association of Canada (NWAC) was a less visible opponent, but no less determined than the NAC in its rejection of the terms of the Charlottetown Accord. The NWAC feared the provision for aboriginal self-government and the proposed exemptions from the Charter that self-government apparently entailed. Implicit in these provisions was official dispensation for a continuation of behaviour that native women perceived to be discriminatory and gender-biased due to the hereditary and patriarchal nature of most band administrations. Although these native women received media coverage for their attempt to legally halt the referendum vote itself, few Canadians were aware of the issues at stake and no nationally recognized spokesperson emerged.

Once again the Yes forces attempted to discredit the concerns of this dissenting group, this time by calling upon aboriginal women who supported the deal to speak out. Of these the most vocal was Rosemarie Kuptana, head of the Inuit Tapirisat, who declared on September 23 that "we are satisfied the equality rights of aboriginal women are not prejudiced by the Charlottetown Accord." Although Ms. Kuptana's personal credibility was extremely high with those she represented, and among the political élites generally, it was not an effective intervention with those native women who went to court to stop the October 26 vote. This was primarily because they were basing their concerns on their different experience from that of Ms. Kuptana and the Inuit.

As status Indians, they constituted only one of four major groups of aboriginal peoples in Canada, all of whom evolved different cultures, traditions, and historical and legal relationships (or non-relationships in the case of the Métis) with the government of Canada. It was precisely these differences between status Indians, non-status Indians, Métis, and Inuit that the accord was overlooking and that were part of the reason for the cracks in the aboriginal community's support for the accord.

The same could not be said for the disabled lobby, which was united in the concerns it initially raised about the accord's perceived failure to protect their Charter rights in the Canada clause. As Carol McGregor of the Coalition of Provincial Organizations of the Handicapped (COPOH) stated in an interview reported in the *Toronto Star*, "We're not even at the same level of equality as women and visible minorities are" in the new Canada clause.

Much publicity was generated on this issue in the early days of the campaign. So much, indeed, that Constitutional Affairs Minister Joe Clark felt obliged to reassure the lobby by indicating that changes could still be made to the accord. (This announcement, in turn, caused Clark innumerable difficulties when opponents began to ask if anything in the deal was fixed in stone, or if instead, many changes could be made after the vote, since the question on the ballot merely said that Canadians were agreeing to an amendment package *on the basis* of the Charlottetown Accord.) In the end, however, a spokesperson for the umbrella association for the disabled announced that they would be supporting the deal on the unwritten understanding that changes would be made in the legal text of the deal.

Although it is possible that these special interests had some impact on the voting intentions of ordinary Canadians, the conclusions of the *Maclean's*/Decima poll suggest that they were not nearly as influential as either the Trudeau federalists or the Reformers. The lack of significant gender gap in national voting behaviour, for example, suggests that Ms. Rebick may have been influential as a credible spokesperson for the No forces, rather than as a spokesperson for the special interests of women. Similarly it is likely that the influence of all these groups was a cumulative one in which most Canadians, already unhappy with the deal for any number of specific reasons, also took into account generally the fact that several categories of disadvantaged citizens perceived themselves to be excluded by the process and harmed by the final product.

Perhaps most important, in those areas where the special interest groups expressed their narrower concerns, the underlying theme of equality was always present, enhancing the arguments of the Trudeau federalists and the Reformers. For those Canadians already concerned with an apparent retreat from the principles of equality of individuals and provinces, this fact could not help but reinforce their belief that the accord, as a whole, was not good for the country.

7

The National Campaign:
The Six-Week Battle for Hearts and Minds

At the unofficial start of the referendum campaign in late August 1992, the Charlottetown Accord enjoyed the support of 70% of Canadians. If a vote had been held at the time, it would have passed by a comfortable majority in every region of the country. Six weeks later that support had evaporated. The accord was solidly defeated nationally, and in all but three provinces and one territory. The decisiveness with which the western provinces rejected the accord was striking, and even in Ontario, once considered to be a sure thing for the Yes side, the result was practically a dead heat.

No single event or individual act was responsible for this astonishing turnaround. Although many incidents increased voter discontent and influenced individual voters, three basic causes can be identified that led to the rejection of the Charlottetown Accord. The first was the disastrous campaign conducted by the Yes forces in which six specific errors or problems can be identified, not the least among them the role played by the prime minister. The second cause was the exceptional effectiveness of the No campaign in which the intervention of Pierre Trudeau may have been the most important factor. Finally, the nature of the referendum itself led to the accord's rejection.

Of the three main causes, the actual structure of the referendum process is the least important, but one that nevertheless bears mentioning. In early September, the government's strategists made the decision to proceed with the referendum in spite of the reservations that had been expressed by some premiers and federal officials. The strategists' first assumption, that there was no other way to legitimate their closed-door consensus, may well have been correct. Their second assumption, that the referendum had to be held on October 26 to accommodate Quebec's timetable, was not. Had they delayed the vote for several months to permit extensive parliamentary hearings, public discussion, and amendments to the package, the result of an eventual referendum might have been very different.

Their third assumption, which also proved to be wrong, was that they had structured the referendum rules and phrased the question in ways that assured them of victory. The brief, six-week campaign, which they began with the support of nearly three out of every four voters, should have worked in the government's favour. They had the advantages of power, money, personnel, and organization. Most important, they had virtually every significant element of the country's establishment on side: political, business, media, and interest-group élites demonstrated amazing unity. In their view, there was every reason to believe that the Yes campaign would roll serenely to victory.

But within days the flaws in the Yes plan became obvious. Virtually every practical problem foreseen by opponents of the deal in the House of Commons debate proved to be justified. A few others, foreseen by no one, also came to light.

The Referendum Process Becomes an Issue

First, the referendum question was criticized by opponents as vague and open-ended. The phrase "on the basis of" seemed to imply that changes could and would be made at a later date, an interpretation the accord's critics emphasized at every opportunity.

Second, the rules did not define what constituted a victory. Having rejected the Opposition's recommendation to use a double majority concept of national total and four or five *regional* totals, Joe Clark and Brian Mulroney found themselves answering questions on this issue for the whole first week of the campaign. Finally, after several false starts and mixed messages, Clark and Mulroney got their act together. They stated categorically that 50 plus 1% would be sufficient at the national level, and that they would need to have the same margin in *every* province or territory. This meant that the number of "wins" they needed had theoretically increased from 5 or 6 to 13!

Third, the referendum question required a simple Yes or No answer to the whole package. The Yes group had refused to consider the suggestions of Clyde Wells and others who argued that the package was too large for one question and should require multiple answers, or at the very least be divided into two sections with two answers (one for the parts of the accord requiring unanimity to be implemented, and one for the parts that could be passed if seven provinces with 50% of the population approved). As a result, the Yes forces found themselves defending every item in the package from attack. In a short time, it had dawned on many of them that rejection of only one element of the deal, if the objections were strong enough, could lead voters to reject the entire package.

Fourth, both the media and the chief electoral officer approached the referendum as if it were an election campaign, in which opponents must receive balanced coverage. As the referendum legislation placed no limit on the number of referendum committees that could be formed, they all — no matter how small, unsophisticated, or unrepresentative — received media coverage and free television time equal to that received by the Yes committees. Individual spokespersons for the No leadership such as Deborah Coyne and Michael Behiels received considerable attention from the broadcast media, who were accustomed to providing such "balanced" coverage of election opponents. At one point, the CBC defended its referendum coverage by producing detailed records documenting to the *second* the equal coverage that the Yes and No leaderships had received.

The result was a disaster for the Yes side. Right from the start, in the first week, five or six No spokespersons received about the same amount of media coverage as the prime minister and a handful of élite spokespersons. The Yes side immediately began to complain that rigid adherence to "balanced coverage" by the media actually distorted the extent of opposition to the accord. As senior Yes strategist Les Campbell lamented in an interview at the end of the campaign, "We didn't anticipate the people on the No side would have such great capacity to get such endless media coverage.... I mean, look at Deborah Coyne. The only thing she isn't doing is cooking shows."

Finally, the fact that the rules were different in Quebec, even though the question was the same, had serious consequences for the Yes side. An estimated 10,000 Canadians residing in Quebec were said to have been disenfranchised because of the different rules that were applied in that province. Most or all of those who were disenfranchised were anglophones or allophones who would probably have supported the deal, given the chance.

The rules respecting the recognition — and financing — of referendum committees in Quebec differed significantly from those in the national campaign. Only two umbrella committees could be formed, one on each side, which meant that the No forces in Quebec enjoyed precisely similar status to Yes forces from the first day. (In the national campaign, the No forces received some free television time but had no access to public financing.)

Although problems with the process were troublesome for the Yes forces, they were hardly decisive. Had other elements of the Yes campaign been effective, these procedural problems would have been no more than minor irritants. That they became significant is testimony to the other major difficulties that the Yes side encountered from the beginning of the campaign. The scope of these difficulties may be judged by the terms in which editorial writers and columnists referred to the Yes campaign on the day it was over, when it was described variously as a "fiasco," a "débâcle," a "comedy of errors," and a "three-ring circus."

The Disastrous Yes Campaign

Given their huge financial and human resources advantages at the start of the six-week battle, it seemed to some to be almost inconceivable that they could have snatched defeat from the jaws of victory. Yet that was exactly what the Yes team managed to do. Although many isolated incidents contributed to this rout, there were six major issues that sealed the fate of the Yes forces. These were the decision to define the question as a matter of loyalty to country rather than focus on the merits of the accord; the decision to pursue a strategy of intimidation directed at all potential sources of dissidence; the failure to produce a legal text until two weeks before the end of the campaign; the failure to prevent splits becoming apparent among the deal's proponents; the inability to control the conduct of the campaign at the provincial level; and finally, the ill-conceived interventions of the prime minister.

The Wrong Definition of the Question

From the start of the campaign, the supporters of the accord attempted to shift the terms of the debate from a discussion of the specific contents to a test of patriotism. Following this strategy, the prime minister and other spokespersons for the élites first labelled opponents of the accord "enemies of Canada" and then, under pressure, softened their characterization to "not proud Canadians."

It appeared, in effect, that the Yes side strategists had learned nothing from the Meech Lake débâcle only two years earlier. In making the case for Meech Lake, Mr. Mulroney had warned of the dire consequences that would surely follow if the deal were not ratified. The consequences of a failure to endorse the Charlottetown Accord were described in similar terms. Rejection of the accord would mean a second "rejection" of Quebec. This in turn would lead, as surely as night follows day, to economic chaos, social instability, and the breakup of the country.

Brian Mulroney began this strategy before the campaign began. On August 22 he declared, "I know that the enemies of Canada will not be happy. And they're going to be out in full force. And they will encounter me and my first ministers at every step of the road, fighting them off and fighting for Canada." Kicking off the Yes campaign on September 22 in western Canada by speaking to a group of students in Vancouver, Mulroney continued in the same vein. He ignored the details of the accord and declared that "without unity we've got nothing. Without the glue that holds Canada together, all of us would suffer great and probably irreparable damage economically." The next day in Saskatoon, he declared that he would "engage in political battle" for Canadian unity since "this is a fight for Canada."

By September 29 he was increasing the stakes. "A No will not mean business as usual," he told a luncheon meeting in Sherbrooke. "It will mean the end of negotiations... the beginning of the process of dismantling Canada." On October 1, he warned Canadians that "voting No would plunge us into the unknown."

These threats did not work. For some, it was a clear indication that the Yes side must already be in severe difficulty. For Deborah Coyne, who launched the national No campaign on September 30, this was an abdication of responsibility. "He's saying that a No means No to Canada," she said at her launch on Parliament Hill. "He's adopting the Quebec nationalist blackmail. What kind of prime minister is this?" For political scientist Guy Laforest of Laval, who reacted to the "fearmongering" in an interview for the *Ottawa Citizen* on October 1, "Mulroney is doing now what we thought he'd do in the last week of the campaign. Everybody was sceptical about the threats because it's too early, too obvious, and too transparent."

Mulroney subsequently toned down the rhetoric, but the essential theme, that the referendum was about national unity, not the terms of the accord, remained unchanged. Speaking in Charlottetown on October 14, he allowed that the separation of Quebec would not automatically follow rejection. "Will Canada fall apart?" he asked. "The answer is no. No is not going to bring a calamity on October 27." But a No victory would "add to economic and political uncertainty and prolong the seemingly endless constitutional debate." In the final week of the campaign, after a brief period in which he soft-pedalled the predictions of imminent catastrophe, Mr. Mulroney picked up the theme again. In Saskatchewan on October 24, he first pleaded with Canadians to "consider your children" and then suggested that if there were a No vote, "Quebeckers could be knocking on the door, asking to separate."

This emphasis on consequences was maintained by virtually all of the Yes élite spokespersons to a greater or lesser extent. While some, such as Clyde Wells, talked of the contents of the deal and then limited their remarks on a possible No outcome to the fact that there would be little likelihood of a return to the bargaining table or a better deal, others, such as Ontario premier Bob Rae, stuck to the threat of Quebec separation throughout the campaign. In fact, as the Yes forces began to lose ground badly in Ontario, the premier's remarks became more extreme. In a province-wide televised speech on October 23, Rae again said he believed "the consequences... will be to encourage the forces in Quebec that want to dismantle the country."

The strategy simply did not work. As the *Maclean's*/Decima poll of October 28 found, some 56% of Canadians outside Quebec believed the failure of the accord would have "no real impact." Among those who voted no, this figure was 65%.

The Failure of the Intimidation Strategy

Consistent with its decision to define the referendum debate as a struggle for Canadian unity, the Yes side adopted a strategy of intimidation rather than positive encouragement. Proponents publicly issued dire threats about the economic consequences of separation and privately attempted to neutralize any organized opposition by interest groups or public servants.

The strategy first came to light when the Quebec Women's Federation released a tape of a discussion with the Chief of Staff of

Secretary of State Robert de Cotret in which they were told their annual grant was being withheld because of their support for the No option. They were further informed that a written statement from the group promising to remain silent in the referendum debate would free up the cheque. Subsequently assuring them that it was "all a misunderstanding," de Cotret met with the group and told them their funding was not at risk. The message, however, had already reached the entire voluntary community network in Canada, and they were not happy with it.

The concern of such groups was heightened the following week when federal officials in the Federal-Provincial Relations Office (FPRO) began calling major social agencies and ethnocultural organizations. According to Sunni Locatelli, the FPRO spokesperson, the calls were to offer information and expert speakers for any meetings the groups might be planning on the referendum issue. For Lynne Toupin, executive director of the National Anti-Poverty Organization, the calls were "all the more intimidating" after hearing of the women's group troubles in Quebec. "They're systematically checking with all the national groups," Ms. Toupin said. She was joined in her concern and anger by George Frajkor of the Slovak Canadian National Council, who said he knew of eight other ethnic groups that had also received calls. "You don't get direct threats," he said, "but it's unspoken that you'd better be in line with the government" if, like most of these groups, you were heavily dependent on federal financing.[1]

In similar fashion, all members of the federal public service in Ottawa — a potent potential group of opponents because of their organizational network and skills — received from Treasury Board Secretary Ian Clarke a letter that stated, "Public servants should ensure that any public involvement or statements about the referendum do not impair their ability to carry out their duties." Although he recognized the right of employees to "participate fully in a referendum" in principle, he went on to stress that "public servants remain responsible in carrying out their duties to provide non-partisan support to the government with respect to the constitutional accord as they would in respect of any other policy of government."

The message was received by public servants loudly and clearly. Since the accord was government policy, Yes activities were permitted. No activities would not be. Although senior Treasury Board officials denied it was meant to be an intimidating letter, the effect was clearly demonstrated by the fact that hundreds of public servants actively worked on the No campaign on their own time, but in secret and in functions that avoided any public contact. As one No organizer in the national capital region declared, "We have had to give [them] back-room jobs doing clerical work or telephone canvassing." In comments on the issue in the *Ottawa Citizen* of October 16, Mario Lamoureux, a No organizer in Gatineau, explained that "some [public servants] are actually worried the government will send someone to check up on what type of signs they have on their lawns."

But the most obvious attempt at intimidation was orchestrated by Yes supporters with the banking community. It began with the release on September 26 by the Royal Bank of Canada of a report on the economic consequences of separation. Royal Bank chairman Allan Taylor noted that the report predicted higher income taxes, a lower standard of living, and the loss of 720,000 jobs if the country split in two. Having already said in his opening remarks that "nothing would do more for economic recovery than a Yes vote," Taylor nevertheless rejected criticism of the report as "fear-mongering" by stressing that neither he nor the report had addressed the consequences of a No vote.

Although the report ostensibly had nothing to do with either the accord or the referendum, media coverage, which was extensive, implied that the supposed consequences of separation were meant to be taken as a warning to potential No supporters. The intervention of the prime minister and other members of the political élite tended to reinforce this message.

Citing political instability as a problem for foreign investment, both the Canadian Chamber of Commerce and the Business Council on

National Issues (BCNI) joined the fray. The intimidation continued with statements by cabinet ministers Michael Wilson and Don Mazankowski in late September. After meeting with trade commissioners who represent Canada abroad, Michael Wilson declared that "millions of dollars" in potential investment had been put on hold until after the referendum results were known.

His colleague, Finance Minister Don Mazankowski, reiterated the theme in Lloydminster, Alberta, when he stated that a Yes vote would "boost the economy." Evidently ignoring two and a half years of severe recession and their underlying causes, Mazankowski declared that "constitutional uncertainty has been a big drag on our economy. You can't have economic security without political security."

None of this produced the desired effect. Few Canadians believed the threat of economic instability, and even more doubted the likelihood of Quebec separation. As for the business community's participation in the debate, one of the most acute critiques on its efficacy came, ironically, from within. Under the title "Business votes Yes but does anyone care?" business columnist Terence Corcoran, a well-known booster of corporate Canada, offered a detailed and devastating analysis of the fallacious arguments that had been presented by two titans of the banking and corporate community — Matthew Barrett of the Bank of Montreal and Tom d'Aquino of the BCNI. Mr. Corcoran concluded: "Neither [of these men] brings any particular constitutional expertise to the debate. Why are [they] speaking on the merits of the aboriginal provisions, the Canada clause, the House of Commons and Senate reforms...?"

As columnist Thomas Walkom pointed out in the *Toronto Star*, the interventions of the political and corporate élite were actually causing some fluctuation in the value of the dollar and in interest rates. But Canadians apparently were not intimidated by any of these tactics. In fact, as the *Globe and Mail* reported on October 30, the Royal Bank in particular saw the graphic results of its interventions. Angered by the attempts at intimidation, many existing and new No supporters removed their money from accounts with the bank, plastered No stickers over automated banking machines, and wrote angry letters to the president. The Quebec wing of the United Steel Workers moved its $6 million account to the National Bank of Canada. And, in the ultimate irony, a portion of the bank's debt was downgraded by Standard and Poor the day after the referendum vote.

Mistakes of the Yes Advertising Campaign

Just about everyone agreed that the Yes advertisements were a disaster. They were too obviously expensive, too slick, and too aggressive. Whether Canadians were seeing the baseball player let the strikes go by, the pot of water boiling over on the stove, or Jacques Parizeau and Lucien Bouchard smile malevolently, the message was the same, and Canadians didn't like it. They felt they were being treated as children, given a lecture, and told how to behave. As one article on the problem concluded, "The Yes campaign had voters seeing red."[2]

How could the Yes side's dream-team committee of strategists have been so wrong? First, as communications specialist Stephen Kline of Simon Fraser University pointed out, their approach was wrong. In an election there is an adversarial approach, and only one side can be a winner. The referendum, on the other hand, was supposed to be a positive, consensus-building exercise, not a contest. "High-impact emotional ads are a terrible way to build a consensus.... This was a selling job, no doubt, but there is more than one way to sell. These strategists are all used to working on political campaigns but this was not an election....They didn't have the tools to use around an issue like this."[3]

Second, by relying on static opinion polls, often asking the wrong questions, they missed the different dynamics of the referendum campaign, and in particular the importance of the two levels of debate. So the content of the Yes ads was wrong as well. What was working for the No side was the fact that they were providing information in their advertising, as they were in their other promotional materials.

As public relations consultant Fraser Likely wrote in the *Ottawa Citizen* of October 22 on the subject of the referendum ads and the need for a more inclusive, consultative approach to public opinion sampling, "Canadians now expect participation. They have learned that their opinion matters and they want to express it. Why should they listen to those in power tell them how to vote.... People want more, not less, substance." By emphasizing consequences and threats over information, "instead of changing No voters' minds the slick Yes commercials intensified their opinions." By the time the Yes side realized the "consequences" strategy wasn't working in the real world, and that they should address the contents of the deal, it was too late.

In addition, as many communications experts observed, the No side's amateurish ads proved remarkably effective precisely because they were so obviously amateur. In a sense, they served to heighten the image of the two sides as David against Goliath, the one with "glitzy" professional ads and the other with home-made efforts. Despite their $5 million budget, the Yes side could not compete with the used-car lot ad in which a sleazy salesman tried to unload a lemon to potential customers by pleading that he would otherwise lose his job, or the talking heads of Deborah Coyne, Michael Behiels, and Preston Manning, who spoke simply and, apparently, from the heart, about the flaws in the deal.

The Legal Text Débâcle

Beside 26 items in the Charlottetown Accord, there were asterisks. These asterisks indicated that further discussion and negotiation were necessary before the issues in question could be resolved. The No forces scored points early in the campaign by drawing attention to these items and arguing, with some justice, that Canadians were being asked to sign a blank cheque.

Doubts mounted when other ambiguities within the document became apparent. Why was the agreement called simply a "consensus document"? Where was the legal text? Why were Canadians not being given a chance to read the fine print? Was it because changes were still being made or contemplated? Concern was heightened when Joe Clark told an audience that a provision to include the disabled might still be added to the accord.

For the No side at the national level, most of them academics or constitutional lawyers by training, the importance of the actual legal wording could not be overestimated. But the political élite attempted to downplay its importance, assuming incorrectly that the general public would not share the concern with details.

When a group of native women who tried to challenge the referendum vote in the courts claimed they knew the legal text would not be ready before voting day, the issue took on a life of its own. Believing the worst about politicians they mistrusted, voters concluded there was a reason that the text was not ready, and they did not believe the eventual explanations of the Yes team about the time and effort required.

Had the Yes forces taken the issue seriously at the beginning and explained their practical limitations clearly, the whole affair might well have come to nothing. But then the prime minister ridiculed the requests of ordinary Canadians, suggesting they were not really interested in the content. "Now we have people saying 'Hey, I want to see a legal text, I want to read every notwithstanding clause on Saturday night after the hockey game'," Mulroney scoffed as he sang the praises of the deal at a luncheon in Halifax on September 29 before a crowd of receptive business persons. The corporate élite may have enjoyed the sarcasm, but for ordinary Canadians it touched a raw nerve.

Finally, Joe Clark recognized that the issue was serious and promised that portions of the document would soon be made public. While it was being prepared, however, Kim Campbell and Barbara MacDougall entered the fray to state that the text would not be changed substantially, so it was irrelevant to the debate. Campbell revealed more than a little of the Yes mentality when she declared in a meeting with the *Montreal Gazette* editorial board that "once you start releasing the legal text, you put it in the hands of lawyers who will argue about what it means."

Apparently trying to be helpful, Premier Frank McKenna of New Brunswick and Liberal MP Sheila Copps chimed in to declare that the legal text issue was a "red herring" created by the No forces to throw the debate off track.

In the end, the more than 100 bureaucrats engaged in the race against time produced a document that the federal government released barely two weeks before the end of the campaign. The government then distributed hundreds of thousands of copies of the "draft" legal text in a vain attempt to restore a modicum of confidence in the contents of the deal, contents that the supporters themselves still did not want to discuss despite the obvious hunger on the part of the general public for information.

Cracks in the Yes Consensus

When the Charlottetown Accord was announced in late August, one of the abiding claims of its supporters was that it represented the "historic" consensus of the political élite, the aboriginal leadership, the corporate élite, and so on. Having made this claim, and having justified the contents of the accord as a reflection of this consensus, the Yes case was obviously damaged when the consensus itself showed signs of crumbling.

While the coalition held at the political level, it was evident to most Canadians that the participation of some of the players, and most notably Clyde Wells, was less than enthusiastic.

Of course, half-hearted support was, from the point of view of the Yes forces, preferable to rejection. In a similar way, the labour union establishment, led by CLC president Bob White, managed to maintain a reasonably solid semblance of unity in spite of a No rebellion by the Canadian Union of Postal Workers.

But when the native community in Canada at the grassroots level began to express concerns about the package, the solid image began to crack. Despite the high credibility that the political élite ascribed to AFN grand chief Ovide Mercredi, he was faced with the same problems as his predecessors. First in Quebec, where the Mohawks refused to recognize the deal or hold a vote in the referendum, and then in Vancouver at the national meeting of chiefs, which refused to endorse the deal, Mercredi faced a steady string of rejections from his own people. When Manitoba MLA Elijah Harper, "hero" of the Meech Lake fight, called on his people to abstain or vote No, the battle was lost.

This disintegration of support among factions assumed to be among the accord's most ardent proponents hurt the Yes side badly precisely because the prime minister, Joe Clark, and others had made so much of the support in the first place. "Say Yes to our native peoples," Mr. Mulroney exclaimed. But the native peoples themselves, apparently, were saying no.

The problem for many Indian band leaders was that the accord was vague on specifics. In particular, it contained no financial guarantees. Based on their previous, mainly unhappy, experience with the Conservative government, few band leaders were prepared to accept its statement of good intentions on faith.

For Canadians, who by a substantial majority had consistently indicated their support for the cause of aboriginal self-government, the fact that native peoples themselves did not seem happy with this deal removed one of the few strong reasons for them to vote Yes.

The Provincial Wild Cards Wreak Havoc

Every week, it seemed, the national Yes campaign suffered serious setbacks because their provincial counterparts were running amok.

First premiers Gary Filmon and Mike Harcourt were unavailable to campaign. Then Clyde Wells made public his demand for changes to the legal text before he would speak out in its favour. To some on the national campaign staff, it began to seem that their friends were more dangerous than their enemies.

Two incidents were particularly damaging to the Yes campaign. In the first, B.C. Intergovernmental Affairs Minister Moe Sihota proclaimed to a small audience in the town of Quesnel that British Columbia had gained in the deal while Quebec had "lost." Bourassa, he said, had faced a "brick wall" of opposition from western premiers. Sihota, it appeared, was unaware that there was a reporter in the hall when he made these remarks. Like the shot that was heard around the world, his off-the-cuff comments were repeated over and over in Quebec in the days that followed, leaving premiers Bourassa and Harcourt to "clarify" them as best they could. As one aide reported, the B.C. premier's furious reaction had been that "there aren't many cabinet ministers who can wound two premiers in one day."[5]

Bob Rae also did as much harm as good to the Yes campaign. Already heading an unpopular government and becoming shriller by the day as the Yes lead slipped away, Rae's references to the No side as "snake oil salesmen" did not help the Yes campaign anywhere. The negative sentiments unleashed by the premier as he escalated his rhetoric during the campaign led at least one columnist to conclude that Rae was becoming almost as much of a detriment to the Yes forces as the prime minister. In an article shortly before the vote, Jim Coyle of the *Ottawa Citizen* felt obliged to recommend to his readers that they "ignore Rae's insults. Trust your gut feeling in deciding yes or no."

The Mulroney Factor

The most unpopular prime minister since polling on popularity first started, Brian Mulroney managed to further alienate Canadians during the six-week referendum campaign. His hyperbole, sarcasm, and excessive rhetoric ("Mother Teresa not being available, I volunteered"); the dramatic ripping up of a document in a speech in Sherbrooke; and his unconvincing attempts at humility in the latter stages of the campaign contributed hugely to the collapse of support for the Yes cause.

As pollster Angus Reid reported in an article for the *Ottawa Citizen* of October 19, his data demonstrated that "the prime minister has emerged as the second most influential figure nationally, but he has done so by unintentionally helping the No side." According to Reid's polling, some 34% of Canadians were more likely to vote No as a result of Mulroney's interventions, while only 16% were more likely to vote Yes and more than 47% said he had made no impact.

Despite the urging of several of the Liberal and NDP handlers in the tripartite Yes committee organization, it did not prove possible to contain Mulroney, who continued to tell reporters that he was obligated to be the "chief salesman" for the deal. By the last third of the campaign, however, his organizers were attempting to focus his interventions in Quebec, where he was believed to still have a positive image.

As the results on October 26 cruelly demonstrated, this was no longer the case. Not only did Quebeckers overwhelmingly reject the accord, but his own riding of Charlevoix defeated the accord by a margin of almost 2 to 1. The extent of the prime minister's personal defeat was probably best summed up by CBC reporter Jason Moscovitz, who recounted several times for his listeners the tale of the reporters herded into a Yes committee headquarters in the riding over an hour before the scheduled arrival of the prime minister. In the time they spent waiting for him, in which the room was "manned" by "volunteers" recruited from a nearby senior citizens' home, the phone rang once.

The Impact of Pierre Trudeau and the No Campaign

If there was one event during the entire campaign that could be said to have influenced the course of history, it was surely the intervention of former prime minister Pierre Trudeau. Having already written an essay in *Maclean's* magazine the preceding week in which he addressed the issue of Quebec nationalism, Trudeau entered more directly into the debate over the accord when he spoke to an audience at a Chinese restaurant, the Maison Eggroll, in Montreal on October 1. Speaking entirely in French without a written text, before a mixed audience of 400 former colleagues and followers who opposed the accord and strong supporters of the deal, with a live radio audience across the breadth of the province hanging on every word, Trudeau elegantly tore the deal to pieces. He also destroyed the Yes argument about the consequences of failure with one simple sentence. "Unfortunately, high-level politicians and even high-level bankers want us to believe that voting YES is a 'yes to Canada' and NO is 'no to Canada.' This is a lie that must be exposed," he said.

Although this was his only public statement — one that was neither televised nor repeated, and not even made in English — the opposition to the accord outside Quebec crystallized around the arguments he had made. Evidence of his impact is irrefutable, despite the attempts of Mr. Mulroney and others on the Yes side to dismiss him as "yesterday's man."

Pollster Angus Reid reported that Trudeau's intervention made him "the most influential national figure in the campaign." According to Reid's poll of October 12-15, fully 41% of Canadians said Trudeau's performance made them more likely to reject the deal. Evidently recognizing this influence, the four major English-language dailies in Toronto, Montreal, and Ottawa showed a picture of Trudeau, not Mulroney, casting his ballot in their October 27 editions.

But the final recognition of the influence that one man had had on the campaign came from columnist Jeffrey Simpson, an articulate and thoughtful opponent of the Trudeau vision who has never underestimated the force of that vision in Canadian politics. In his column of October 29 analyzing the referendum results, Simpson summed up the campaign succinctly in three words — "Trudeau's vision triumphed."

Of course Trudeau was not alone in the fight. The effectiveness of the academic élite, grassroots organizations, and rare media opponents of the deal has been documented earlier. Together with Trudeau, their success could be attributed to their steadfast criticism of the contents of the deal.

Supporters of the accord complained that the No side could bring about its demise simply (and unfairly, in their view) by focusing on a single weakness. In fact, the No side's critique was always wide-ranging. The majority of the deal's opponents in the national campaign spoke from a consistent set of principles and beliefs. And it was to their enunciation of principle that Canadians responded.

As Jeffrey Simpson correctly concluded, the referendum debate was not, in the end, about the personality of the prime minister. It was, to some extent, about the political élites who joined him in sponsoring the accord. Their show of unity appears to have inspired distrust rather than reassurance among a majority of Canadians. But for these same Canadians, the referendum was primarily about the future of the country. On the evidence of the referendum's result, Canadians outside Quebec, at least, shared a common vision of what the country should be. And they did not see that vision reflected in the Charlottetown Accord.

8

The Quebec Campaign:
The Distinctly Different Battle

When Robert Bourassa announced in early 1992 that his government would hold a referendum on the question of sovereignty later that year, politics in the province of Quebec had come full circle. Only 12 years earlier, another referendum had been held on the sovereignty question, but it was sponsored by the separatist government of René Lévesque. Its decisive rejection was supposed to have resolved the matter once and for all.

The reason for this second referendum in little more than a decade was painfully evident. Bourassa, who had frequently been faint in his praise of federalism and often defended it as merely "profitable," was responding to the recommendation of the Bélanger-Campeau Commission on Quebec's Future. Bourassa had appointed the commission in the wake of the Meech Lake débâcle in the hope of defusing growing nationalist sentiment within his own party. Far from putting out the nationalist fires, however, it fanned the flames.

Bourassa was clearly uncomfortable with the referendum question, and he delayed taking up the commission's recommendation as long as he dared. As time passed and his anxiety mounted, he devised a strategy of encouraging the federal government and the other premiers to go back to the bargaining table to come up with a federal "offer" to Quebec. This would allow him to hold the referendum on the offer, rather than on sovereignty.

When the first ministers finally came up with a package, Bourassa announced with obvious relief that the provincial referendum scheduled for October 26 would now ask Quebeckers to approve or reject the federal package, known to the rest of the country as the Charlottetown Accord.

The roots of Bourassa's predicament were once again grounded in the way the political élites had responded to the failure of Meech Lake and the process that had since evolved to produce the Charlottetown Accord. But they were also grounded in the 1980 campaign, an event that had led to the 1982 constitutional amendment and Quebec's rejection of it. The importance of this sequence of events can hardly be overestimated; nor can the difference in perspective with which Quebeckers viewed them.

In 1992 the major political actors in Quebec were different. With the manoeuvring of Bourassa, the question in the 1992 referendum would also be different. But many argued the real issue in 1992 would be the same as in 1980. Was Quebec's place in Canada or as an independent country?

Déjà Vu

The Quebec referendum campaign of 1980 was an emotional battle between two titans who had dominated the political landscape for nearly three decades. The fiery rhetoric of René Lévesque, the populist, was pitted against the Cartesian logic of Pierre Trudeau, the aristocrat, in a battle to determine once and for all whether Quebeckers wanted to remain within Canada. It was a passionate and hard-fought battle that divided friends and families. When it was over, the majority of participants on both sides of the debate agreed on one thing: they wanted never to live through another experience with direct democracy.

The question posed to the voters by Premier Lévesque's separatist government was whether they would authorize him to begin negotiating with the federal government with a view towards eventual separation. Although the question was more tentative than many people had expected, Lévesque made it clear that a yes vote would be the first step on the road to Quebec independence.

Then - prime minister Pierre Trudeau and his Quebec cabinet ministers, of whom the populist justice minister, Jean Chrétien, was the most visible and effective, campaigned hard across the length and breadth of the province. Tirelessly, they sang the praises of federalism and the many benefits that had accrued to Quebec as a result of its participation in Confederation. While they spoke of the benefits, however, backroom organizers on the federalist team were orchestrating a "dirty tricks" campaign of fear and intimidation. Armoured Brinks trucks were seen leaving the province supposedly bound for Toronto with all of Quebec's corporate wealth. Phoney dollar bills were circulated, allegedly worth 50 cents in the new state of Quebec.

The positive campaign of the politicians and the dirty tricks of the backroom organizers combined to deliver a substantial victory for the No side. Sixty per cent of Quebeckers chose renewed federalism over separation, and the belief took root that the matter was settled. Only Premier Lévesque, whose graceful speech acknowledging defeat concluded on a wistful note with the phrase "Until next time," appeared to believe that the issue was not closed.

Two years later, when Trudeau's commitment to renewed federalism resulted in the constitutional amendment package of 1982, Quebec was the only province not to sign. Lévesque himself never forgave the federal government's decision to proceed without the agreement of Quebec. He draped the legislature in black crêpe and flew flags at half mast the day Queen Elizabeth formally signed the document on Parliament Hill in April 1982.

Quebeckers took a much more sanguine view. As Gallup reported in June, some 49% believed Trudeau's amendment package would be a "good thing" for Canada, and only 16% saw it as a bad thing. Even more important, only 28% thought that separation was "inevitable." Subsequent revelations by former Quebec cabinet ministers and bureaucrats from the era have shown that the federal government was right to think that the Lévesque government would never have signed an agreement, no matter what the contents.

For the next three years, Lévesque boycotted federal-provincial meetings as a protest. For the next three years, the Quebec economy prospered. Opinion polls during the 1985 provincial election campaign in June consistently showed that Quebeckers were not interested in the Constitution and did not consider changes to be necessary.

Nevertheless, barely a year after Robert Bourassa and his Liberal Party regained power in June 1985, they proposed a set of five conditions that would meet Quebec's "concerns." Resolution of these concerns, they assured the federal government, would allow the province to return to the federal-provincial meeting table, where issues such as aboriginal reform and cost-sharing programs were waiting to be resolved.

The fact that Brian Mulroney had now replaced Pierre Trudeau in Ottawa no doubt convinced the Bourassa government that the effort was worthwhile. A pragmatist and master of brokerage politics whose contradictory election statements on the Constitution suggested he held no strong views on the subject, Mulroney was far more likely to acquiesce to Quebec's demands than the dogmatic Trudeau.

"The Quebec Round" was expressly undertaken by Mulroney to accommodate Quebec's five concerns, despite a level of public anxiety in the rest of the country about their implications, and despite the fact the public in Quebec had not expressed any interest in the subject.

As described in an earlier chapter, the prime minister utilized all his negotiating skills and wove his spell on several provincial premiers who were new to the game, to reach an agreement in June 1987 that came to be known as the Meech Lake Accord. Emerging from the follow-up meeting in Ottawa a few weeks later to iron out the details, an elated Premier Bourassa announced to the world that he had received more than he had asked for.

And so he had. But the trade-offs that the prime minister had agreed to in order to bring about this deal soon caused as much trouble as the original five conditions. When neither he nor the premiers was prepared to consider any changes to the "seamless web" he had woven, the accord's fate was in doubt.

For the next three years, Brian Mulroney and Robert Bourassa rewrote history, telling Quebeckers they had been "humiliated" in 1982. They also assured Quebeckers that only the country's acceptance of the Meech Lake Accord could right this "wrong." Misjudging entirely the public mood in the rest of the country in the final few months before the accord was due to expire, Mulroney and Bourassa began to invoke doomsday scenarios. The failure of the accord would lead to economic chaos. Pitting one group of Canadians against another, the prime minister told Manitobans and Newfoundlanders that it would be their fault if Quebec were to separate as a result of yet another "rejection" by "the rest of Canada."

The accord died in spite of their efforts. In Quebec, where many citizens were now under the impression that they were not even a part of Canada since they had not agreed to the 1982 document, the nationalism that had been quiescent since 1980 returned to virulent levels. Polls throughout the fall and winter months showed that support for "sovereignty-association" was back up to the levels of the pre-1980 referendum period.

Meech Plus (the Charlottetown Accord)

Alarmed by this nationalist upsurge, the political élites soon decided to return to the bargaining table. This time, however, they prefaced their closed-door meetings with a series of public consultations.

Apparently unaware or unconcerned by the fact that support for the sovereignty option in Quebec began dropping in 1991 and had returned to its more traditional 40% level by spring of 1992, Mulroney and the first ministers continued to believe they had a mission to resolve the Quebec issue. At the same time, the western premiers were demanding that new items be added to the constitutional agenda if they were to participate in yet another round of negotiations.

In the rest of Canada, the "Quebec Round" of Meech Lake became the "Canada Round" of all the premiers, in order to respond to these new demands. Yet in Quebec both Mulroney and Bourassa referred to the negotiations simply as the prelude to "Meech Plus." This different approach was essential, since Bourassa had already given in to the prevailing wisdom and declared many times that he would never settle for less than Quebec had already achieved in the Meech Lake agreement.

By the time the Charlottetown Accord was announced in late August of 1992, it contained many more provisions than Meech, most of which had nothing to do with Quebec's original concerns. Among these were the elected Senate and the provisions for aboriginal self-government. As a result, although it could be said that the agreement addressed all Quebec's five demands, they were so deeply buried among other provisions that they were difficult to see and even more difficult to appreciate.

Bourassa Takes the Plunge

In a now-famous interview given before the start of the referendum campaign, Robert Bourassa carefully explained that he would never call an election he could not win. As if to reinforce that point, he referred to the polls showing substantial popular support for the deal not only in Quebec but also in the rest of the country. He pointed out that the referendum was being run on Quebec's terms. The province even had its own referendum rules and chief electoral officer, a fact the national Yes campaign was to stumble over many times in the succeeding weeks, particularly on the language issue.

Yet even at the start of the referendum campaign in Quebec, there were signs of trouble ahead. On September 16 the National Assembly approved the question. Having changed the referendum question from a vote on sovereignty to one about the federal "offers" — a question that was now being asked throughout Canada on the same day — the premier spent most of his National Assembly speech fending off accusations by the Parti Québécois opposition that Quebec actually received less in Charlottetown than in Meech Lake.

After outlining the elements of the accord that responded to Quebec's original demands, Bourassa then tried to reassure Quebeckers that the Senate changes and other provisions would not be harmful to Quebec. This was a tough sell, given that Quebec would in fact lose Senate seats. Having concluded that the "gains" made by Quebec in this deal were "without precedence," the premier set the tone for the Yes campaign by ignoring the contents entirely and turning to the "real" issue — political stability. "By voting yes," he said, "Quebeckers will more than ever assure their future."

But the PQ and its leader, Jacques Parizeau, had inside information up their sleeves to refute these claims. Parizeau referred to a series of private letters between Bourassa and Prime Minister Mulroney that he had obtained from the daily newspaper *La Presse*. In these letters, disagreements between the two first ministers on the meaning of several provisions were spelled out. Since the correspondence was dated from August 25 to September 7 there was every indication that these disputes remained unresolved.

Bourassa in turn accused the PQ leader of trying to confuse and mislead Quebeckers. He then returned to his theme that economic prosperity and political stability were the real question before the people.

Defining the Question

As in the rest of Canada, the real meaning of the referendum question was very much an issue in Quebec. Like their fellow Canadians, most Quebeckers ignored the arguments of the Yes campaign and decided that this was a vote on the deal, not a vote on the future of the country. Nor did they believe Premier Bourassa's arguments about the need for a Yes vote to ensure economic stability. "There's no risk in saying yes," Bourassa argued, "but there are lots of risks in saying no."

As the campaign progressed, voters were telling pollsters in Quebec that they were planning to vote no although they were also planning to support Bourassa and the Liberals in the next provincial election. What clearer way to demonstrate that the vote was not a message of support for either Jacques Parizeau or Lucien Bouchard, but rather a rejection of the accord?

Parizeau himself assisted voters in coming to this conclusion. He stated almost from the beginning that a vote against the deal would not be taken by him or his party as a vote in favour of sovereignty. This strategy was necessary partly for the obvious reason — to attract as many voters as possible to the No side. It had a second and more immediate purpose, however: to bring into the fold the dissatisfied nationalist federalists who had broken with the Liberal Party over its failure to adopt the Allaire Report.

Both the youth wing of the provincial Liberal Party under Mario Dumont and a number of disgruntled nationalist Liberals led by lawyer Jean Allaire agonized over their position on the referendum question until Jacques Parizeau made it easy for them. A No vote was not a vote for sovereignty. And although the Quebec legislation insisted that all registered groups work under one umbrella Yes and No commit-tee each, Parizeau also told the disaffected Liberals they could form their own group and in reality work independently from his commit-tee. They took him at his word.

As pollster Claude Gauthier of the Quebec polling firm CROP later indicated, Allaire's decision to enter the debate was a key element of the No victory. "Mr. Allaire allows people to be Liberal, vote no and not feel guilty," he said.[1] Without fear of economic chaos, and with-out guilt at partisan desertion, voting no became acceptable. Even for Liberals it was okay.

The anglophone and ethnocultural communities in Quebec never had any doubt what the referendum meant. It was a matter of survival. A No vote would lead to chaos, rejection, and inevitably to separa-tion. A Yes vote, however, would allow them to continue to live and work in Quebec without losing their status as Canadians. This point of view was held strongly throughout the campaign by all but a few dissident intellectuals and academics within the minority communities. Powerful interest group representatives such as Alliance Quebec, the Canadian Jewish Congress, and the Italian Canadian Congress all supported the accord. So did the leadership of the Equality Party. It was these groups that prevented the No vote from becoming a rout.

The No Team:
Separatists and Nationalist Federalists Join Forces

Outside Quebec the three main groups that opposed the accord disagreed on their precise reasons for rejecting the deal but they all agreed that the deal "went too far." For the No campaign in Quebec, the problem was the opposite: the deal "did not go far enough."

Even in Quebec, however, the No forces were subject to the "strange bedfellows" syndrome. On the one hand, there were the separatists. They were led by not one but two people: the provincial Parti Québécois's Jacques Parizeau, and the oxymoronic "federal separatist" Bloc Québécois party's Lucien Bouchard. The package was not expected to satisfy the demands of these two groups, since they were dogmatically committed to Quebec's separation from Canada.

The approach the two leaders took in hopes of achieving separation had already become something of a controversy, however, and the internal struggles of the parties meant that a co-ordinated approach to the campaign was difficult to achieve. The two men were evidently not comfortable together and preferred to fight the campaign each in his own way. Parizeau favoured media events such as the debate with the premier. Bouchard spoke to meetings of supporters, made a number of major speeches, and wrote several critiques of the accord for publication.

Added to the separatists, whose opposition to the accord was to be expected, were the Quebec Liberal Party's "nationalist federalists."

They were led by Jean Allaire, the obscure lawyer and party militant who had chaired the party's own internal committee on the Constitution and produced the extremist Allaire Report that the party had, in effect, rejected by supporting the Charlottetown Accord. Allaire was joined in his defection by Mario Dumont, head of the party's youth wing, and an influential number of like-minded dissidents.

For these nationalists, however, the ultimate objective was not separation. Federalism continued to be their preferred option. While the separatists were urging Quebeckers to vote no because no acceptable deal could ever be reached, the Allaire group was arguing that this particular deal should be rejected as unacceptable, after which a better deal could be achieved in a new round of negotiations.

During the course of the campaign, the PQ and BQ organizations joined forces at the riding level and were remarkably effective in "getting the vote out." Jean Allaire, whose credibility and visibility increased throughout the campaign, organized a parallel grassroots operation. Ostracized by the official Liberal Party machinery, he and his cohorts nevertheless managed to pull together a significant operation. Their success was due, in no small measure, to the provincial referendum legislation's stricter limits on spending and scrupulous assistance to both sides in the campaign. These conditions allowed the No forces to campaign on an almost equal footing with the Yes side's advertising and promotional materials. This factor was particularly important in Montreal, where the decisive votes were to be won, and where the main efforts of the No forces were successfully directed.

As for strategy, the No team had an easier task than the Yes forces, who by now had fallen victim to the Meech Plus mentality and were obliged to convince Quebeckers that this was not just the best deal possible but one that was a "victory" for Quebec. Meanwhile, the No forces had to persuade Quebeckers only that the deal could have been better.

Seen in this light, the only thing that stood between the No forces and victory was likely to be the high credibility that Robert Bourassa enjoyed with the electorate. Unfortunately for the premier, this credibility quickly fell victim to a series of mishaps, none of which were orchestrated by the No forces, but rather by his own supporters and allies.

The Yes Campaign: A Comedy of Errors

Canadians in the rest of Canada could hardly fail to notice when the Yes campaign in Quebec was launched by Premier Bourassa with a speech that made no mention of Canada, on a platform draped with fleurs-de-lys and no maple leaves. Strategists for the Yes side seemed scarcely to notice the effect such symbolism would have in English Canada. In these terms, the launch of the Quebec Yes campaign was the exact analogue of the national campaign's unilingual launch in an Ottawa high school. Both emphasized that, for the Yes forces, the two campaigns were entirely divorced.

Quebeckers were witnessing, in effect, a pale rerun of the campaign of 1980. Neither Robert Bourassa nor Brian Mulroney was Pierre Trudeau. Neither Jacques Parizeau nor Lucien Bouchard was René Lévesque. And Quebec was not the same province it had been a decade earlier. Plagued by a recession as deep and unemployment as high or higher than most other parts of the country, the enthusiasm of Quebec's entrepreneurial class that had supported sovereignty in 1980 was decidedly missing from the No campaign of 1992. Luckily for Parizeau and Bouchard, the Yes side aroused even less enthusiasm. Their official launch inspired little attention and less interest. As columnist Lysiane Gagnon noted sarcastically in the early days of the campaign, a crowd of 200 was a huge turnout for the Yes forces.

From then on it was all downhill. In a campaign that never got off the ground, Robert Bourassa and the Yes team saw their slight advantage in the polls melt away within days of the official launch. Like their counterparts at the national level, the Yes side stood complacently by in the first week, allowing the No forces to have the media coverage all to themselves. When they did enter the battle, it was not to make strategic errors as the experts in Ottawa were doing. The Yes forces in Quebec apparently never enjoyed the luxury of pursuing a game plan, even one that was fatally misconceived. Instead, they lurched from one accident and disastrous revelation to another.

To begin with, the Yes side never recovered from the defection of Jean Allaire and the nationalist wing of the provincial Liberal party. Their departure from the party's convention had been one thing. Their decision to campaign actively for the No side was another, and the Yes forces seemed totally unable to cope with it. It was a stunning blow — a clear and evidently sincere repudiation of Robert Bourassa and the party leadership. Having encouraged the nationalist element by his own actions over the past several years Bourassa, in turn, had no one to blame but himself for the evident lack of appreciation of the federal system that a large proportion of his party membership were now demonstrating.

A second blow to the premier's credibility was also delivered from within his own ranks. As one federal member of Parliament from Quebec with a somewhat jaundiced view of the referendum campaign commented privately, only in Canada would an obscure public servant become a household name because of the Constitution. Yet this was precisely what Diane Wilhelmy achieved.

On September 17, in the first of a series of revelations that rocked the Bourassa government and the Yes campaign, the private conversation of Mr. Bourassa's two top advisers on the constitutional portfolio became the topic of newspaper headlines and gossip columnists. Despite a lengthy attempt to prevent the release of the taped telephone conversations, the entire exchange between Diane Wilhelmy, the deputy minister of intergovernmental affairs, and André Tremblay, Mr. Bourassa's top political aide, became the subject of debate in the National Assembly and across the country.

"We just caved in, that's all," Wilhelmy reportedly told Tremblay. And with the publication and endless repetition of those words, the entire effort by Bourassa to base the Yes strategy on his personal credibility was left in tatters.

The day was not saved when Prime Minister Mulroney rushed to Quebec to defend Bourassa as a "skilled and effective" negotiator. Warming to his task, he attacked the comments of the two aides as "one of the most preposterous and fraudulent charges ever made" by "people who were not only not in the room, they were not even in the province while the negotiations were taking place." Mr. Mulroney then defended the accord, rather surprisingly, as not only Meech Plus, but as an agreement that met all of former premier René Lévesque's demands. Lucien Bouchard, who declared that Bourassa's credibility had been one of "the few things the Yes side had going for it," mocked Mulroney's defence of the beleaguered premier by saying, "It's a bit like the lion who eats the lamb and then compliments the lamb for tasting so good."[2]

Evidently Quebeckers agreed with Bouchard. By September 20, less than a month after the accord had been agreed to, polls in Quebec were showing the No forces with a lead of more than 13 percentage points.

The blows to Bourassa's personal credibility did not stop with the Wilhelmy affair. A month later, on October 17, the Quebec magazine *l'Actualité* published what it claimed were confidential briefing notes of senior officials of the Quebec delegation — notes highly critical of the final accord. Declaring that the notes were dated and easily discredited, Bourassa also argued that such anonymous documents should not be given precedence by the media over formal statements by lawyers and constitutional experts who supported the deal. But the damage was done. By now the polls were placing the No vote at 48%, with the Yes at 32% and only 16% undecided.

Meanwhile the premier's political allies outside Quebec had not been helping his cause. The prime minister's ripping up of symbolic papers in Sherbrooke set off a chain reaction of criticism and also a self-fulfilling prophecy of panic reflected by the polls. The Sihota affair in B.C. followed. That minister's unfortunate comment and Ontario premier Bob Rae's reference to opponents of the deal as "snake oil salesmen" were widely reported in Quebec to little advantage.

Although the support of the Quebec élites was more evenly divided between the Yes and No camps than at the national level, like their national counterparts a very large percentage of those supporting the accord in Quebec appeared to come from the ranks of the Establishment and closed ranks in their support of the deal. The corporate élite, much of the labour leadership, and various leaders of the multicultural and artistic community joined forces with the political élite to fight for the "historic" consensus. Also like their counterparts in the rest of Canada, their intervention was not well received.

The statement by the chairman of the Royal Bank and the bank's doomsday report about the costs of Quebec separation reminded people of the 1980 campaign. But this time it failed to intimidate. Jacques Parizeau made fun of the whole affair while ordinary Quebeckers expressed outrage. Many people withdrew funds from the bank and took their business elsewhere.

When the corporate élite in Quebec jumped in to help out the Yes team, the effect was as unhelpful as it had been in the national campaign. Bombardier CEO Laurent Beaudoin's attempts to influence his employees through pamphlets distributed to workers and speeches at special meetings were not only scorned but examined by the Quebec chief electoral officer as a possible violation of that province's referendum legislation.

The referendum legislation provisions for equal media time and free advertisements for both sides once again helped the No side in Quebec as they had done for the national No team elsewhere. But in Quebec a defining moment in the campaign was the debate between Premier Bourassa and Jacques Parizeau for which there was no national equivalent. (Audrey McLaughlin debated Preston Manning at Guelph University, but they were secondary players and attracted relatively little attention.)

Most observers agreed that Bourassa won the debate on points, but he scored no "knockout punch," which, at this point in the campaign, was what he needed. Despite the fact the debate had been viewed by unprecedented numbers of attentive Quebeckers, the Yes forces received only a minor and temporary boost in support as a result of the confrontation.

The Yes side also tried its version of the national campaign's honorary "eminent persons" chairs, with a similar lack of success. Epitomized by the two-day intervention of hockey great Guy Lafleur, who quickly realized that sports and politics do not mix, the array of performing artists and literary and business élites who were drawn into the Yes network failed to impress voters.

As the polls reflected a steady deterioration in support for the Yes side, proponents of the deal, including the prime minister, Premier Rae of Ontario, and Bourassa himself made more dire warnings about the consequences of rejection. The possibility was raised that the Americans would abrogate the free trade agreement. But, perhaps because the province was suffering from the effects of the depression that had gripped much of the country for two years, the warning had little effect.

A number of defections from the Yes side by groups such as the powerful teachers' union seemed to make the No option more politically acceptable, but the half-hearted nature of endorsements by some key interest groups such as the Equality Party and the Conseil du patronat may have actually *encouraged* more potential Yes voters to reject the deal. Indeed the comments of Robert Libman, head of the anglophone rights Equality Party, that the accord did not provide "a rock-solid guarantee of any kind" on minority language rights but instead offered "some potential protection," which was better than nothing, were hardly reassuring. Coupled with Mr. Libman's statement that the party would therefore be "willing to hold our noses and support it," and the defection of several of his members as a result, the support of the Equality Party provided cold comfort to the Yes side.[3]

When Premier Bourassa began to speculate over a week before voting day on the possibility of calling a provincial election, Quebeckers knew the Yes side had thrown in the towel. As the premier carefully repeated for the next seven days, No would not be the end of the world. No would not mean that he would resign. After all, René Lévesque had not resigned when he lost the 1980 referendum. And last but not least, he would lead the party in the next provincial election, which he expected to win.

Explaining the Results

The referendum was defeated in Quebec by a 13% margin: 55.4% to 42.4%. The size of the No vote led virtually all observers to conclude that the separatists had been joined by a sizeable number of federalists. In general, it also appeared that francophones had rejected the deal while the anglophone and allophone community had supported it. Former prime minister Trudeau's largely anglophone riding of Mount Royal had voted yes. Although Robert Bourassa's riding narrowly supported the deal, those of many of his ministers and many of the federal MPs who had supported the deal were awash in No votes.

Despite the ongoing debate between Premier Bourassa and Jacques Parizeau as to whether Quebec had received "enough" in the Charlottetown Accord, most voters indicated this was not their prime concern when they rejected the deal. While 44% who voted no indicated that Quebec did not get enough concessions, some 56% said they did so because it was a poor deal.

In spite of the predictions of imminent doom that Mr. Mulroney and several provincial premiers had made before voting day, some 22% of Quebec voters believed the Constitution should now be put on the back burner, and nearly 50% did not describe it as a pressing issue. The majority who voted no also believed a better deal was indeed possible in future negotiations.

The victorious separatists were careful to play down the meaning of the No victory. In his victory speech, Jacques Parizeau avoided claiming that the province had moved closer to sovereignty, but spoke of working gradually towards "the next stage." This speech did much to comfort those federalists who had voted yes for fear of the consequences of a No vote. More importantly, the relatively low-key campaign devoid of personal attacks on either side had avoided the degree of tension and enmity that developed in 1980, leading many observers to speculate that the public's "recovery" from this referendum would be a matter of days or weeks.

As for the fortunes of Robert Bourassa, his party's standing increased steadily during the referendum campaign. If an election had been held on October 26, he would have defeated handily the Parti Québécois and Jacques Parizeau. In what many of his federal and provincial counterparts must have viewed as the ultimate irony, the man whose position they had attempted to buttress with the calling of the referendum campaign was perhaps the only one among them not likely to suffer from its defeat.

Bourassa understood, however, that the defeat of the accord required him to make some adjustments to his re-election strategy. The direction he appeared to be taking in the winter of 1992 was not without its own irony: the man who took Quebeckers to the brink of sovereignty in the days following Meech Lake and who opened the Yes campaign in Quebec without once mentioning Canada began to speak almost enthusiastically about the benefits of federalism for Quebec.

9

Putting the Genie Back in the Bottle

On the surface, at least, the referendum vote appeared to have unleashed a number of demons that would be hard for politicians to contain. A greater number of constitutional issues than ever before had been raised, intensely debated, and then left unresolved by the defeat of the Charlottetown Accord. The clear distinction between the Trudeau and Clark visions of federalism had once again been put under the microscope. The differences between separatists and federalists in Quebec had been reinforced.

Perhaps even more important, a profound and deep-seated disenchantment with the entire political process seemed to have seized hold of the electorate in all regions of the country. The nation's élites — the national leadership of political, corporate, labour, and special interest groups — appeared to have been repudiated. By the end of the campaign many dejected supporters of the accord were asking themselves whether the country could survive such a devastating public dissection of its differences and the apparent lack of faith in politicians and institutions.

The decision Canadians made on October 26, 1992, will clearly have both short-term and longer-term consequences for the political process and the players in it. In reality, however, many of the perceived problems flowing from that decision were a mirage. Some were simply misunderstood; others were confused and lumped together with unrelated problems. Once disentangled and properly understood, many of these problems may be relatively easily resolved.

Despite the dire predictions of the Yes forces, there was no panic in the days and weeks that followed the accord's defeat. As Liberal

MP Brian Tobin remarked, "The [only] people who are running around feeling stunned, in fact, are in large measure the leadership of the country — politicians, journalists, labour, business and so on. The reality is the people are not feeling stunned. They're not feeling in crisis. They're saying the system works."

The panic of the political élites, in turn, came from the realization that their leadership of the nation had been repudiated. There could be no doubt that pent-up frustration with politicians, and prolonged economic misery, led to an unprecedented degree of hostility and cynicism on the part of voters during the campaign. Although it did not, as many of the élites believed, play the decisive role in determining voters' choices, this underlying hostility certainly motivated many Canadians, and particularly those on the No side who resented being described as unpatriotic, to express their rejection of the accord in vocal and active rather than passive ways. The ferocity of some elements of the No campaign — a very "un-Canadian" approach to politics — caught the Yes side off guard. This backlash, however, was merely a side-effect rather than the driving force of the No campaign.

This disenchantment with the political élites had actually begun well before the referendum. It can be traced to the period immediately after the 1988 federal election, when the effects of globalization of markets, the free trade agreement, and the introduction of the GST combined to wreak havoc on the Canadian economy. Job losses, the decline of the manufacturing sector, and record levels of personal and business bankruptcies left many Canadians wondering who was minding the store. This level of unhappiness increased dramatically as a result of the 1990 Meech Lake débâcle. In subsequent provincial elections in Manitoba, Ontario, British Columbia, and Saskatchewan, the incumbents paid the price for this widespread dissatisfaction.

At the national level, unable to vent their frustration at the ballot box for several more years because of the Mulroney government's secure majority, voters listened attentively to those who suggested changes in the political process itself. Canadians appearing before the

Spicer Commission in 1990-91 vividly reflected the prevailing dis-enchantment when they recommended everything from the removal of members of Parliament by petition to the impeachment of the prime minister. When constitutional reform returned to the political agenda, the calls for an open and participatory process, and for mechanisms such as a constituent assembly of citizens, intensified.

By insisting on consultation during the formulation of the Charlot-tetown Accord, Canadians simply were reacting to the perceived lack of legitimacy of the political élites of the day. When that consultative process was cut off in mid-stream, moving from closed-door sessions to a referendum without an intermediary stage of parliamentary delib-eration, Canadians rebelled. Many voters agreed with Professor Michael Behiels (who was a leading force in the No campaign) when he wrote in the *Globe and Mail* of August 30 that "only an open and democratic process will do."

Responding to polling on the question in early September in antic-ipation of the referendum call, Canadians stated categorically that "not enough consultation had taken place" to proceed with such a vote. Bemused supporters of the accord and the proposed referendum mis-takenly concluded that the population was either confused or contrary. They completely failed to recognize that they had put the cart before the horse — holding consultations in advance of their closed-door deliberations, and then moving directly to the referendum.

The Fate of the Political Élites

The popular hostility towards the élites may be expiated in a most direct manner in forthcoming provincial and federal elections. Leaders and organizers at both levels of government, evidently recognizing their peril, took stock of their position in the aftermath of the rejec-tion of the Charlottetown Accord.

Clearly the individual most affected by the soul-searching was the prime minister. So great was his personal unpopularity that some pollsters concluded his interventions in favour of the accord were only slightly less effective than Pierre Trudeau's in achieving the opposite result. Having committed himself on two separate occasions to a package of constitutional reforms that were broadly rejected by the population, it would have been difficult if not impossible for Brian Mulroney to attempt any further modifications to the existing Constitution, despite his longstanding desire to be the prime minister who would "reintegrate" Quebec into the Canadian constitutional family. Indeed, the repudiation of his proposals seemed to indicate that his approach to constitutional reform and national unity was one that was simply not shared by the vast majority of Canadians, in either Quebec or the rest of the country.

At the height of the campaign, on October 13-15, a Gallup poll found more than 70% of Canadians expected the prime minister to leave the federal scene if the accord were defeated. Some 42% wanted to see a federal election called in the near future, while another 31% indicated they believed he should step down as prime minister and leader of his party.

Of course, Mulroney neither stepped down nor disappeared. On the contrary, he met with his cabinet and caucus to assure them that he would be staying on to champion the cause of NAFTA and the other economic priorities of the government. This pronouncement was followed by a period of two weeks in which there were neither economic initiatives nor the recall of Parliament: it was apparent that the government was attempting, in some haste, to decide what its economic priorities were.

In the interim, a variety of long-serving cabinet ministers such as Jake Epp, Michael Wilson, and Don Mazankowski quietly let it be known that they were unlikely to stand again for public office. Intergovernmental Affairs Minister Joe Clark, a man without a department or mandate and already in danger of defeat in his Yellowhead riding in Alberta, had quietly disappeared from view to consider his options.

In light of these developments, Mulroney's political future could not help but be called into question. Several ministers, including Justice Minister Kim Campbell, Communications Minister Perrin Beatty, Environment Minister Jean Charest, and External Affairs Minister Barbara McDougall, soon began to test the waters in a possible bid for the leadership of the Conservative Party, should Mulroney decide to leave.

None of these contenders was without some political credibility, but none appeared likely to be able to sustain the fragile coalition of westerners and Quebec nationalists on which Tory success in the Mulroney years had depended. Tory spirits, in the fall of 1992, were accordingly decidedly glum. As columnist Leonard Shiffrin wrote in the *Ottawa Citizen* of November 14, "The Tories' election strategy is struggling to survive."

Mulroney's performance in Parliament over the course of the fall sitting, which began two days later in mid-November, proved a further factor fueling speculation. In the days immediately preceding the return on November 16, the prime minister cancelled a scheduled major address on the economy, two intensive cabinet meetings failed to decide on a course of action concerning proposed cutbacks to the public service, and various government ministers speculated openly on the possibility of the federal budget deficit exceeding its projections for the fiscal year by more than $5 billion.

With the Conservative government in disarray and no economic agenda on the horizon, the opposition parties might well have been expected to take the upper hand. However, they were in little better shape. Discontent in both Liberal and NDP ranks over the failure of their leaders to seize the constitutional agenda from Mulroney during the campaign lingered on after the return of Parliament. Having chosen to support the accord, both leaders had proceeded to conduct a low-profile campaign that left their parties on the sidelines.

On the other hand, the implicit decision by voters to separate the referendum issue from partisan politics also meant that neither opposition party suffered a devastating setback as a result of the referendum débâcle. However the Reform Party, under the leadership of Preston Manning, had staked a lot on its opposition to the referendum and appeared to have suffered for it. Shortly after the referendum vote, a number of national polls revealed virtually no change in popular support for the three mainstream federal parties: the Liberals remained 20 percentage points ahead, in the low 40% range, while the Tories trailed at 19%, and the NDP had stalled at 18%. But the Reform Party had actually lost support, dropping from nearly 12% to 9% by voting day.

All three opposition leaders attempted to switch their attention to the economy on the return of Parliament, but with only a modicum of success. Building on her attendance at provincial NDP meetings in the preceding weeks, NDP leader Audrey McLaughlin emerged from a national caucus meeting in Ottawa before the return of Parliament to announce that job creation and opposition to the NAFTA would be the focus of NDP attention in the coming months. "The referendum is over," McLaughlin said. "It didn't pass, and so we move on." Despite their third-place standing in the polls behind the unpopular Mulroney government, no public comments by McLaughlin's caucus members were made regarding her leadership.

On the Liberal benches, discreet grumbling about recent unpopular decisions of the leadership, notably in the appointment of candidates without nomination meetings, took the place of open criticism of the leader. Emerging from his own national caucus meeting in the wake of the accord's defeat, Jean Chrétien outlined a proposed economic strategy that focused on infrastructure repair and expansion, a proposal that the government had already announced it would be pursuing with the provinces. On the return of Parliament, the Liberal strategy was clearly designed to force the government to release a major economic strategy paper or mini-budget before Christmas, rather than wait for the New Year, but when Don Mazankowski obliged with a mini-budget on December 2 the Liberals had few alternative proposals for action.

Meanwhile Preston Manning, demoralized by the poor showing of his party in the polls, wasted no time in returning to the attack by releasing a proposal for dramatic cuts to the public service and junior ministries of cabinet, a proposal that left the Conservatives scrambling for a response in light of their fears of Reform strength in western Canada.

At the level of staff and officials, the Yes forces suffered a number of blows to their credibility and integrity in the weeks immediately following the vote, as one story after another emerged relating to the contracts paid to Yes organizers with public funds. A leaked internal strategy document written by former Mulroney adviser Bill Fox during the campaign confirmed many critics' worst fears, revealing as it did a concerted strategy of fear and blackmail, particularly in Quebec, to sell the accord. A parliamentary committee chaired by a Conservative backbencher began investigating conflict-of-interest charges concerning the wife of a Yes organizer, who had worked for Senator Lowell Murray and FPRO while her husband received large polling contracts. Les Campbell, Audrey McLaughlin's Chief of Staff and Yes organizer, resigned after caucus criticism of his handling of the leader's role.

In short, with the return of Parliament in mid-November it appeared, for the time being at least, that it would be business as usual in Ottawa.

This was not the case at the provincial level, where many political élites were undergoing significant changes. Even before the vote was held, the premier of Alberta, Don Getty, had stunned other supporters of the accord when he indicated his intention to step down and call a leadership race in the middle of the referendum campaign. Led by Joe Ghiz, the popular premier of Prince Edward Island, a number of other leaders decided the referendum vote was an appropriate watershed on which to complete their public careers. Liberal leader Sharon Carstairs of Manitoba, fresh from an exhilarating success as a prominent leader of the No forces nationally and in her home province, announced within days that she would be stepping down as party leader in the spring. Although rumours were well-founded of fierce infighting between

Carstairs and federal Liberal Lloyd Axworthy, the Manitoba lieutenant who supported the accord, the one-time opponent of Meech Lake appeared sincere in her declaration that her departure was voluntary and based primarily on a sense of accomplishment. With obvious pleasure, she also indicated that she felt her role in the accord's demise was a vindication of her last-minute acquiescence, after months of opposition, to the Meech Lake Accord in 1990, a decision she had always regretted.

In British Columbia and Ontario, premiers Mike Harcourt and Bob Rae were in trouble. Their prominent participation in the Yes campaign was only partly to blame. They also were experiencing problems that were caused by tough economic times in their respective provinces. But Rae's intemperate cheerleading in favour of the accord, and the widespread perception that Harcourt had been bamboozled at the bargaining table, made their situations worse. In both cases, the NDP party philosophy was also clashing head on with economic realities, providing for considerable discontent among rank-and-file party members who were witnessing the sacrifice of more than one cherished party platform on the altar of deficit reduction.

But perhaps the most interesting developments were taking place in the province of Quebec. Neither Jacques Parizeau nor Lucien Bouchard appeared to have benefited from the victory of the No forces. Columnist Lysiane Gagnon underlined the point in two articles written after the defeat of the accord, the first of which was entitled: "A no vote does not mean that sovereignists have won" and the second: "The no vote was a shallow victory for the sovereignists." Gagnon noted that no one in Quebec was calling for more discussions on the Constitution and concluded that Liberal premier Robert Bourassa could well win the next provincial election (due within the following eighteen months). A number of opinion polls appeared to support the claim.

The fate of Parizeau and Bouchard also remained unresolved by the No victory in terms of the leadership of the separatist cause. Given the disintegration of the Conservative vote in Quebec federally, the major players now appeared to be the federal Liberals and the BQ, which Bouchard led. At the provincial level, Parizeau's PQ separatist party had not managed to increase its support. Instead, several polls indicated that support for separatism was dropping even as support for the No option rose during the campaign.

Within the Quebec Liberal Party, a purge of some prominent No supporters was taking place, but with little public effect. Mario Dumont, dissident president of the youth wing of the party, was suspended from the provincial executive as a result of his formal participation in the No campaign, and 20 of his cohorts left with him. His "nationalist federalist" line, it appeared, was no longer acceptable to the party that had initially endorsed the report of Jean Allaire.

In a similar vein, the premier and several of his leading cabinet ministers, including deputy premier Lise Bacon and veteran minister John Ciaccia, were declaring almost immediately after the vote that the party would quickly move to a more ardent defence of the current federal system. "We're going to have to make a choice," Ciaccia said. "We're either going to *become* [emphasis added] federalists or we're going to go to the Parti Québécois. I don't see a third option."

Indicating that the party grassroots shared the optimism of their leadership for their political fortunes in the next election, Health Minister Marc-Yvan Côté referred to the 1976 defeat of the Liberals by the Parti Québécois as a disaster that had overwhelmed him for "a long time." This time, he said, reaction to the defeat of the accord "lasted one night."

In Quebec, then, the message also appeared to be business as usual. Just as René Lévesque had lost a referendum and then won a renewed term of office, so the politician least likely to be affected personally by the defeat of the accord was Robert Bourassa. With the announcement in January of Bourassa's renewed battle with skin cancer, and the possibility of a liberal leadership race looming, politics in Quebec became much less predictable, but the constitution was hardly the reason. At the same time, the tendency of Quebeckers to hedge their bets may lead, in the next federal election, to a strong showing by the Bloc

Québécois, who have now apparently replaced the Conservatives as the only opposition to the federal Liberals.

The Immediate Prospects of the Interest Group Élites

The political élites were not the only ones to be affected by the referendum results. In the short term, their eagerness to side with the political élites may cause problems for some of the interest group leaders, but the long-term consequences of their alliance for the special interests they represent are not significant. The referendum campaign appeared to have little or no effect on the overall credibility of the groups in question, just as it did not affect the relative standing of the main political parties. Unhappiness with the position taken by a particular group or special interest was limited to the membership of the groups themselves, with the direct effect that some in leadership positions may lose their jobs.

Within the business community, the failure of the accord had little effect, except perhaps at the Royal Bank. The bank suffered significant withdrawals of funds by voters protesting its intervention in the referendum debate. Although its chairman, Allan Taylor, had the support of his board at the time, criticism of his initiative by other leaders of the banking community continued for some time afterwards. Still, there was no evidence to suggest that Taylor himself was in difficulty.

For others on the Yes side, it may be a different story. Ovide Mercredi, the most prominent of the aboriginal spokespersons, was in obvious difficulty when the accord went down to defeat. With some 70% of Indian voters on reserves rejecting the deal, and fully 81% outside of Quebec doing so, Mercredi, in effect, was left without a mandate as grand chief of the Assembly of First Nations.

His difficulties were compounded by the fact he was obliged to apologize publicly for his outbursts on the night of the election, in which he mistakenly accused ordinary Canadians of rejecting the accord because of racism and bigotry. Speaking the following day, Mercredi recognized that "five million voted in favour of the package," and that "the approach I took that all Canadians rejected us is not a good approach to take."

Having called a meeting of the Grand Council for mid-November, Mercredi nevertheless denied that his leadership was in doubt. Responding to questions in a press conference on November 4, he stated, "It's not on the agenda. I don't think my leadership is an issue at all." Instead he pointed out that technically a vote of 60% of the national assembly of chiefs would be required to replace him, and no such meeting was scheduled for the following six months. His three-year term of office, meanwhile, was not due to expire until 1994.

When he was asked about the opposition to the AFN's stand on the accord that was mounted by some native women's groups, Mercredi allowed that in future a more grassroots-oriented approach and greater consultation would be in order.

Soon after, Mercredi announced plans for a "quiet revolution." Sensing that he had been perceived by many Indians as too flexible and accommodating, Mercredi apparently intended to reassert control by adopting a strategy of tough bargaining and more radical demands. He raised the possibility that Indians on reserves would unilaterally assert their rights and pass their own laws, a theme to which he returned after meeting on October 27 with other members of his executive. Describing the persecution of Mohawk cigarette smugglers at Oka as victimization by invalid "foreign" laws, Mercredi said, "It is only illegal if you don't recognize our rights." He then indicated he would also be taking his people's complaints to international forums such as the United Nations. Commenting pointedly that 1993 would be the International Year of Aboriginal Peoples, he cited various areas of concern in which he believed the federal government could act unilaterally to remedy problems if it chose.

Announcing that he would be meeting shortly with Joe Clark to request that the federal government implement the section of the

Charlottetown Accord related to treaty promises made in the 19th and 20th centuries in northern Ontario and the Prairies, Mercredi declared, "There has to be some demonstration of good faith that these treaties will be respected. The federal cabinet has the power to go ahead with this commitment, regardless of the lack of a constitutional deal."

Among No supporters, the most significant difficulties emerged for the leadership of the women's movement and that of the labour unions, both of which were split between Yes and No camps. In both cases, internal dissension and leadership were complicated by the fact that traditional linkages with the NDP were also badly frayed. Although Judy Rebick of the NAC emerged from the debate with greater credibility and a higher public profile than before, her organization had endured a number of nasty behind-the-scenes altercations with its traditional left-wing political allies. These disagreements soon became public. At a party to celebrate the publication of NDP leader Audrey McLaughlin's autobiography, Rebick was isolated from the majority of those attending, literally left standing in a corner.

Ironically, Ms. McLaughlin had earlier said that "a hunt for blame would be a negative force.... We have to search for common ground." As reported by the *Globe and Mail* of October 26, Ms. Rebick had admitted, "A lot of women at the grassroots level are pretty upset at the NDP.... People feel there's been some disrespect for our position, not taking our position very seriously." Citing a common concern of all groups that campaigned on the No side and that also receive federal funding, Rebick noted, "There were veiled threats that groups could lose their funding, and I didn't hear anyone from the NDP protesting."

All interest groups, however, were bound soon to turn their attention to the issues of the day and the practical requirements of fund raising. An extended bout of finger pointing and blame was in nobody's interest. The NDP, trailing the federal Tories, could hardly afford to lose the support of the women's movement, nor could the women's movement afford to alienate their most significant political ally. Similarly, the labour unions could not afford to remain divided in the face of the threatened layoffs and plant closures that continued to dominate the economic scene.

The most obvious conclusion to be drawn from the experiences of the interest groups involved in the campaign was that no group on either side of the issue was likely to benefit directly from the outcome, with the possible exception of the aboriginal peoples. For many, the decision to intervene in the process was a costly and painful one that they would have preferred to avoid. For the élites of these umbrella groups, the difficulties involved in articulating a common message exceeded their abilities to forge an internal consensus. These splits within such large, broad-based interest groups were likely inevitable, and the effect of their lobbying was dissipated by the competing loyalties of individual Canadians, most of whom in the end ignored these narrower interests and voted in what they believed to be the best interest of the country as a whole.

The Fate of Issues Dealt with in the Accord

There are several elements of the Charlottetown Accord on which no movement can be expected for some time. Changes to the Senate, House of Commons, and Supreme Court can be formally accomplished only by constitutional amendment. Similarly, the addition of a "distinct society" provision is an entirely constitutional matter, regardless of whether it is placed in a preamble or in the body of the constitutional text.

Chances are, these and other institutional concerns are going to remain unresolved for a while. The loss may be of little consequence. The measures relating to the House of Commons, for example, were introduced only as part of a trade-off relating to proposed Senate reform and were never an issue in their own right.

Pressure from the west for an elected Senate could be met informally as it was when the late Stan Waters was elected in Alberta to a Senate seat. The process was one not recognized by the Constitution, but conceded by the federal government in deference to provincial demand. Although there are some problems with this approach, in practice a variation on the Alberta model could be worked out to accommodate the concerns of western Canadians. Instead, the prime minister indicated in statements in late December 1992 that he was in no mood to make such concessions. Accusing the people of Alberta of having rejected an elected Senate when they rejected the accord in the referendum, Brian Mulroney perversely insisted that he would utilize his powers under the existing system to make his own appointments, and proceeded to do so.

It is worth noting, however, that the drive for a triple-E Senate and for Senate reform generally was led by Premier Getty and supported only half-heartedly by the premiers of Saskatchewan and Manitoba. Premier Harcourt became a supporter of Senate reform primarily out of a desire to achieve a consensus. Seen in this light, the issue of Senate reform, an idea that had not been seriously advanced in federal-provincial negotiations before the Quebec Round of 1987-90, may yet prove to be a passing phenomenon.

Similarly, the proposed constitutional changes to the Supreme Court were driven by Quebec's desire to institutionalize an already established practice. By continuing to maintain a presence of three Quebec judges on the Supreme Court and by increasing the level of federal-provincial consultation on the appointments, the federal government may be able to alleviate pressure regarding the issue for some time to come.

The Quebec government has itself demonstrated that the distinct society clause may be superfluous, at least for the protection of cultural autonomy and identity. Since its inclusion in the 1982 constitutional amendment package, the Quebec government has used the notwithstanding clause repeatedly to achieve the same objective.

Quebec's need to avail itself of even this tool has become less obvious with several recent and broad-based interpretations of the Supreme Court based on Section 1 of the Charter of Rights and Freedoms, which accepts limitations on the rights protected therein if these limitations can be demonstrably justified in a free and democratic society. In the case of Quebec's Bill 101 and the infamous sign legislation case, the Supreme Court in effect advised the provincial government how to draft legislation that would be found acceptable, despite some limitations it might impose on freedom of linguistic expression. Approval would be possible through the Court's generous interpretation of section 1 to reflect the distinctive character of Quebec society and the government's need to preserve and promote this distinctiveness.

Rather than take the Court's advice, however, the Bourassa government chose once again to invoke the notwithstanding clause and introduce Bill 178, legislation that permitted English-language signs only on the inside of commercial enterprises, while French was to be the only language visible on the outside. Since then, public opinion in Quebec has swung dramatically away from this rigid approach to cultural identity. Recent pressure to remove the restrictions of Bill 178, motivated as much by public embarrassment as it was by concern for the protection of human rights, appeared to have had an effect on the Bourassa government.

In short, as both Lysiane Gagnon and Michael Bliss suggested in the course of the campaign, pressures from the population at large may lead to a reduced interest in formal recognition of distinct status for Quebec. Ms. Gagnon also noted that the demand for special status was not historically grounded and could easily be replaced by resolution of the more longstanding of Quebec's constitutional concerns, such as the veto.

Another measure related to language rights could be dealt with immediately, because only federal and New Brunswick consent were necessary. In December 1992, the Mulroney government tabled legislation to implement a minor provision of the Charlottetown Accord guaranteeing minority language rights in New Brunswick. The McKenna government had already approved the provision and it was expected to pass through Parliament quickly, despite vocal opposition by some No supporters.

Other issues dealt with in the Charlottetown Accord could be addressed readily by non-constitutional means. In many cases, the accord did not actually resolve the issues it raised, but merely committed the parties involved to further discussion. In such cases, nothing was "lost" with the defeat of the accord. The proposed elimination of inter-provincial trade barriers is a case in point. The provisions for aborig-inal self-government may be another, inasmuch as funding and the definition of key issues were left, by the accord, to be settled in future negotiation.

And despite the claim made by the Yes forces that the "Social Charter" represented a significant achievement, most constitutional experts disagreed, saying that it was weak and unenforceable.

The social charter, originally suggested by Bob Rae as a response to the current federal government's continued assault on Canada's "social safety net," was ill-advised. There simply was no way to entrench the federal government's spending obligations in the Constitution. In effect, the social charter merely affirmed Canadians' commitment to the idea. Its utility as a determinant of federal policy would likely have been nil.

The programs that constitute the social safety net can best be pro-tected by the continued vigilance of the federal opposition parties and the provincial political élites. A more immediate result may be attained if voters remove the Mulroney Conservatives from office at the first opportunity.

As discussed above, the aboriginal leadership has already initiat-ed a number of measures to accomplish some of the objectives of the self-government provisions. In practical terms, movement towards self-government has always been within the purview of the federal government, at least with respect to the Indians on reserves, which it administers through the Indian Act, and in the territories.

As Ovide Mercredi made clear on several occasions following the accord's defeat, much can be accomplished through legislative and administrative arrangements, the transfer of additional funds (the current federal government having actually reduced funding for a variety of native programs over the past eight years), and the negotiation of land claims settlements. The recent approval of the Nunavut proposal by the Inuit population has also demonstrated the alternative possibilities for other native peoples with a land base.

In many respects, the degree of progress that native peoples can achieve through non-constitutional means is directly related to the degree of political will exhibited by the governing élites. Given the renewed interest that has recently been demonstrated in the Royal Commission on Aboriginal Rights, and the high level of popular support for the legitimate claims and aspirations of native peoples that continues to be demonstrated in public opinion polls, both the federal and relevant provincial governments should be more receptive to such initiatives. In fact, the provincial governments of Ontario and British Columbia have both indicated their intention to move as quickly as possible to resolve some of their outstanding issues.

Interprovincial trade barriers can, and probably should, be eliminated through administrative agreements rather than by constitutional fiat. The fact that the accord left the issue to future discussion reflects the lack of political will to bring about change. Some provinces remain concerned that their ability to protect affirmative action programs and social benefits would be impaired if provincial boundaries are opened. These and other concerns are impeding progress. While several provinces have committed themselves in principle to a lowering of barriers, only the Atlantic provinces have taken concrete steps to move towards this objective.

Similarly the issue of the transfer of powers is one that need not be constitutionalized and, traditionally, has been accomplished through "administrative federalism." Although it is unclear which powers provinces other than Quebec would be most intent on reclaiming, and although there is certainly no consensus among Canadians on the degree of decentralization that should be tolerated, it is nevertheless possible for the federal and provincial governments to arrive at administrative arrangements to accommodate some degree of decentralization if they choose to do so. In addition these arrangements, since they are not constitutionally entrenched, can more easily be changed to reflect new economic and other realities.

Indeed, a number of prominent economists have argued that this less formal type of arrangement is ideal in the rapidly changing global economy in which Canada finds it must now operate. Albert Breton and André Raynauld, two former chairs of the Economic Council of Canada, and former finance mandarin Sylvia Ostry have all argued in the recent past that Canada's competitiveness and productivity depend on a practical restructuring of powers that allows Ottawa, not the provinces, to assume greater responsibility for some areas such as education and labour adjustment programs. Pointing to the model of the European Community, they note the need for larger, not smaller, economic units and greater co-ordination of effort to function successfully in the post-industrial marketplace. Breton has also stressed the lengthy tradition of "competitive" administrative federalism and the way in which it has served to accommodate changing realities in a more flexible and responsive fashion than constitutional change could ever hope to do.

Future Directions:
The Longer-Term Consequences of October 26

All the short-term implications discussed above result directly from the failure of the Charlottetown Accord. With few exceptions, they could have been predicted before the start of the campaign, in the event of a No vote. Clearly the defeat of a proposal that enjoyed the support of virtually all the country's élites would have significant repercussions for the careers of those individuals. Clearly the failure to approve the specific provisions would lead to further questions about the best way to accomplish the same objectives.

But the profound cynicism and mini-revolt of the population against not just the élites but the political system as a whole, which appears to have taken place during the course of the campaign, raises other questions about the long-term implications for the political process and institutions of government.

The defeat of the accord has also called into question Canadians' core values, exposed the profound division between two competing visions of federalism, and raised concerns about the apparent lack of a unifying common vision.

Some observers have argued that the globalization phenomenon has reduced the effectiveness and authority of all élites, so that Canadians' expectations of their governments and leaders are now totally unrealistic. For others, the referendum process was not a victory for democracy but a victory for narrow special interests and entitlements that will make the country ungovernable. Still others would argue that the referendum has put in motion an irreversible move towards the eventual separation of Quebec.

Yet, as the referendum results themselves make clear, the widespread rejection of the Charlottetown Accord outside Quebec provides evidence of a broad-based and coherent *national* vision that virtually ignored or repudiated special group and regional interests in favour of the principles of equality of provinces and individuals. This vision, in turn, appears to run directly counter to the view of federalism and the Canadian nation-state that was supported by the No forces in Quebec.

10

Finding Common Ground

The deafening silence on the part of much of the political, inter-est group, and media élite following the October referendum came as a surprise to many Canadians, albeit a welcome one. What happened? Was disaster not, after all, imminent? What of the Yes side's awful predictions? As columnist Carol Goar put it in an arti-cle for the *Toronto Star*: "How can a nation be on the brink of cri-sis one day and go back to business as usual the next? How can an issue so important that it crowds everything else off the national agenda abruptly disappear?"

The answer, of course, was that the crisis existed only in the mind of the political élites. Ample proof of this was to be found in the Angus Reid poll conducted between October 28 and November 2, 1992. Across the country, support for "national unity" was extremely strong. Not only was Quebec's separation from Canada not imminent, it was not even on the menu. Support for the sovereignty option had actually *lost* ground in that province, and it had not increased anywhere else.

Only 38% of those surveyed in Quebec agreed that "it would be better in the long run if Quebec were to simply separate," while slightly more than 53% disagreed. In the rest of Canada, 74% dis-agreed with that statement. If a vote on independence had been held in Quebec, it would have been rejected by a margin of 54% to 34%; only 24% of respondents even indicated they wanted such a vote to take place.

Just as they were wrong about the public's state of mind during the referendum campaign, the political élites were wrong about the reasons for the accord's defeat. Instead of recognizing that the contents of the accord were the primary cause of its demise, many who have spoken out since, including the prime minister, have blamed the unreasonable expectations of both special interest groups and ordinary Canadians for its failure. Both of these explanations are wrong.

First, the No vote of October 26 did *not* represent a victory for special interests and the politics of "entitlement," making future compromise impossible and the country ungovernable. Second, it is not true that the élites bear little responsibility for the negative results because public expectations are unreasonably high, while events on the international scene have rendered the élites much less powerful and able to effect solutions than they once were.

It is difficult to know which of these proffered explanations of the referendum's failure is the most pernicious.

As the referendum results and subsequent polling have conclusively demonstrated, the accord was not rejected by most Canadians because of narrow self-interest or regional bias. It was rejected by a substantial number of Canadians in six provinces and all regions of the country. In the two most populous provinces, Ontario and Quebec, half of the electorate rejected the deal.

Individual Canadians who voted no consistently indicated to pollsters that they rejected the accord as a package; they disliked many if not most of the provisions in the deal, not simply one or two items, and they also considered much of it to be simply too vague and incomplete — the so-called "blank cheque" phenomenon. Polls also demonstrated that neither gender, ethnic origin, nor language played a decisive role in voting behaviour.

In addition, the stated positions of most special interest groups during the campaign belie the élite's claims. Most interest groups spoke in *favour* of the accord. Labour, business, aboriginal groups, the ethnocultural community, linguistic minorities inside and outside of Quebec — all were strong supporters of the deal, even though many of these groups' leaders articulated very specific concerns about the potential implications of some provisions for those they represented. Indeed, several leaders made a point of saying they would support the deal *despite* their self-interest concerns.

The disabled and environmental groups, both of whom perceived significant problems with the accord and were highly disappointed with the political élites' failure to respond positively to their concerns before the vote, nevertheless expressed public approval for the deal. The Green Party and other environmental groups actually sponsored broadcast ads for the Yes team. While some small pockets of dissent emerged at the level of the environmental rank and file, as it did with the labour unions, it was the prevailing impression of the general public that the vast majority of special interest groups supported the deal in the same way that corporate Canada and the media élite did.

In fact, only representatives of the women's movement could be considered to have publicly and aggressively opposed the deal. And the Yes campaign wasted no time or effort in trying to demonstrate to Canadians that Judy Rebick and the National Action Committee did not speak for most Canadian women. Voting behaviour analyses after the fact confirm an absence of gender bias, which suggests that the NAC campaign, while prominent, had little or no effect on the end result.

Similarly the élite's claim that the disparate groups and interests that formed the No campaign rejected the deal because they did not "get enough" are largely unfounded. Women, Trudeau federalists, and others who rejected many provisions of the accord had not even asked for another round of constitutional negotiations in the first place. They had accepted, in effect, the status quo. Their opposition to the accord arose because they believed that its provisions would have *taken away* existing rights and established a measure of *inequality* or *special status* where it had not existed before. In particular, the attempt by the accord's creators to add a Canada clause that excluded some individual rights already established in the Charter aroused much opposition. The élite's refusal to make modifications to the accord that took these objections into account was fatal.

What, then, are we to make of the refrain of the political élite that "special interests" have "captured" the constitutional agenda in Canada and have made, or will continue to make, further reform impossible?

In part, the élite's failure to understand the dynamics of the No vote stems from their failure to understand the criticism levelled at the *process* by which the accord, like Meech Lake before it, had been negotiated. Although they appeared sensitive to the need for consultation and inclusion at the beginning of the process, the accord's drafters eventually returned to closed doors and then moved directly to the referendum. Thus many groups of Canadians who wanted to feel included in the process did not. As consultant Andrew Cardozo, former head of the Ethnocultural Council of Canada, complained in an article for the *Ottawa Citizen*, the élites still "just don't get it." Most groups were not asking for special provisions but for representation and consultation. They asked only to be included in the process *after* the deal was struck, so that their input might actually be seen as meaningful.

The first major problem, then, was the political élite's decision to return to executive federalism as the principal format for achieving constitutional reform. As an earlier chapter has demonstrated, this format worked well in the post-war era when 11 first ministers were negotiating highly technical issues of little interest to the general public. After 1982, however, executive federalism was perceived to be an unacceptable approach, not only because the public expected to participate in some way, but also because the content of the discussions had changed. The issues being addressed in Meech Lake and the Charlottetown Accord had obvious implications for all Canadians, and they wanted their views to be heard.

There were, of course, other mechanisms available to the élites to legitimate the consensus they achieved through executive federalism, but they either failed to take advantage of them or misused them. As the 1982 process demonstrated, the use of the special parliamentary committee can be extremely effective in forging a broad-based public consensus and conferring legitimacy on a political agreement.

In the case of Meech Lake, however, the élites ostensibly followed the 1982 procedure by establishing a special parliamentary committee to examine the agreement, but then adopted a steadfast position that "not one comma" could be changed in the "seamless web," so that in reality the whole committee exercise was a sham. Those few witnesses who actually testified before the committee — hastily set up and ordered to conduct hearings over the summer of 1987 and report back to Parliament in two months — emerged disillusioned and angry. Canadians saw Meech Lake's "consultative" process for what it was — a travesty of participatory democracy.

The lesson to be learned from the failure of the Charlottetown Accord process is not that the political system is flawed but rather that the incumbents in the political élite abused it.

As if the emphasis on executive federalism were not bad enough, it was combined with a new type of constitutional deal making that Brian Mulroney brought with him into the political arena, fresh from his days as a corporate labour lawyer negotiating with the unions. Mulroney's new approach of "brokerage politics," applied to constitution-making when he took office, was one from which he seemed unable to part despite its obvious failings. His attempt to respond to all demands from all sectors, and to please all elements at least a little, proved disastrous. It led to a dog's breakfast of political deals that pleased no one in the end and offered no national vision to Canadians as a whole.

It is difficult to overestimate the importance of Mulroney's brokerage approach to federal-provincial relations and constitutional affairs. Its effect was to remove the national government from the playing field in any capacity except that of referee. Instead of a national vision, Canadians were treated to the spectacle of provincial élites carving up the country. Contrary to what members of this élite have maintained since the accord's defeat, it was *provincial* and *regional* demands, encouraged by the executive federalism format and Mulroney's brokerage approach, that made the negotiating process hopelessly complex and the final product unsaleable, *not* the entitlement claims of special interests and groups in society. Indeed, a majority of citizens rejected the deal precisely because they believed it reflected narrow, regional interests rather than the national interest.

This in turn leads to a third major problem of the Meech Lake and Charlottetown Accord processes, namely, the marginalization of elected officials and legislatures. Part of the problem of executive federalism, as Pierre Trudeau had recognized, was that it reduced major decisions to the whims of 11 men, who might or might not be representative of their electorates. Without a return to Parliament and the provincial legislatures to validate the agreements they reached, the perceived legitimacy of the exercise would be minimal. Yet after the Charlottetown Accord was struck, the élites moved directly to the referendum, bypassing Parliament and provincial legislatures.

Lastly, both opposition parties at the federal level, and most parties at the provincial level, threw their support behind the Charlottetown Accord from the beginning, further limiting Canadians' sense that their elected officials had given the agreement the benefit of careful scrutiny and sober second thought. In a parliamentary system, the image of opposition parties happily joining forces with the government of the day is one that rightly or wrongly makes many Canadians uneasy and sceptical. By contrast, in 1982 both federal opposition parties expressed significant reservations about the government's proposal, demanded and received changes, and then agreed to the revised version, thus enhancing its legitimacy.

Just as the flawed process of the Charlottetown Accord was a major issue, so too the unrepresentative nature of the élites was another problem during the referendum campaign. The obvious question is why the political leadership came to be seen as unrepresentative and therefore not credible. In part this can be explained by the long series of scandals and blunders within federal and provincial governments in recent years, but it was much more than that.

Over the years, successive generations of federal governments have articulated a national vision. From Macdonald's National Policy to

Pearson's view of Canada as international peacekeeper, Diefenbaker's dream of the north as the New Frontier, and Trudeau's Just Society, our most effective leaders have defined an image of Canada that all its citizens, regardless of their linguistic, ethnic, or other differences, could share.

With the coming to power of a neo-conservative regime with an economy-driven agenda of deficit reduction, free trade, and greater competitiveness, Canadians have not been given a new image or vision of the country — a new *projet de société* for the 21st century — on which to focus their constructive energies. Instead, they have seen the old vision of social justice demolished with each cut to the social safety net and the welfare state. They have witnessed the dismantling of the national infrastructure, the diminution or outright elimination of the outward and visible symbols of the country from Via Rail and Air Canada to the CBC, Canada Post, and many significant cultural, scientific, and economic advisory bodies. They have seen the merits of bilingualism, multiculturalism, and the Charter of Rights questioned by the Mulroney government. *And nothing has been put in their place.*

The free trade debate in the 1988 election offered a perfect example of this failure. Canadians were asked by the Mulroney Conservatives to support the free trade initiative of 1988 because it would be good for the economy and for business. Ultimately, it would lead to more and better jobs, they argued. Put another way, the federal government's entire argument was playing to individual self-interest and economic motives. There was no attempt to articulate a new direction for the country or its citizens as a whole. Free trade was not placed in the broader context of a bold new experiment that would lead to something more significant for Canada than profits and an improved bottom line.

Another argument made by several premiers and members of the corporate élite on referendum night and shortly thereafter was that Canadians expect too much from their élites, who are no longer in a position to control either the political or the economic state of the nation in the way they once did because of the overriding effects of globalization. Nothing could be farther from the truth.

International forces can hardly be regarded as a satisfactory explanation for a made-in-Canada constitutional crisis. On the contrary, this is perhaps one of the few remaining areas directly under the control of the political élites and their supporters. If international forces *had* been at work, the elimination of interprovincial trade barriers — long decried by all supporters of free trade and the neo-conservative agenda — would actually have been achieved in this round of constitutional reform, rather than simply discussed and put off for further deliberation.

Put another way, the federal government and all provincial governments are responsible for the very real economic and social policy choices they have made. Perhaps their options have been more limited than those of other governments at other times. But the Mulroney government's decisions to move forward with the GST and NAFTA, to eliminate much of the social safety net, and to put off any attempt at introducing a national child-care program, clearly reflect real choices with real consequences.

Similarly at the provincial level it is perhaps more significant than might originally be thought that the Liberal governments of Joe Ghiz, Frank McKenna, and Clyde Wells were able to retain a margin of credibility with voters during the referendum campaign while the Conservative governments of Don Getty and Gary Filmon, closely aligned in voters' minds with the federal government's policies, were not. As for the NDP governments of Bob Rae and Mike Harcourt, it would appear that any number of locally driven policy decisions (such as the doctors' strike in British Columbia and a string of unpopular insurance, labour, and employment equity provisions in Ontario), to say nothing of ministerial demonstrations of incompetence, greatly diminished the credibility of those élites.

This attempt by the Yes side to blame much of the reason for their failure on external forces beyond their control was not limited to the political élite; it is instructive to note that they were joined in expressing this view by the corporate sector. Both élites have one overriding concern in Canada, a concern shared by their counterparts in Britain, the United States, Japan, and other western democracies that have been managed for the past decade by a neo-conservative agenda, namely, the withdrawal of government from the marketplace. After ten years of this agenda, few citizens in any of those countries are unaware of the consequences.

As journalist Michael Ignatieff and economist John Kenneth Galbraith both have argued recently, the general public and especially the middle class in Britain and the United States are engaged in a battle to reclaim their political heritage and force their governments to return to more intervention in the affairs of the nation, not less.[1]

If the vote of October 26 was indeed a rejection of much of the current political élite, does this mean, as many analysts have suggested, that the traditional Canadian process of élite accommodation is also endangered?

In a highly pluralistic country such as Canada, where every citizen is a member of several subgroups by virtue of race, ethnicity, language, region, or religion, the emergence of spokespersons for their various interests is a practical necessity. In theory, the élites representing these interests then work within the political system to achieve compromise and consensus. This process of élite accommodation is, of course, dependent on two things: a willingness on the part of ordinary citizens to allow the political élites to make decisions once chosen or elected (implying a minimal level of public participation apart from the electoral process), and second, a prior consensus on who the legitimate élites are.[2]

What has emerged over the past five years in Canada is a decreased willingness on the part of citizens to recognize the legitimacy of the current élites. This, in turn, has led to increased demands for citizen participation to counteract the decision-making authority of these "illegitimate" or unrepresentative élites.

In short, by getting rid of many of the individuals in the current political leadership, the major concern of Canadians about their élites will likely have been addressed, provided acceptable alternatives are presented to them.

Once this is accomplished, it is unlikely that most Canadians will want to participate actively and aggressively in all areas of public policy making. It is rapidly becoming the conventional wisdom that the well-educated baby boomer generation in technologically advanced societies will demand an increasing role in governance. While there is some evidence to suggest that their knowledge and attitudes towards authority make them less inclined to tolerate poor performance, it is much less clear that their high expectations for politicians will in fact translate into a desire to intervene directly themselves. In Canada it appears more likely that the *perception* of being consulted on important matters, and the actual ability to influence politicians' behaviour through public opinion, are the real concerns of most citizens. Indeed, there is still considerable evidence available to suggest that, for many, the act of voting no was a sufficient degree of intervention.

However, the Constitution will no doubt remain a horse of a different colour. Canadians' participation in the constitutional process, if it should resume at some point in the future, appears an entrenched expectation stemming from the 1982 exercise. To that degree at least, élite accommodation in Canada has been modified and the new political élite will need to recognize this essential point.

Clearly neither the prime minister nor any of his key ministers recognized that Canadians' expectations were being dashed by their élitist approach to constitutional reform. This miscalculation becomes even more important when placed in the context of Canada's unique political culture, another matter that the current political élites seem to have completely misjudged. In their attempts to forge a "historic compromise" in the Charlottetown Accord, many of the key players attempted to downplay or dismiss the very real and deeply held difference of opinion that exists on the nature of the federal system and the Confederation bargain. Simply put, there are two very different views of the world held by most Canadians living in the rest of Canada, and many of those Canadians living in Quebec.

In the terminology of cultural anthropology and communications, societies can be placed on a continuum from "high-context" to "low-context" cultures. High-context societies are usually ones that have been in stable existence for a long period of time, have a nearly homogeneous population, and often occupy a small or isolated geographic base. African and North American Indian tribes, the Japanese, and a number of western European democracies such as Italy, France, and Sweden can be placed in this category. In these high-context societies, the rules of the game and the appropriate behaviour of the players are known to everyone, almost automatically. There is little need to write down the rules or externalize them.

By contrast, low-context societies are newer, are far more heterogeneous or pluralistic, and often occupy physically larger areas. Not surprisingly, the United States and Australia, as immigrant-receiver countries of the new world, both fall into this category. In these societies, as cross-cultural training expert Edward Hall has noted, "there is a widely shared assumption — and behaviour to support that assumption — that the amount of stored (common) knowledge ... is minimal. That is, there is a need to tell everybody everything in great detail." Hall notes that this particularly applies to instructions and legal texts. He then goes on to underline that communication between high- and low-context societies is fraught with difficulty and the potential for misunderstanding.[3]

Applying these insights to Canada leads many observers to conclude that we are more than a plural society in the way the United States and Australia are. There is, above all, our obvious English-French duality, which is reinforced by geography: French Canada based primarily in Quebec, English Canada largely outside Quebec. Moreover English Canada received the lion's share of the immigrants who came to Canada over the past 125 years. While large communities of immigrants formed in major cities, allowing them to preserve their language and culture easily, those new arrivals who chose Quebec either spoke French to begin with, or were more aggressively integrated into Quebec society through provincial government policies. This in turn created a far more heterogeneous society in English Canada. In these terms, then, Canadian political culture may be best explained as a unique mix of a high-context society in Quebec, married to a low-context society in the rest of the country.

The success of the Confederation bargain was that much of the detail was left out of the Constitution, avoiding the need to reconcile the two contradictory views of the world. Instead, the federal system left Quebec to manage most of its own affairs while building a common *national* identity and values to bridge the gap. One hundred and twenty-five years later, when the "rest of Canada" is an even more pluralistic society in which the multicultural mosaic, not the melting pot of the Americans, has continued to prevail, any attempt to broker a new compromise on some of the most fundamental elements of the country's Constitution is a nearly impossible task.

The recent inclusion of native peoples — an extremely high-context society — in the constitutional equation could only confuse the issue further. Seen in this light, the ongoing differences of opinion among the various élites over the perceived need to define such terms as "inherent" rights and "aboriginal self-government" become much more comprehensible, but no less difficult to resolve. For native peoples, the ultimate high-context society, in which little was ever written down and an entire series of land claims and constitutional arrangements were represented for the Iroquois nation by the famous "two-line wampum belt," the élite's debate on semantics is incomprehensible.

All of this would seem to lead to some inevitable conclusions. Since the vaunted Canadian trait of compromise has historically been demonstrated *outside* the Constitution, massive changes or additions to the basic elements of the existing Canadian Constitution are never likely to be feasible. In fact, no constitutional reform is ever likely to be successful if it involves more than minor, incremental changes to discrete elements. Even then, it is a precarious exercise that may be better left alone, particularly since many other avenues of change are available to the political élites under the existing rules. A constitution that provides the basic outlines for the rules of the game, and an élite which practises the art of compromise through administrative flexibility rather than brokerage politics, may well be the most appropriate solution for the Canadian political culture.

As columnist Lysiane Gagnon wrote in the *Globe and Mail* of November 21, 1992, "Canadians cannot seem to accept a compromise written on paper and enshrined in the Constitution, but their actual behaviour is based on accommodation." *Montreal Gazette* columnist Josh Freed came to a similar conclusion intuitively when he wrote that "constitutions are like marriage contracts... impossible to renegotiate when you've lived together too long. Imagine trying to spell out the unspoken rules of your relationship after 10 years with your partner." Freed optimistically concluded: "I've been to nice countries like England that don't have a constitution at all. I've also been to lousy countries that had wonderful written constitutions."

The example of the United States, a low-context society with a predictable, highly detailed constitution, is also instructive. The Americans experience extraordinary difficulty altering the rules of the game in even minor ways. The attempt to enshrine an equal rights amendment to protect women's rights in the American constitution failed. But following that failure, virtually every significant political actor acknowledged that gender equality is now, for all intents and purposes, a core American value.

As an earlier chapter demonstrated, historically Canada too has adopted an informal approach in lieu of rule changes. The success of various versions of administrative federalism over the years, particularly in accommodating changing economic realities to the structure of power-sharing between the two levels of government, should not be dismissed out of hand as no longer relevant. Our existing Constitution, and the sensitivity of the political élites of the past, is what made this flexibility possible.

In addition, federalism itself offers a degree of flexibility that many would argue is highly appropriate to Canada's cultural diversity. It is no accident that many other low-context, plural societies (such as the United States and Australia) have a federal structure. As proponents of federalism have always emphasized, it is the ideal solution for a plural society because it allows for a degree of cultural autonomy at the regional (provincial, state, canton, etc.) level of government while providing a national political unit sufficiently large to function in the world. In an era of globalization of markets and economies of scale, most Canadian economists agree with the prevailing international wisdom that the larger the political unit the more effective it will be in its economic competitiveness and political power.

The flexibility of federalism is also ideal for testing new ideas and accommodating the emerging concerns of regionally based political cultures. Medicare first emerged in Saskatchewan, and state financial enterprises such as SIDBEC were pioneered by the government of Quebec. Human rights legislation at the federal level evolved only after several provinces led the way with their own laws identifying various discrimination and equality issues.

In the same way, Canada's federal system should be able to accommodate by administrative means a variety of practical arrangements with the provinces regarding their present concerns about cost-sharing programs and the division of powers. As even Jacques Parizeau has been forced to admit on occasion, almost all of the original demands raised by René Lévesque in his 1968 separatist treatise, *An Option for Quebec*, had been achieved by Lévesque and his successor, Robert Bourassa, within the federal framework, long before Meech Lake. The Cullen-Couture immigration agreement was, after all, an existing administrative agreement negotiated between officials of the federal and Quebec governments, and so successful that Quebec requested its inclusion in the Meech Lake Accord.

In reality what has historically been less flexible and adaptive than the federal structure is Canada's *parliamentary* system of government. Yet several non-constitutional reforms of our political institutions could be carried out in the near future if the political élites wished to do so. The procedures of Parliament, and in particular of the House of Commons, could be greatly improved to enhance their credibility and increase Canadians' sense of representation in the democratic process.

Among other changes that have been proposed and could easily be implemented are a reduction in the number of parliamentary committees and a greater use of those committees, with real power to examine and recommend changes to legislation, and the mandate to approve, rather than review, patronage order-in-council appointments. Suggestions have also been made that a decrease in party discipline should be encouraged, an idea that is less easy to implement and contains a number of substantial drawbacks for the opposition in a parliamentary system. Alternatively, the decreased observance of the non-confidence motion in voting on government legislation might provide a real possibility for greater accountability of parliamentarians to their constituents.

Political parties must also make significant changes in their structure and operation if they are to become more accountable and representative of the Canadian public, and ultimately regain their credibility. The report of the Lortie Commission on Electoral Reform, released in 1992, offered a number of practical recommendations that would go a long way towards accomplishing these objectives. In particular, changes to the nomination process in political parties — to ensure fairness, equity, and real equality of access for women and ethnocultural and other minorities — should include a redefinition of the rules on party membership and voting rights to conform with the Elections Act, strict limitations on spending, and a reasonable time requirement for membership before voting privileges are granted. Once again the political will of the party élites will be crucial to the success of such reforms.

As the election of a 40-something president and an unprecedented number of female candidates in the United States demonstrates, a party's concerted efforts to better reflect its constituents can make a real difference in a relatively short space of time.

Along similar lines many improvements could be made to the operation of government, and especially the practice of patronage appointments and contracting, to enhance the credibility of politicians and the political system. After nearly a decade of high public expectations and low levels of performance, especially at the federal level, the concepts of transparent and accountable government are more important than ever. Changes to conflict-of-interest legislation and its enforcement, and greater openness through a more co-operative approach on access to information and human rights issues, could significantly improve Canadians' respect for their elected officials, currently at an abysmally low level.

In the final analysis, however, the most important non-constitutional reform may be that of renewed national leadership. The common values that Canadians and their political élites have shared since Confederation have not disappeared, they have merely been overridden by the focus of the current élites on their differences during the past five years of constitutional wrangling. These differences were highlighted by a prime minister who not only lacked an overarching national vision, but pursued a destructive strategy of divide-and-conquer brokerage politics that pitted regions and special interests against one another. In the end it led to an ill-fated referendum campaign fought on both sides by a bizarre coalition of groups and interests — strange bedfellows indeed. For many on the Yes side, the distinction between compromise and deal-making remained elusive. It was left to the Canadian people, through the referendum, to put a halt to this divisive treadmill and reassert their commitment to those fundamental values.

Ironically, it may be the "yesterday's man" so despised by the Yes forces, former prime minister Trudeau, who best articulated these common values and forged a consensus around concrete measures taken by his national government to further them. It is often said that his was a unique and strongly held vision of Canada to which

Canadians responded, but it seems likely in retrospect that his vision was successful primarily because much of it was already shared by most Canadians. His articulation of that vision struck a responsive chord precisely because it reflected a set of common values already present, to which he gave both voice and government initiatives. Far from being yesterday's man, he may yet prove to have been a man ahead of his times.

The referendum of October 1992 demonstrated, as nothing else could have done, the awful chasm separating Canadians from their current political élite, but this chasm may be bridged fairly easily if a new generation of political leaders emerges with a better understanding of their country and its citizens.

Clearly Canadians are awaiting a political rebirth similar to the one that has recently taken place in the United States with the election of Bill Clinton. After more than a decade of the politics of privilege and individual selfishness, Americans have returned a party whose platform speaks to their core values, and a new generation of politicians that promises a renewed effort to legitimize the political process.

In Canada, where the crisis of leadership has endured for almost as long as in the United States, all eyes will now turn anxiously to the next federal election to learn which party will present a new and compelling national vision. A strong message from the electorate about the direction they want to see the country and the national government take on economic and social policy issues will have important consequences for the future of regional unrest and Quebec nationalism. A prosperous, tolerant, and caring society is surely the most likely to foster unifying common values, and to weather the storms of future conflicts and competing claims among the diverse interests that comprise the Canadian cultural mosaic.

NOTES

Chapter 1

[1] A good summary of these developments can be found in Jackson et. al. *Politics in Canada* (Toronto: Prentice-Hall, 1986) pp. 77-209

[2] Adie and Thomas, *Canadian Public Administration: Problematical Perspectives* (Toronto: Prentice-Hall, 1987) pp. 425-470

Chapter 3

[1] P. Blaikie, "While Canada is my Country, Quebec is my Home," *Montreal Gazette*, September 24, 1992.

[2] See, for example, Andrew Cohen, *A Deal Undone* (Vancouver: Douglas and McIntyre, 1991)

[3] D. Coyne, "A Dozen Reasons for Saying No," *Ottawa Citizen*, September 18, 1992

[4] *Globe and Mail*, October 1992

[5] *The Network*, Vol. 1, No. 5, October 10, 1991.

[6] *Globe and Mail*, October 28, 1991.

[7] Special Joint Committee on a Renewed Canada, *Minutes of Proceedings* 32 December 17, 1991.

[8] Ibid.

[9] B. Schwartz, *Still Thinking: A Guide to the 1992 Referendum* (Hull: Voyageur Publishing, September 1992.

[10] *Montreal Gazette*, October 2, 1992.

[11] D. Coyne, *Roll of the Dice: The Final Act*, (Toronto: Lorimer 1992). See also D. Coyne and R. Howse. *No Deal*, (Hull: Voyageur Press, September, 1992.

[12] R.Jackson, "A Rubik's Cube," *Ottawa Citizen.*

[13] *Toronto Star*, September 6, 1992.

[14] D. Coyne, *Roll of the Dice.*

[15] "The Constitution Proposals and the Canada-Quebec Dilemma" (unpublished document) November 12, 1991

[16] *Globe and Mail*, October 8, 1992.

[17] *Toronto Star*, October 6, 1992.

[18] *Ottawa Citizen*, September 19, 1992.

[19] R. Tassé, "Finding the Balance," *Network,* Analysis No. 6, October, 1992; R. Howse. "Comments on Analysis No. 6," October, 1992

Chapter 4

[1] See for example Library of Parliament, Research Branch, "Referendums: The Canadian Experience in an International Context," BP-271E, January 1992; P. Boyer, *Lawmaking by the People*, (Toronto: Butterworths, 1982); and Canadian Unity Information Office, "Understanding Referenda: Six Histories," Ottawa 1978.

Chapter 5

[1] *Globe and Mail*, September 20, 1992.

[2] *Ottawa Citizen*, September 23, 1992.

Chapter 6

[1] *Globe and Mail*, September 28, 1992.

[2] *Ottawa Citizen*, October 26, 1992.

Chapter 7

1 *Globe and Mail*, September 18, 1992.
2 *Ottawa Citizen*, October 27, 1992.
3 Ibid.
4 *Maclean's*, November 2, 1992, p. 28.

Chapter 8

1 *Montreal Gazette*, October 20, 1992.
2 *Toronto Star*, October 4, 1992.
3 Globe and Mail, September 8, 1992.

Chapter 10

1 J. Galbraith, *The Culture of Contentment*, (Boston: Houghton-Muffin, 1992).
2 R. Presthus, *Elite Accommodation in Canadian Politics*, (Toronto: Macmillan, 1973). See also K. McRae (ed.) *Consociational Democracy* (Toronto, McClelland and Stewart, 1974).
3 A. Thomas and E. Ploman (eds.), (*Learning and Development*: Toronto) O.I.S.E., 1986.

BIBLIOGRAPHY

Abele, F. (ed.). *How Ottawa Spends 1991-92: The Politics of Fragmentation*. Ottawa: Carleton University Press; 1992.

Aucoin, P. "The Machinery of Government," in Taras and Pal (eds.), *Prime Ministers and Premiers: Political Leadership and Public Policy in Canada*. Toronto: Prentice-Hall, 1988.

Behiels, M. (ed.), *The Meech Lake Primer*. Ottawa: University of Ottawa Press, 1989.

Boyer, P. *Lawmaking by the People: Referendums and Plebiscites in Canada*. Toronto: Butterworths, 1982.

Campbell, C. "Mulroney's Broker Politics: The Ultimate in Politicized Incompetence," in Gollner and Salee (eds.), *Canada Under Mulroney: An End of Term Report*. Montreal: Vehicule Press, 1988.

Cohen, A. *A Deal Undone*. Vancouver: Douglas and McIntyre, 1991.

Coyne, D. *Roll of the Dice*. Toronto: Lorimer, 1992.

Coyne, D., and R. Howse, *No Deal*. Hull: Voyageur Press, 1992.

Government of Canada, Department of Supply and Services, Citizens' Forum on Canada's Future. *Report*. June 27, 1991.

_____ *Shaping Canada's Future Together: Proposals*. September 1991.

_____ "Responsive Institutions for a Modern Canada," "Canadian Federalism and Economic Union," and "Distribution of Powers and Functions in the Federal System": Background

Papers for the five "Renewal of Canada" Constitutional Policy Forums (F.P.R.O.), January 1992.

_____ Special Joint Committee on a Renewed Canada. *Report.* February 28 1992.

Galbraith, J. *The Culture of Contentment.* Boston: Houghton-Mifflin. 1992.

Government of Ontario. Ministry of Intergovernmental Affairs. *A Canadian Social Charter.* September 1991.

Gregg, A., and M. Posner, *The Big Picture.* Toronto: Macfarlane, Walter and Ross, 1990.

House of Commons. *Debates* Volume 132, nos. 143-6, 148-52, 166-7 (May 15, 19-21, June 1-5, September 9, 10).

_____ Bill C-81. (An Act to Provide for Referendums on the Constitution of Canada), June 4, 1992.

Jackson, Jackson and Baxter-Moore. *Politics in Canada.* Toronto: Prentice-Hall, 1990.

Jeffrey, B. *Breaking Faith: The Mulroney Legacy.* Toronto: Key Porter, 1992.

_____ "Constitutional Reform in Canada from 1971 to 1985," Library of Parliament, BP 102-E, 1985.

_____ "The Charter of Rights and Freedoms: Some Positive Benefits," Acadia University, National Conference on Human Rights, October 1983.

_____ *The Constitutional Amendment Process 1980-82: A Case Study.* Carleton University, December 1983.

_____ "The Protection of Human Rights in Canada," *Canadian Regional Review* 2/37-54 (August 1979).

_____ "The Recognition and Obligations of a New State," in D. Rowat (ed.), *The Referendum and Separation Elsewhere: Implications for Quebec*. Ottawa: Carleton University Press, 1978.

Johnston, D. (ed.) *With a Bang Not a Whimper: Pierre Trudeau Speaks Out*. Toronto: Stoddart, 1988.

Latouche, D. (ed.). *Allair, Bélanger, Campeau et les autres: Les québécois s'interrogent sur leur avenir*. Montreal: Editions Québec/Amerique, 1991.

Lévesque, R. *An Option for Quebec*. Toronto: McClelland and Stewart, 1971.

_____ *Attendez que je me rappelle*. Montreal: Editions Québec/Amerique, 1986.

Maclean's. Special Constitution/Referendum Editions (January 6, September 28, October 19, November 2, 1992).

McRae, K. (ed.). *Consociational Democracy*. Toronto: McClelland and Stewart, 1974.

Monahan, Patrick J. *Meech Lake: The Inside Story*. Toronto: Unversity of Toronto Press, 1991.

Presthus, R. *Elite Accommodation in Canadian Politics*. Toronto: Macmillan, 1973.

Research Branch, Library of Parliament: "The Pre-Referendum Campaign in Quebec," CIR 80-1E, April 1980.

_____ "The Sovereignty Option of the PQ in Abeyance," MR 85-4E, January 1985.

_____ "Quebec's Constitutional Proposals, 1986," MR 86-20E, September 1986.

_____ "The Meech Lake Accord: A Constitutional Conundrum," BP-186E, January 1989.

_____ "The Belanger-Campeau and Allaire Reports," BP-257E, May 1991.

_____ "The Constitutional Proposals of the Federal Government, September 1991," BP-274E, September 1991.

_____ "Referendums: The Canadian Experience in an International Context," BP-271E, January 1992.

Ranney, A. (ed.). *The Referendum Device*. Washington, D.C.: American Institute for Public Policy Research, 1981.

Schwartz, B. *Fathoming Meech Lake*. Winnipeg: Legal Research Institute, University of Manitoba, 1988.

_____ *Still Thinking: A Guide to the 1992 Referendum*. Hull: Voyageur Press, 1992.

Sheppard and M. Valpy *The National Deal*. Toronto: Fleet Books, 1982.

Simeon, R. (ed.). *Toolkits and Building Blocks*: C.D. Howe Institute, 1991.

Smith, D., et al. (eds.). *After Meech Lake*. Saskatoon: Fifth House Publishers, 1991.

Thomas, A., and E. Ploman (eds.). *Learning and Development*. Toronto: O.I.S.E. 1986.

Trudeau, P. *A Mess That Deserves A Big NO*. Toronto, Robert Davies Publishing, 1992.

_____ *Federalism and the French Canadians*. Toronto: Macmillan, 1968.

Van Loon, R., and M. Whittington *The Canadian Political System*.

Watts, R. (ed.). *Canadian Constitutional Options*. Toronto: BCNI Conference, January 1991.

APPENDIX A: REFERENDUM RESULTS

	Yes	No
NATIONAL	44.8 (6,185,902)	54.2 (7,550,723)
NFLD.	62.9 (133,649)	36.5 (77,587)
N.B.	61.3 (234,450)	38.0 (145,096)
N.S.	48.5 (230,182)	51.1 (230,182)
P.E.I.	73.6 (48,626)	25.9 (17,124)
QUE.	42.4 (4,032,856)	55.4 (2,232,280)
ONT.	49.8 (2,409,414)	49.6 (2,398,945)
MAN.	37.9 (198,143)	61.7 (323,062)
SASK.	45.5 (203,655)	55.1 (252,410)
ALTA.	39.6 (482,659)	60.2 (730,738)
B.C.	31.9 (512,712)	67.8 (1,098,157)
NWT	60.2 (14,476)	39.0 (9,371)
YUKON	43.4 (5,354)	56.1 (6,922)

APPENDIX B: KEY CONSTITUTIONAL DEVELOPMENTS 1931 TO 1982

1931 Statute of Westminster

1949 Supreme Court of Canada becomes final court of appeal

1961 Diefenbaker Bill of Rights

1964 Fulton-Favreau formula rejected by Quebec

1968 First ministers' meetings on the Constitution

1971 Victoria Charter rejected by Quebec

1976 Election of PQ government in Quebec under René Lévesque

1978 Bill C-60

1980 (May) Quebec referendum on sovereignty defeated

1980 (September) First ministers meet at Château Laurier

1980 (October) PM Trudeau tables unilateral resolution in House of Commons

1981 (February) Parliamentary committee and witnesses approve resolution package

1981 (September) Supreme Court rules resolution is constitutionally correct but violates convention

1981 (November) FMC makes three significant changes to resolution; package rejected by Quebec

1981 (December) Resolution passed by Parliament

1982 (April) Queen Elizabeth II signs Constitution Act, 1982

APPENDIX C: CHRONOLOGY OF EVENTS

Part I: Public Consultation

June 24, 1990 Meech Lake Accord dies

Summer 1990 Formation of Bloc Québécois, rise of Reform Party, Oka Crisis

November 1, 1990 Announcement of Citizens' Forum on Canada's Future (Spicer Commission)

January 28, 1991 Report of Constitutional Committee of Quebec Liberal Party (Allaire Report) issued

February 1991 Interim Report of Spicer Commission released

March 27, 1991 Report of the Commission on the Political and Constitutional Future of Quebec (Campeau-Bélanger Report) issued

April 21, 1991 Federal cabinet shuffle creates "Unity Cabinet" and appoints Joe Clark as Minister for Constitutional Affairs

May 13, 1991 Federal throne speech promises proposals for a renewed federation, tabling of referendum legislation

May 15, 1991 Premier Bourassa tables referendum legislation (Bill 150)

June 27, 1991 Spicer Commission Report released

Summer 1991 Federal "Unity Cabinet" meets several times debating a set of options for a federal proposal; deep internal divisions exposed

September 24, 1991 Federal constitutional proposal tabled in the House of Commons

September 25, 1991 Special Joint Parliamentary Committee on a Renewed Canada (Dobbie-Castonguay Committee) created with mandate to examine federal proposal, tour country to hear witnesses, and gather public input

November 6, 1991 Dobbie-Castonguay Committee returns to Ottawa in disarray after chaotic first week, opposition charges of patronage, Senator Claude Castonguay resigns as co-chair of the committee, citing ill health

November 13, 1991 Joe Clark announces series of five "public" policy conferences in wake of committee fiasco and increased public cynicism

November 26, 1991 Parliamentary committee regroups under new co-chair, Senator Gérald Beaudoin, resumes hearings as Beaudoin-Dobbie Committee

January 17- February 14, 1992 Five policy conferences held in Halifax, Toronto, Montreal, Calgary, and Vancouver

February 28, 1992 Beaudoin-Dobbie Committee tables report with all-party approval

Part II: Return to Closed-Door Negotiations

March 12, 1992 First federal-provincial meeting on the Constitution since death of Meech Lake (Quebec absent) to consider Beaudoin-Dobbie Report

April 18, 1992 Quebec Premier Robert Bourassa announces the provincial referendum will now be held on the "federal offers" and not sovereignty

May 15, 1992 Federal government tables referendum legislation in the House of Commons

June 24, 1992 Prime Minister Mulroney tells premiers he will table a package in the House of Commons and proceed "unilaterally" if they are unable to reach a consensus

June 29, 1992 First ministers meet in Ottawa (except Quebec) but fail to agree on a package; agreement to hold further meetings among nine premiers and Joe Clark

July 7, 1992 Premiers reach tentative agreement based on Senate reform

July 30, 1992 Bourassa demurs, finally agrees to come to table

August 4, 1992 First Ministers' Conference with Bourassa at Harrington Lake; no agreement. Further meetings in Toronto among nine premiers with eventual agreement on a deal

August 28, 1992 First Ministers meet to iron out details in Charlottetown; Draft Consensus results

September 9, 1992 House recalled to debate question for referendum; vote on Chalottetown Accord called for October 26

APPENDIX D: REFERENDUM CAMPAIGN CHRONOLOGY

August 28, 1992 Charlottetown Accord announced by federal government, 10 premiers, 2 territorial leaders, and native representatives; PM Mulroney refers to opponents of the deal as "enemies of Canada"

September 1 Deborah Coyne and Professor Michael Behiels launch the "Canada for All Canadians" national No Committee on Parliament Hill

September 3 Quebec Liberal Jean Allaire announces he will vote no

September 9 House of Commons meets to approve referendum question

September 10 Reform Party announces it will campaign for the No side

September 13 NAC announces it will campaign for the No side

September 16 Wilhelmy affair in Quebec; leaked conversation of senior Bourassa aides suggest premier "caved in"

September 20 *Maclean's* publishes an editorial by former PM Trudeau condemning Quebec separatists as "master blackmailers"

September 21 Official referendum campaign begins

September 22 National Yes "Canada Committee" has official launch with seven "eminent Canadian" co-chairs in an Ottawa high school; lack of material in French widely reported as major faux pas

September 26 Royal Bank chair Allan Taylor releases report saying No vote disastrous for economy, based on assumption breakup of Canada follows

September 29 Canadian dollar's drop greatest since Depression; banks raise interest rates more than 2 percentage points

September 29 PM Mulroney rips up document at Yes rally in Sherbrooke

October 1 Former PM Trudeau declares for No side in speech at Maison Eggroll

October 6 NDP Leader Audrey McLaughlin debates Preston Manning

October 7 Nfld. Premier Clyde Wells begins tour of western provinces for Yes forces after his legal text concerns are resolved

October 8 Television advertising begins

October 8 B.C. Intergovernmental Affairs Minister Moe Sihota tells audience Premier Bourassa faced a "brick wall" at the bargaining table and "lost"

October 12 Televised debate between Premier Bourassa and PQ leader Jacques Parizeau

October 18 Assembly of First Nations has meeting in Vancouver; chiefs refuse to endorse accord

October 16 L'Actualité magazine publishes leaked documents of Quebec officials criticizing the accord

October 19-22 PM Mulroney begins three days of interviews in support of accord

October 22 Manitoba native MLA Elijah Harper calls for native boycott of vote

October 26 Referendum Day

INDEX

Pepin, Jean-Luc, 125
Peterson, David, 63, 81, 100
Peterson, Jim, 6

Quebec: Charlottetown Accord, 72,
78-82; different rules for referendum, 107, 158; failure to sign
1982 agreement, 33, 56-60; fate
of issues in Charlottetown
Accord, 203-05; federal government driven by agenda, 47-49;
immigrants, 220-21; 1980 referendum, 175-76; 1992 referendum, 174-90; Meech Lake
Accord, 60-61, 177-78; referendum results, 2, 8, 9, 189-90, 198-
200; rejected Victoria Charter, 26
Quebec Round, 58-60, 177, 204
Quebec Women's Federation, 161-62

Rae, Bob, 50, 52, 63, 81, 86, 100,
123, 138, 161, 170, 198, 217
Raynauld, André, 208
REAL Women, 150
Rebick, Judy, 5, 87, 89, 151, 202
referendum on Charlottetown
Accord, 10-11, 50; advertising,
165-66; different from an election, 97-98, 118, 157, 165; disenchantment with political process,
191-93; government's legislation, 101-08; historical prece-
dents, 95-96; meaning of results,

211-15; Mulroney's decision to
hold, 95, 99; national campaign,
155-59; No campaign, 171-73;
partisan politics, 110-12; prob-
lems with referendums, 96-101;
Quebec campaign, 174-90; refer-
endum question, 108-10; "refer-
endum stress," 134; structure of,
155-56; support for
Charlottetown Accord at start,
155; wrong definition of question,
159-61; Yes campaign, 159-71
Reform Party, 38, 145-48, 196
Reid, Angus, 172
Reid, Tim, 128
Rémillard, Gil, 59, 61
Robertson, Gordon, 85-86
Robinson, Michael, 116
Rochon, Louis-Philippe, 141
Romanow, Roy, 51
Royal Bank of Canada, 127, 163-65, 200
Ruby, Clayton, 74, 76, 142
Ryan, Jim, 117

Sarault, Guy, 141
Schwartz, Bryan, 77-78, 84, 88, 142
Scott, Stephen, 36, 90, 142
Segal, Hugh, 116
Senate reform, 62-63, 65, 80-83,
203-04
Shiffrin, Leonard, 195
Sihota, Moe, 12, 123, 170
Simard, Michel, 141